Over the Edge

Over the Edge

A Regular Guy's Odyssey in Extreme Sports

Michael Bane

WILDERNESS PRESS
BERKELEY

FIRST EDITION April 2000

Copyright ©2000 by Michael Bane

Design and typesetting by Terragraphics/Margaret Copeland
Cover design by Jaan Hitt
Cover photo: Tawhai Falls, New Zealand ©2000 Denise E. Jackson

ISBN 0-89997-265-9
A catalog record is available from the Library of Congress.

Manufactured in the United States of America

Published by   **Wilderness Press**
                  1200 5th Street
                  Berkeley, CA 94710
                  (800) 443-7227 • Fax (510) 558-1696
                  mail@wildernesspress.com

Visit our website www.wildernesspress.com
Contact us for a free catalog

To My Beloved Parents—

*Bob Bane, who never once suggested there might be
anything I couldn't do, and*

*Barbara Bane (1930-1995), who couldn't wait
to read this book.*

I hope you like it, Mom.

Acknowledgments

There are times when this book has seemed a Herculean effort. But it has been the enthusiasm of so many people that kept me plodding along. Below is a probably incomplete listing, but be assured that each and every one of you have a special place in my heart. Thank you for joining me along the way.

Guides: Steve and Deborah Ilg, Myrna Haig, Rachelle Roberts, Milt Bedingfield, Lisa Jaimison, Nancy Frederickson, Clark Man, Michael Powers, Mimi Borquin, Bill Lawrence, Steve Dunbar, Angela Hawse, Hal Watts, Wings and Ani Stock, Gary Gentile, John and Shelley Orlowski, Dick Eustis, Carolyn Reed, and Sonny the Bricklayer.

Fellow Travelers: John and Sandi Rodolf, Richard Lewis, Susan Smith, Dave and Deb Johnson, Alden Cockburn, Kelby "I Can Scam It For You" Roberts, The Denali crew (Rich, Tom, Roger, Dr. Jim, and Tommy), David Feeney and the Scuba Network gang of lunatics, Michael Menduno, Mary Ellen Moore, Bob "It Won't Hurt, Really" Potter, Natalie Bayol, the Dud Thames Bicycle Shop staff, Walter Brown, and so many others.

A special thanks to Roger Borthwick, for one hell of a Big Day: *I didn't win, Roger, but I finished.*

Finally, to my girlfriend, partner and cohort on so many of these adventures, Denise E. Jackson, whose selfless love and caring have opened up a world of new possibilities. Thank you.

Contents

1

To The Edge

*"You cannot learn to fly by flying. First
you must learn to walk, and to run, and
to climb and to dance."*
—Nietzsche

It is 10 degrees below zero outside my tent, and it has been snowing steadily for three days. I keep trying to think of new, inventive ways of keeping warm, but, ultimately, they all boil down to just one—stay in my purple sleeping bag as long as I can, try to will my mind to blankness.

The wind roars, and the tent pops like a piece of rawhide on the end of Indiana Jones' bullwhip.

It is, I think, Indiana Jones who has gotten me into this. At least, he's got to be partially responsible. Him and his keyword, "adventure."

In a few minutes, I will have to crawl out of my marginally warm sleeping bag, punch a hole up, through the snow, crawl out and start digging my out my tent. Welcome to Denali, Mt. McKinley, Alaska, Land of Adventure. I have come to this undefrosted refrigerator of a land to check an item off a list. No, make that, The List. Thirteen items, activities, events that have come to define the outer limits of my life; heck, the outer limits of any life.

It is an over the edge list, a collection of events that nightmares are made of:

Trapped in underwater caves . . .

Trapped on a frozen waterfall . . .

Trapped in Death Valley . . .

Trapped in Alcatraz . . .

And now, trapped on the highest mountain in North America, pinned in by a brutal blizzard and temperatures almost beyond comprehension.

"Wind chill? How about *real damn* cold?"

I twist into as much of a ball as you can twist into in a mummy sleeping bag, avoiding the inevitable.

I am not supposed to be here . . .

I am in my 40s, well past the derring-do years. I am a couch potato; well, maybe I *was* a couch potato. But I know, emphatically, I am not supposed to die in a blizzard on this mountain.

Or am I?

I don't remember the first time I saw the picture—Ansel Adams' flawless black-and-white Denali, standing over the remote and unforgiving Alaskan tundra like some Athabascan god. The great mountain seemed them, as now, as distant and as reachable as the moon, a part of a world that exists only in myth. I remember looking at the picture, at its fine, seamless grain, and imagining the gravity of the great mountain, pulling me north.

What was it like, I think, looking at the tranquil picture of the mountain, to fight your way to the top, through the snows and the killing winds and the endless, bottomless valleys of ice?

What was it like to go to the very edge of the world, and look over?

I remember shrugging. I would never know, would I?

2

The List

Disclaimer: Iditasport is difficult and hazardous under the best of conditions. You could be on your own in an area of Alaska where coastal storms meet the frigid cold of the Alaska Range and the Interior. No rescue can be anticipated. The appropriate knowledge of snow camping, frozen river travel, animal confrontations, illness, injury, gear failure or loss, self rescue, bad weather, hypothermia, frostbite and the like must have been acquired before entering Iditasport. All too often, those not experienced in these conditions underestimate both the dangers and difficulties to be encountered.

This notarized release is designed to relieve everyone involved in Iditasport from any liability. This prevents you, or your next of kin, should the worst happen to you, including death, from blaming or suing Iditasport, its sponsors, or the land owners of the course, whether private, state, or federal. Any decision you make is your own, and you are responsible for it.

—Liability release for the Iditasport 155-mile bike race

Sign Before You Climb! Rock climbing is inherently dangerous . . . You could die . . . Have a great day!

—Liability release for climbing, scrawled on a napkin

"But we're never gonna survive
Unless we get a little crazy . . . "
—Seal

Here is the exact moment when I realized that things had begun to spin out of control: It is a west wind, a 55 mile-per-hour freight train from the Midwest. Palm trees rock and snap; live oak branches the size of a kid's waist bounce off the highway, spinning into the boiling air. Miniature whirlwinds dance through the sand and gravel, pelting the car like a furious dry hailstorm.

Roger just grins.

"It's do-able," he says, watching a sailboat break loose from its storm anchors and head for the beach. A garbage can bounces by, just missing the car, only to flatten itself against a chain link fence. "Besides, what's the worst that can happen here?"

So we huddle alongside the rocking car, rigging two sailboards, slithering into our wetsuits like we have good sense. We haul the boards to the edge of the water, fighting the wind, the blowing sand, struggling to hold the tiny sails back in the face of the gale. A real sailor, in heavy weather gear and carrying a rope, runs down to the water's edge, shouting to be heard over the wind.

"You're not serious!" he bellows in his best real sailor voice. "You can't be serious, you crazy shits!"

"No!" I start to yell back, and then the wind, all 55 miles-an-hour of it, catches the sail. From the corner of my eye, for just a millisecond, I see Roger's board and sail explode out of his hands, blowing into the bay.

And then I am gone, a red and white rocket trying desperately to avoid skewering the rocking sailboats; the sailboard making a hissing sound like water slashing across a red-hot skillet as the board claws for the horizon.

The first drop on a roller coaster . . . The first corner of a haunted house . . . The first fumbled groping in the backseat of a borrowed car . . . The pure, cold amber of crazy . . .

Chain lightning and adrenaline, salt water and the bitter taste of bile.

But that's not when I knew things were unraveling. The exact moment comes an hour later, back on the beach, throwing up dirty salt water and looking at the red raw blisters across my palm. I am calm and happy, and it all makes perfectly good sense to me. I sit down behind the car, out of the wind, take a roll of silver gray duct tape, and tape my hands, double layers over the blisters. My elbows feel disconnected, my back a solid throb of pain. A muscle in my right knee twitches uncontrollably. Flexing my duct-taped hands, I reflect that I feel better than I have in ages.

The first drop on a roller coaster... The first corner of a haunted house... The first fumbled groping in the backseat of a borrowed car... The pure, cold amber of crazy...

Somewhere out there are the extremes, ringing the fringes of the sports world we're familiar with, a black hole for the imagination, with the power to draw and hold even the most stalwart soul.

And they are booming.

Call them extreme sports, risk sports, adventure sports, whatever, the fact is that the extreme fringe of the sporting world is going through an unprecedented boom. Fueled by a virtual mania for bungee jumping—leaping off a platform with a rubber "bungee cord" attached to the ankles—such sports as rock and ice climbing, endurance ultramarathon running, snowboarding, downhill mountain bike racing, skydiving and parasailing, radical in-line skating and the more extreme versions of multi-sport events are all off the charts, the more bizarre the event, the more enthusiastic the participation.

The question is, of course, *why?*

Or, maybe, *why not?*

My strength, I will later learn, is my ignorance. I sit in my car, the wind rocking my windsurfer, now lashed to the roof racks, and begin making what my friends will eventually refer to as The List, a series of athletic events out on the pale. Later, The List will take on a life of its own; dominating not only my life, but my friends' lives as well. The List will change everything it touches, take me places I've only imagined. It will allow me to reach out and touch... something. Something desirable; something mythical. But as is true in all fairy stories, it will extract a price.

Of course, I don't really know this yet, as Roger and I pack it in and head for a pizza joint, Paranelli's, near the beach in Tampa. We get there, call some friends, order a pitcher of beer, and do what windsurfers do when they finish windsurfing—talk about windsurfing.

Friends arrive, and the conversation keeps swirling around the wind. Finally, I turn to Roger.

"I have an idea," I say, a slight bit off kilter from the beer.

Roger nods.

"It was really...different...out there today," I begin.

"Yeah," says Roger. "We didn't drown."

"Yeah, yeah," I agree. "I liked it, you know?"

He nods.

"I liked the feeling."

He nods. By now, other people are paying attention.

"I bet you can get that feeling doing other stuff."

Roger agrees.

"So my idea is to make a list of extreme sports..."

Roger is really brightening up now.

"The List..."

"Thirteen things," Roger says. "An extreme list ought to have 13 things on it..."

"Then go do everything on The List."

"Damn good idea!"

Everyone agrees.

So I get a cocktail napkin, borrow a pen from the waitress and clear off enough space around me to write.

"Number 1: Windsurf big air, like in Maui or the Gorge in Oregon..."

"That goes without saying, man," Roger replies.

"Number 2—what's that bicycle race where they go downhill at like 60 miles an hour, in California or somewhere?"

"The Mammoth Mountain Kamikaze Downhill," someone chimes in.

"Okay," I say, "that's 2."

Three is a popular one, the Escape From Alcatraz Triathlon...

"...Where you gotta swim with all those sharks..."

"Take like a canoe off a waterfall," someone says, and I dutifully write, "Whitewater off a waterfall."

"Rock climb!" Number 5.

"Diving in underwater caves...That's some loony shit..." Number 6.

"Climb frozen waterfalls." Number 7.

"Jump outta airplanes!" Number 8. "And do those parachute thingies, or kites, or whatever."

"I read," someone begins as we order another pitcher of beer, "that there's some roller skate race that's been going on for ten years, through the hills outside Atlanta..."

Skates. Cool. Number 9.

I need another SCUBA (Self-Contained Underwater Breathing Apparatuses) thing..." I start to say.

"Hell," someone answers. "Why not? You can't even swim, much less dive."

"...Maybe really deep, like 200 feet or something," I say.

"Sounds good to me," answers Roger, starting on the new pitchers. "Is that 10 or 11?"

"That's 10," I reply.

"Badwater," a marathon runner says. "It's an ultramarathon, like 150 miles or something, that starts in Death Valley and runs up Mt. Whitney."

Number 11.

"As long as we're talking crazy, how about the bike race in Alaska on the Iditarod sled dog trail in February..."

"Bicycling in Alaska in February?" asks Roger. "That's seriously stupid."

Number 12.

"How about Big Number 13?"

"I know what 13 is," I say quickly. "Denali."

"Denali?"

"Mt. McKinley," I say. "The highest point on the continent. In Alaska. An expedition to Denali is Number 13." *Thank you, Ansel Adams...*

"Sold," says Roger.

The next morning, on the desk in my office, lies a cocktail napkin with 13 items scrawled across it.

Suppose I really did the list? No, The List, upper case. Suppose I really did it? How crazy is this stuff, anyway? Who are the people who think these things are *fun*?

I mean, it's easy to understand why a person might want to run three miles; harder to understand what drives a person to train to run almost 150 miles across one of the most godforsaken spots in the world, where the asphalt, I will learn, is hot enough to cause the air pockets in the runners' sneakers to explode and the final 13 miles of climbing will bring them from scorching heat to cold approaching freezing.

It's easy to understand the urge to swim a couple of times a week for fitness at the local "Y"; harder to grasp the dark appeal of the Alcatraz swim, the bitter cold waters sluicing in and out of San Francisco Bay, the fog and swirling currents, the real or imagined torpedo-like shapes patrolling the deep channels.

So I come to the risk sports looking, I think, for Indiana Jones. Or, at least, someone like him. Some part and parcel of our mythology, cowboy or samurai, riding the edge jaggies for all they're worth.

Instead, I will find a group of puzzled people with a tiger by the tail, interested not so much in mythology as in touching and holding an experience as ephemeral as spider silk, ghostly as morning mist over a Montana river, an experience made of equal parts of muscle, adrenaline, and a mind that echoes a sneaker commercial...just do it...do it...do it. An experience I touched, however briefly, on a piece of fiberglass in a windy yacht basin.

"I think I know where you're going," one of my many instructors will tell me as we hike along the frozen waterfalls of New Hampshire's Frankenstein Cliffs, named not for Mary Shelley's monster, but for an artist. The temperature will be below zero, and the winds from the valley below will scour the ice, turning it as brittle and fragile as an old window pane. "But how do you plan on getting back?"

But that is still a ways in the future; out of sight; out of reach.

I stare at my cocktail napkin.

Why not? How hard can it be?

I spend an afternoon at the library, looking up events. There is precious little hard information. I can turn on the television and see all manner of this stuff, but hard information is lacking. The more I search, the more extreme sports seems to be terra incognito, the place on the map where there's nothing but a hand-drawn dragon. There are secrets here, I think, a world over the edge of the map. Secrets . . .

Here is what I will learn, somewhere over the edge:

The extreme sports, I think, change the people who participate in them. While a bungee jumper might feel a certain rush of immortality, the other extreme sports offer something far less tangible—and far more rewarding. University of Chicago psychology professor Mihaly Csikszentmihalyi writes of what he terms *flow*, a sense, to borrow Eastern terminology, of flowing with the universe. The flow state, he says, comes when we ask our body and mind to reach for the limits; it arrives when everything "clicks," and we are *doing* without *thinking* about doing. Our best moments, continues Dr. Csikszentmihalyi, occur when "a person's body or mind is stretched to its limits in a voluntary effort to accomplish something difficult and worthwhile"

"Stretched to the limits . . ."

"Difficult and worthwhile . . ."

I go back to my office and stare at my cocktail napkin:

1. Windsurf Big Air

2. *Kamikaze Downhill*

3. *Escape From Alcatraz*

4. *Whitewater off a Waterfall*

5. *Rock Climb*

6. *Cave Dive*

7. *Ice Climb*

8. *Skydive; whatever those parachute thingies are.*

9. *Skate Marathon*

10. *Dive Really Deep.*

11. *Badwater Death Valley Run*

12. *Iditarod Bike Race*

13. *Denali*

I need a plan. At first, the plan seems easy—I'll scrape up what money I have, go out to Death Valley and tag onto that nightmarish run. Then I'll head on up north to do the Kamikaze Downhill. I'll learn to rock climb, then mountain climb and get certified to SCUBA dive while I'm at it. I'll even learn to swim, something I've been avoiding. The wind howls, and nothing seems impossible. I drive home, clean my equipment, take a handful of aspirin, shower, and bandage my hands. Then I get the morning paper and turn to the classifieds—I'm going to need a mountain bike, I think . . .

3

Strength and Muscle
and Jungle Work

Flush with the concept of The List, I start doodling around real plans—just how, exactly, do I plan to pull this stuff off?

I actually don't have a clue.

In the cold light of day, and without the lubricating experience of pitchers of beer, The List looks pretty stupid sitting there on my desk.

There are a couple of problems that jump right out at me. Take the Alcatraz Triathlon, for example, Item Number 3 on The List. First and foremost is the fact that I can't swim; I am, in fact, slightly afraid of water. It's always been a joke among my windsurfing buddies. I can't afford to be thrown too far—beyond dog-paddling distance—from my board, since I swim like a concrete block.

Secondly is the fact that my bicycle, a fat-tired beach cruiser with a little chrome bell and a carrier for a can of cola, has just been stolen. Assuming I use the pittance from the insurance company to buy another beach cruiser, I suspect that is not the type of bike used in triathlons.

Thirdly, I haven't run a mile since high school, after which I had vowed to never run again unless I was being chased by something large and particularly nasty.

The Kamikaze, Item 2?

I didn't own a mountain bike; had never, in fact, even seen a mountain bike except for photos in *Mountain Bike Action* magazine. Aside from the bike, I had a critical shortage of one other element—mountains. One of the highest points in Florida is, if memory serves me, a few hundred feet high, and it's a garbage dump outside of Ft. Lauderdale.

Cave diving?

I wasn't certified to SCUBA dive at all, and I wasn't even sure how to go about getting certified.

Ice climbing?

Get real. The only ice I was really familiar with was in my refrigerator. The closest I'd come to a frozen waterfall was on a Discovery Channel special.

Denali?

That stops me. What do I really know about Denali? That it's the highest mountain in North America, sure. That it's in Alaska. That Ansel Adams took pretty good pictures of it; that Inuits worshipped it; that, real or imagined, it calls to me. But climbing it? I'd seen *all the movies*. I knew that mountain climbing looks cold, unpleasant, and decidedly dangerous.

I thumbtack The List to the whitewashed wall of my office, next to the window looking out on the palm trees and neat lawns of my Florida neighborhood.

The List might have stayed there forever, except for one of those little quirks of fate that periodically comes spinning into peoples' lives, spreading chaos and unintended consequences. As it happens, my sometimes workout partner Susan Smith doesn't have a lick of rhythm, and, about a week after I'd thumbtacked The List to the wall, she proves it by stumbling in the middle of an aerobics class we were both taking. Within a day, she's hobbling around pitifully on a grossly swollen, black ankle.

Over coffee at the gym the next morning, she gives the medical update, basically a long list of things she couldn't do for a long time.

"What can you do?" I ask.

"Swim and bike, the doctor says," Susan replies. She sits there and plays with her coffee spoon for a while before speaking again. "You know your stupid list?"

"The one thumbtacked to the wall?" I say.

"The one you talk about, yeah. Triathlon's on there somewhere, isn't it?"

I nod.

"Well, there," she says, as if everything is now clear. "*That's* what we'll do. There's this short triathlon two months away, if we start training for it right now, we ought to be able to do it no problem, and that way, you'll get a start on The List..."

"Susan," I say, interrupting. "I can't swim. Your bicycle has a baby seat on it."

"We can *get* bikes," she says with the passion of a true exercise junkie looking at six weeks of rehab. "We can *learn* to swim. I've checked into everything, and it'll work. It *will*."

"Sure," I say—not for the last time. "We'll do a triathlon. In two months."

Susan beams.

The first trip to the bicycle shop is telling. We both show up the next Saturday morning, respective spousal units in tow, at one of those shops that specializes in Lycra tops with color schemes resembling smashed bananas. Everyone in the shop is rail thin with legs the size of sumo wrestlers. They have odd sunburns, from wearing those strange bike clothes. There is a subtle shuffling in the store; the serious bikers head for the back. The last guy left standing has to wait on us.

"We'd like to buy bicycles," I say brightly.

"Ah," says the clerk.

"For triathlons," I add. the clerk looks us up and down.

"Really?" he says.

"Really," I reply.

I start walking toward the brightly colored, sleek looking machines hanging from the ceiling, but the clerk directs us to a different part of the store.

"Back here," he says. "I think you'll find more of a . . . price range . . . you'll be interested in."

In the end, we buy bottom-of-the-line Cannondales, $449.

"Excellent frames," says the clerk, "but the components are, well, compromised."

"No problem, I say, writing out the check. It is, I think, the first check I've written in support of The List. There should have been organ music in the background—it will not be the *last* check I write.

With the Cannondale, I figure I'm halfway—well, one-third of the way—there. There is my small problem with the water. We respond to this by hiring, for the sum of $7.50 an hour, a swim coach who, by his own admission, specializes in three-year-olds. He's a little puzzled about why I want him in particular, but I tell him it will soon become clear.

We meet at a pool later in the week.

"Okay," he says. "What I want you to do, Michael, is swim a couple of lengths of the pool so I can get a feel for your stroke."

"I can't swim," I say.

"Everybody says that," replies the kiddy coach. "But go ahead and show me."

I shrug and start dog-paddling. As soon as the water is over my head, I move smoothly to my second stroke, thrashing. The kiddy coach stands on the side of the pool scratching his chin.

"You can't swim," he says.

"No kidding."

He brings us back to the side of the pool. Susan, who can swim, strokes back. I climb out of the water and walk.

"What do we want to accomplish here?" the kiddy coach asks. "Do you want to feel comfortable in the water? Feel safer with your kids"—nodding to mommy Susan—"or just have fun?"

"I want to be able to swim half a mile in open water in six weeks," I say, smiling happily. The kiddy coach actually starts to laugh before he glances over at Susan, who is nodding in agreement.

"You're serious?" he says, a phrase I will become very familiar with.

I nod.

"Why half a mile?"

"It's a triathlon; that's the swim distance."

He nods.

"So you're not just talking about half a mile," he says. "You're talking about racing half a mile, with other people kicking and thrashing and knocking your goggles off."

"Right," I say.

"I think we'd better get started," he says.

I'm already started in the final third. We have successfully completed a one-mile run, although I did have to walk a little bit, maybe half. I realize that coaching myself isn't going to work. And not just for this triathlon. I am staggered by how much I don't know—and this is running, biking, and swimming. The implications for the rest of The List are sobering indeed. If I know so little about biking and running—forget swimming—how much *less* must I know about diving and rock climbing? I am unlikely to die in a local triathlon. I may wish I was dead, but, really, the risk is very low. I sit in my office and look at the 13 items on The List thumbtacked to the wall. I can't say the same for all those items.

So Michael's Rule Number One emerges—get instruction from people who know what they're doing.

Accordingly, I attend a lecture on nutrition at the local YMCA by one Myrna Haig, who is reputed to be the best triathlon coach in the area. She has bulled her way through all the local races and even competed successfully in the legendary Hawaii Ironman. Instead of the expected Amazon, I find a petite, dark-haired woman with a blaring voice and a spectacular sense of humor. After her talk, I hang around.

"I'd like to do a triathlon," I say.

"Cool," says Myrna. "Next season, you'll be rarin' to go."

"In six weeks."

She stares at me, but, amazingly doesn't blurt the expected.

"It's going to hurt," she says.

"But is it possible?"

"Like I said, it's going to hurt."

The problem, as it turns out, is one of start-up. It's not that I'm in bad shape, it's just that those particular words don't mean anything. There is no mythical "in shape." Being in shape, says Myrna, depends totally on what one wants to do.

"For example, you're obviously in shape for windsurfing, because you windsurf just fine. All that extra weight doesn't bother you," she says. Tact is perhaps not her strong point. "But for running, any extra weight hurts. And triathlon is that much worse. The whole is much worse than the sum of the parts."

She explains this while I sit on a stationary bicycle in a gym, seemingly hours before dawn, spinning like a hamster on amphetamines. I will spin on the stationary bike for an hour. Then I'll stretch for 15 minutes and head for the weights, which will occupy my time until the sun grudgingly comes up. On alternate days, I'll either bike or run with my workout partner. Three days a week, at lunch, I get my swimming lessons. In the evenings, I swim—or occasionally run a short distance.

Strength and muscle and jungle work, I chant from an old Warren Zevon song. *Strength and muscle and jungle work . . .*

On Monday, my "rest day," I will stay in my bed and hurt like a horse beaten by a savage owner. My shoulders will ache; my tendons will cry for mercy; the muscles of my legs will quiver like frightened birds, even when I am sitting down. I will get up only long enough to start the coffee and get a handful of aspirin.

"Well, it's your stupid list," says Susan. "You don't *have* to train this hard, you know."

But I do, I think. The List is becoming real in my mind, or, rather, I'm starting to sneak up on it. With each endless bike lap around Davis Islands, a residential development near my house, I seem to be a little closer to the jumping off point. *Well, they're not totally impossible.*

Slowly, but surely, I learn to swim, just like any happy three-year-old.

"I'm going to try this with you, Michael, and I don't want you to be insulted," the kiddy coach says one day. "The problem is you want to hold your breath when your face is underwater, which is causing you to run short of air, which is causing you to panic."

This is, I admit, a problem.

"So we'll try this. I tell my kids to actually say, 'blow bubbles' when their face is under water," he says. "So I want you to say, 'Mikey blow bubbles,' all the while blowing bubbles. See?"

Mikey blow bubbles?

I nod. I put on my goggles—the first pair I've ever owned; yet another check—take a deep breath, and head toward the deep end of the pool.

Mikey blow bubbles... Mikey blow bubbles... Mikey blow bubbles...

To my complete surprise, it works.

Later that night, at dinner with my friends, one leans across the table and grins: "*Mikey blow bubbles,*" he says.

Suppose, I think, I do the entire List. How does it have to work? In addition to training like a lunatic, I am poring through books on sports training. Unfortunately, what I'm finding is they're all very sports specific.

"Well of course they are," says Myrna one morning after I point this insight out. "The best way to train for running is to run; the best way to train for biking is to bike. That's the way the body works."

But what if, I persist, you don't want to just run or bike or even just do triathlons? What if there's a broad range of activities you have planned? Don't you need to be able to, somehow, shift gears?

"What is it you plan to do," she asks suspiciously.

So I start telling her about The List, about windsurfing big air, about the Kamikaze, about Alcatraz and climbing Denali and sky-diving and all the rest of it."

"Holy shit," she says. "I knew you were crazy from the start."

What's crazy about it, I persist?

"About half of that stuff is fatal," she says. "The other half is real hard."

Okay, I say. It's a training question. Can I train for a range of outdoor sports?

"Yeah," Myrna says, "but it's going to hurt."

This is, I think, *not news.*

The triathlon is two weeks away, and that knowledge has settled into the pit of my stomach. I have actually been able to swim 8 lengths of the pool without grabbing onto the side. My excitement at this fact is slightly tempered by the fact that a half-mile is 32 lengths of the pool. And, secondly, I wonder who is going to paint a black line along the sand floor of the Gulf of Mexico so I'll know which direction to swim.

"No time for finesse, Michael," says the kiddy coach finally. "You're just going to have to stop and look."

The biking and the running, though, are going just fine. Your body bitches and moans and whines about the load, then, one morning, you notice that it's no longer bitching and moaning and whining. It's as if your body is a totally separate entity from your mind. It wants to do what it wants to do, and it doesn't like your pesky mind telling it what to do. So it tries every trick in the book to make you stop doing what it doesn't like, and start doing what it likes.

"It's like there's a little guy inside you," says Myrna, "and you're always negotiating."

Okay, I think to my body, *I'll deal. We have a long way to go, and we're going to be pushing very hard. I'm going to ask you to do stuff you're not going to like, but, afterwards, we can rest, hit the beer, whatever. I won't break you, won't do any permanent damage.*

You just gotta go with me when I need it. Unscientific as hell, I think, but it's all I got. There is no response from my body, at least, none that I can tell.

If I'd been sleeping the morning of the triathlon, the thunder would have woken me up. Lightning arcs across the sky as I load the bottom-of-the-line Cannondale on the back of Susan's car. Before we're halfway to the race site, before the sun has even considered coming up, it is pouring down rain.

"Maybe they'll cancel," I say.

"Naw," says Susan. "Our luck's not that good."

We join a long line of cars, and while we're waiting to park, the rain stops.

Shit, I'm actually going to have to do this...

First you swim half-a-mile, then you bike 15 miles, then you run three miles. In between the three events, you stumble around the transition area and pretend you know what you're doing. I lay out my running shoes and a towel next to the bike, then I take my goggles and a swim cap and go stare at the water. It is about 20 minutes before dawn, and the water is black and cold.

It's your stupid List...

We line up by age groups, and, on the sunrise, we go into the water. It is, I imagine, much like being in a blender with 500 of your closest friends. Arms and legs are thrashing, the water is boiling, there's the occasional curse. Eventually, I'm able to swallow my panic and start some semblance of swimming.

Mikey blow bubbles... Mikey blow bubbles... Mikey blow bubbles...

I raise my head, and I am swimming at a 90-degree angle to the rest of the swimmers.

Whoops...

But the swim passes much faster than I had expected (and, luckily, the water at the turnaround point was shallow enough to allow me to stand up for a minute while the crowds passed), and the bike and run went slowly, but good. Neither Susan nor I finished last, which was our clever pre-race strategy.

"I knew you could do it," says Myrna, toweling off the dirty salt water.

"How?" I ask.

"Because you're crazy," she says, not particularly joking.

And for the first time, The List is real to me. It's do-able, as my friend Roger is fond of saying. Not easily do-able, but not totally out of reach, either. And I am beginning to think the deal with my body is do-able as well. You deliver when I need it, and I'll never abuse you. On the way home, I start laying out another training program, just as hard, but without such a specific goal.

"That was the hardest thing I've ever done," says Susan, and I agree. "You're gonna do The List, aren't you?"

"I think so," I say.

"Who's going to coach you?" she asks. "I think you're out there by yourself on this one."

"I'll find someone."

"Good luck."

4

Brain Aerobics

SUPPOSE, I THINK, I JUST TREAT THE LIST as a long triathlon? I've already gotten past the first step (I think), which is always alleged to be the hardest. If I just train and train and train, I should be okay.

Okay?

Maybe not so okay. The more I plow into the research for extreme sports, the more I find an interesting vacuum. I can find lots of older material under the loose heading of "adventure." These stories read, roughly, like: "Headhunters! How I Crossed Borneo With A Camel Between My Lips And A Babe On My Arm." This is, I suspect, not what I'm looking for. There's also the deluge of sports specific books—how to train for practically everything. But each one I read seems rooted in the premise that the sport described is going to become your primary avocation, your religion, your entire life.

What is missing is that ephemeral feeling I had windsurfing big wind; that feeling of having the nonessentials stripped away by the wind, until nothing remains but the pure processing machine. Yes, that feeling is tied into the physical; but it's tied into the mental as well. When I reorient myself toward sports "psychology," most of what I find is along the lines of "Visualize Your Way To A Faster Six Mile Run!" Specificity again, with a different spin.

The windsurfing experience haunts me. I spend some time trying to divide out what was physically hard—holding a sail in a 60-mile-per-hour wind, bouncing the board over the fierce wind-driven chop—and what was mentally hard—controlling a level of fear that I was totally unfamiliar with, a fear so profound and so powerful that it threatened to reduce my brain to nonfunctioning gray Jell-O. Yet the most frustrating thing to me is that this physical stress/mental terror produced the most sublime of experiences that had nothing to do with either stress or terror. Instead, the combination of the two seems to kick me to a whole different level, a whole different experience. The question seemed to be, what was that experience?

"Oh," says a friend of mine who's been sharing the now-standard early morning runs, "you mean The Fear."

"The fear?"

"No, no," she says. "Not, the fear, lower case, but The Fear, upper case."

What's the difference?" I ask.

"Let me give you an example," she says. "Each year, my family does some sort of camping trip together. Last year, we decided to learn to rock climb. So I'm out there on this ledge, maybe 50 feet above the ground. And I've got a rope on and everything, but I look down, and I just seize up. It's like a system malfunction or something. I couldn't go forward; I couldn't go backwards; I couldn't go up; I couldn't go down. When I closed my eyes, all I could see was this white light. That's The Fear."

What, I ask, had she done?

"Nothing," she says. "There was nothing I could do. I stood on that ledge for an hour with all these people talking to me telling me it was okay. Then I climbed down."

But it's more than The Fear, I persist. It's like The Fear kicked in some kind of accelerator, maybe caused me to go out and recruit some additional brain cells that were just hanging around doing nothing.

She shrugs.

"You had a good day," she says.

But I am convinced it is more than a good day. The List, I know, is all tied up in that singular experience, that sense of everything *working*, of being caught up in an experience bigger than I am. Since The List began growing in importance in my own mind, I've been regularly asking the same questions of friends and acquaintances: Why do some people feel obligated to go to extremes? What is the appeal of the edge?

The answers have a boring monotony about them:

Because some people are stone crazy, or *because some people are addicted to adrenaline.*

That can't, I think, be all there is to it.

My friends shrug.

What I really need, I think, is a guide to brain aerobics. I start in the dojo, the gymnasium of the martial artist, where I have spent more than a few years. What I remember is an interesting fact about sparring, fighting. The more you think about fighting while you're in the circle, the more you tend to get your chimes rung. This I learned through painful repetition. Instead, I fight best when I am not there, the personality, the *me*, strictly along for the ride. It took me years to figure out that when I got mad, I kept getting bopped on the head. But being absent didn't mean I wasn't aware. On the contrary, I was never quite so aware as I was when I stepping into the dojo's fighting circle.

"Awareness," wrote Bruce Lee, the patron saint of all martial artists, "has no frontier; it is a giving of your whole being, without exclusion."

I was coming to accept that, at least for me, awareness and fear seemed pretty chained together. After all, in the dojo, it was a fear of seeing stars and spending the next six weeks taping my ribs that seemed to move me to a different state; in windsurfing, it was the fear of sleeping with the fishes that tripped my experience.

It is also clear to me that time itself seems chained to those elements of awareness and fear.

One of the first things I learned—which I had already learned intuitively—is that time is not what we think it is. When we think of time, we see a linear beast; it starts in the past, and it goes to the future. A minute is a minute is a minute.

But somewhere out on the edges, a minute is no longer a minute. Time stops making linear sense and becomes something much more subjective. In 1982, Larry Dossey, a Texas medical doctor and professor, wrote a book called *Space, Time & Medicine*, where he touched briefly on an interesting point:

"Many athletes have described experiences of time that resemble nonlinear, nonflowing spacetime," he wrote.

The book has a number of anecdotes aimed at showing time not as the spinning hands of a clock, but as some plastic pseudosubstance that changes, depending on our experience.

Dossey sums it up this way:

"In baseball, the bat and the ball are one; the batter can't miss. For the pitcher, the curve ball breaks perfectly, the fast ball is alive and hitters are retired in effortless sequence. For the basketball player the ball and the net form an arc of oneness from the moment of the ball's release. In all these moments there is an inexplicable and ineffable sense of perfection and flow."

Hummm...

Much of the early research on risk concentrates on a phrase I am coming to hate, "thrill seeking." I am not sure what this means, and it doesn't seem to me that the researchers are that far ahead.

"People," Melvin Konner writes in *Why The Reckless Survive*, a 1990 book, "don't think clearly about risk."

He then cites earlier research that lumps "sensation seekers" into four dimensions—thrill and adventure seeking, experience seeking, disinhibition, and boredom susceptibility. Sort of the collected pathology of high risk. Sensation seekers, he notes, also seem to have an inordinate amount of sex, presumably with each other.

And don't forget, Myrna Haig reminds me, "flee or fight."

Ah, yes, flee or fight, that chemical leftover from our ancestors' days on the veldts of Africa. At its very basic, flee or fight is really very simple—when presented with a threat, our body gears up to either fight the threat, or get us the hell out of the way.

There are a whole series of well documented physical changes as our body revs up. Adrenaline gets us ready to lift cars off babies; endorphins, pain blockers, prepare to insulate us from the consequences of lifting that car. More importantly, there proves to be a body of new research suggesting that fear heightens our learning ability—something that scares the hell out of us is more likely to be lodged permanently in our memory cells.

"If you touch a scalding radiator when you are three years old," says Michael Davis, who studies so-called "fear learning" at Yale, "You never touch a radiator again."

We're getting somewhere, but it takes yet another psychologist to put it together for me. The link that Dr. Mihaly Csikszentmihalyi provides is to get beyond the negative connotations of fear learning to suggest that things that are hard, things that are scary, things that push us to our limits and beyond can create a unique mental occurrence.

He calls such occurrences *flow*, optimal experiences.

"When all a person's relevant skills are needed to cope with the challenges of the situation, that person's attention is completely absorbed by the activity. There is no excess psychic energy left over to process any information but what the activity offers," he writes in *Flow: The Psychology Of Optimal Experience*. "As a result, one of the most universal and distinctive features of optimal experience takes place; people become so involved in what they are doing that the activity becomes spontaneous, almost automatic; they stop being aware of themselves as separate from the actions they are performing."

The concept of flow—defined by Dr. Csikszentmihalyi as *joy, creativity, the process of total involvement with life*—is hardly new. The great Japanese swordsman and Zen master Takuan wrote hundreds of years ago:

The mind must always be in a state of "flowing," for when it stops anywhere, that means the flow is interrupted and it is this interruption that is injurious to the well-being of the mind. In the case of the swordsman, it means death.

The Chinese sage Chuang-Tzu wrote, "Flow with whatever may happen and let your mind be free. Stay centered by accepting whatever you are doing. This is the ultimate."

Whenever we hear from our top sports figures or artists or performers, they consistently talk about "flowing with the universe," "going with the flow," "being totally involved." Yet we continue to think of risk in terms of *rush*. As if the adrenaline is the entire experience. And is such a cheap experience worth having?

Dr. Csikszentmihalyi's contribution to my own thinking is that he doesn't look on risk-taking as a pathology, a disease.

I stumble on some of the last pieces of the puzzle in an odd place. Massad Ayoob isn't a psychologist or an athletic trainer, although he's actually a little of both. What he is is a cop, a cop who teaches self defense strategies, both armed and unarmed, to cops and civilians. When we first start talking, he quickly takes over the conversation. People in high stress situations, such as cops, he says, have to learn how to function in those situations. That includes dealing with the huge chemical dump triggered by flee or fight.

"You know how time changes, usually slows down," he asks.

I nod.

"You can use that," he says. "If time is slowing down, and you expect time to slow down, you have more subjective time to act. But you've got to be ready for it if you're going to be able to use it."

Life-threatening stress, Ayoob adds, also triggers a whole series of perceptual narrowing—tunnel vision, acute hearing, loss of fine motor control of the muscles.

"You're body's giving you a different set of tools," Ayoob says. "Like any tools, they have their limitations. But if you learn to use them, you've got a hell of a better chance of coming out of this stuff alive."

And so we try to avoid risk. Our current culture of cynicism masks a deep-seated fear of change and of the risks that drives the change. In our personal lives, we accept the government's (and the legal system's) position that life should be free of risks—hence the proliferation of liability laws. Our businesses have been hampered— even crippled—by steadfastly clinging to a status quo that clearly isn't working.

"Rather than encourage the type of cautious experimentation that defines good management," says Daniel Kehrer, "many American companies have so far spent their greatest resources trying to *avoid* risk."

And yet there is, always, a hunger.

The urge for risks in sports, writes sports philosopher and martial artist George Leonard, runs counter to the tendency in modern industrial society to reduce or eliminate risks from every aspect of life. "The arena of sports," he writes, "has provided a place for people to take calculated risks without breaking the law."

My experience on the windsurfer is even more complicated than I'd imagined, warping the very limits of time and space. But as people, aren't we more complicated than we'd imagined? As I think more and more about The List, there is one more quote that stays in my mind. It is, again, from George Leonard, in his small book titled *Mastery.* "Whatever your age, your upbringing, or your education," Leonard wrote, "what you are made of is mostly unused potential. It is your evolutionary destiny to use what is unused, to learn and keep on learning for as long as you live... How to begin the journey? You need only take the first step. When? There's always now."

There is still one last building block I need to discover. I come across a reference to an athletic trainer named Steve Ilg, of Santa Fe, New Mexico. Ilg teaches what he calls "Wholistic Fitness," and his basic mindset is that people are whole units and need to approach training from that perspective.

"Specialization," he writes, "is for insects."

I find a copy of his book, *The Outdoor Athlete*, and I am struck by his beliefs about training, about mental training and about the edge.

"For the most part," Ilg writes, "the mainstream regards multi-sport athletes as oddities, like we're some eccentric aberration of the gene pool. As close to the multisport wilderness that the orthodox sports media will venture is the triathlon. But here's where the problems begin. Triathlon is not a good example of a multisport. It's still a specific sport, all endurance oriented. Genuine multisport performance requires fitness at the extremes... At the elite level, the true multisport athlete should be able to run or cycle at an ultra distance, back squat two and a half times bodyweight, climb at a 5.12 level and do it all with spiritual depth... "

Okay, I'm not sure what he's talking about, but it's starting to make sense. I give him a call and, without preamble, launch into an explanation of The List. He listens, asks a few questions, and finally comes out with the best comment I've heard in a long time: "Cool."

I have found a guru for the edge.

5

Hanging Out
in Death Valley

THE FIRST CLASH WITH REALITY comes when the rubber meets the road, or, more honestly, when the sneakers meet the dirt. I am methodically (and painfully) turning myself into the slowest runner in the world. Train though I might, in the end, I suspect running will have the upper hand. Still, it's a necessary step, I grudgingly admit, if I am ever going to get anywhere. I can see the edge, and it seems far off in the horizon.

This obsession with running is triggered by the first contact between The List and the obstacles. I have decided, for reasons that are not totally clear to me, that the Death Valley run, Item 11, would be a good starting point to get me out in training and into doing. It takes me a couple of weeks of phone calls to find out anything about that Death Valley race, which turns out to be the Hi-Tec Badwater 145-miler, sponsored by a sneaker company, Hi-Tec. I learn this from an ad in an old magazine someone loans me, which is a font of information. I learn, for example, that the race, 145 miles of living hell, across Death Valley, over two mountain ranges and up the highest peak in the continental U.S., was created to promote a trail running sneaker, which is no longer being manufactured. Upon seeing a picture of the sneaker, I understand why it is no longer being manufactured. In a world of sleek, high fashion athletic shoes, the Badwater sneaker is butt ugly.

I call the toll-free number listed on the old ad, and eventually end up talking to Dave Pompel, the genial Hi-Tec exec who handles the race. Can I, I ask, just jump in and run the next race, which happens to be a few months away?

"No," Pompel says.

"Why not?"

"Because," he continues, "this is one of the hardest running races in the world, and—correct me if I'm wrong—you don't strike me as being an elite ultramarathon runner."

Well, I reply, there's something to that.

"Also, the race requires a sag wagon carrying your water and medical support," he says. "I don't suppose you have a sag wagon lined up?"

Well, I say, not exactly.

I think about the situation for about a minute while Pompel patiently waits. I need to do something, or The List is going to die before it even gets started.

"Can I come watch?" I hear myself asking.

"By all means," says Pompel. "And bring a bicycle."

Perfect!

I have already purchased a battered mountain bike from the classified ads, which I'm going to use in the Kamikaze Downhill. Death Valley, two mountain ranges, and the climb up Mt. Whitney ought to get the kinks worked out of the bike.

"I'll be there, " I say. "Death Valley in July sounds wonderful."

"Bring water," Pompel adds. "And lots and lots of sunscreen."

The cheapest airfare is into Reno, which is, of course, nowhere near Death Valley. Nonetheless, my bicycle and I arrive in the ratty gambling town late at night, where we pick up the rental and head through the relentless neon into the cool dark of the desert. I camp out in a cowboy motif motel near the desert town of Lone Pine, and head into Death Valley the next morning.

Did I mention the heat?

By 10 a.m. it is skillet-hot, the whole world taking on the smell of glowing iron, while the temperature of the rental car climbs perilously into the red. I look at the first rising hills, and I realize that the air conditioner, never perhaps an optimum piece of machinery, wouldn't make the climb. I shut if off and roll down the windows.

There is only one radio station I can find as I creep into the blistering mountains, and the disc jockey is performing an on-air exorcism on one of Satan's minions, a 16-year-old fan of Dungeons and Dragons.

"I want," the announcer shouts, "to speak to the demon! Speak to me, demon!"

The boy makes a choking noise. "I can't!" he screams, although it comes out something like, "Ah caned! Ah caned!"

Suddenly, the boy's voice changes.

"Damn you!" the boy shouts in a new voice. "Damn you and your Jesus!"

Amazingly, the announcer cuts to a commercial for Diet Coke. The car is moving about 10 miles per hour up the steep grade. Every few miles there's an iron water tank for overheated radiators, and the rising heat creates a twisted carnival mirror effect. The distant mountains dance and twist, and I wonder how far we are from the Charles Manson homestead.

"We now join live, on the air, a battle for a man's soul," the radio announcer is whispering, breathlessly. "There's some rough language, but, people, we are dealing with Satan himself, right now, live!"

We creep on.

"It was Satan, Beelzebub, the Beast Himself that made you kill those little animals, wasn't it! Wasn't it!"

"Damn you! Damn you! Damn You!"

I am beginning to wonder whether this is such a great idea after all when we top the last hill and I see the long roller coaster ride into Death Valley proper. It looks... hot.

I roll on through the desert, past ghost towns and moving sand dunes, until I come to a sign that reads: "Ahead—Dates!"

After hours of steady exorcism, the idea of a date in Death Valley is a little frightening. *Date palms, of course*—the oasis in the middle of the desert. When I arrive, the place strikes me as hell's own Holiday Inn, a flashy stone building resort surrounded by date palms. There's even a pool, filled with German and Japanese tourists who appear to have all been dipped in the last existing batch of Red Dye #2. Welcome to Furnace Creek, and pass the sunscreen. This is race headquarters.

"Be gone, demon! Back to The Pit! Be gone!"

When I shut off the ticking, clanking car, the demon is still hanging on, but I sense it's a close battle.

I check in, stow the bike in my room, and head for the mandatory prerace meeting. There are 15 entrants this year, and for the privilege of running across the desert and up assorted mountains, each entrant will receive a plastic water bottle and a t-shirt. Finishers will receive the coveted Badwater belt buckle.

The race is simplicity itself. At 6 P.M. tomorrow, the contestants will travel the few miles to Badwater, at 282 feet below sea level, the lowest point in the United States. It's called Badwater because there is, in fact, a pool of water there, so laced with alkalis of various sorts that it's a nasty, poisonous chemical stew. Badwater is south, deep into the valley, past the Devil's Golf Course, in the shadow of 11,000-foot Telescope Peak.

The temperature at the race start will be around 125 degrees. Six feet above the blistering, shimmering asphalt—roughly at head level—the temperature will be closer to 160.

"Last year," one of the racers chortles, "some peoples' air pockets in their sneakers blew up!"

The runners will head north onto U.S. 190, the main two-lane blacktop that carves across this Road Warrior landscape. The runners will pass Furnace Creek, heading toward Stovepipe Wells, a wide spot in the road on the edge of the great migrating sand dunes.

With luck, the runners will hit the first of the mountain ranges, the Panamints, around dawn. They'll creep up the road I coasted down, headed toward 5,000-foot Towne Pass, where they'll have a relatively straight shot down into the brilliant salt flats of the Panamint Valley. The runners will have another climb into the tail end of the Inyo Mountains, before heading down onto the long, flat stretch into Lone Pine and the entrance to Mt. Whitney. The run to the entrance to the Mt. Whitney park is 13 miles, with almost a 9000-foot elevation gain. At the portals, the clock stops, and the race formally ends, because the Park Service doesn't allow races to be run on public land. Most runners, though, Pompel confides, will continue informally to the top of Mt. Whitney, elevation 14,494 feet.

The temperature at the portals will probably be in the 40s, although it could easily dip to below freezing. Snow is a possibility.

There is no water on the course, no medical care available, no food and supplies for the hottest part of the run. There is also a 60-hour time limit. The fastest runner will hit the portals in under 30 hours.

"Is this a great race, or what?" says Pompel.

I have decided to follow, mostly, Marshall Ulrich, a 30-something Colorado runner who has made the race his own. When I call his business to let him know I'm coming, his secretary tells me he's not in.

"He's out running across the state," she says without a trace of irony. "He'll be back in a few days."

When Marshall and I finally meet, he is what one would expect from a person who thinks running across a state—any state—is fun—thin, wiry, and intense. He takes me aside to tell me his finely honed strategy for the race.

"If I can run flat seven-minute miles for the first 35 miles, it'll get me through the hottest part of the run with a minimum amount of contact between my feet and the pavement," he confides.

Makes sense, I say. I have run a seven-minute mile—exactly *one* seven-minute mile, and then I had to lay down on the track. I am beginning to think very kindly of Dave Pompel's foresight.

I meet some of the other racers—a rodeo cowboy turned banker turned ultramarathoner, a phys ed teacher whose husband "gave" her this race as a wedding present, a doctor who has just finished the Markleeville Death Race bicycle ride, and whose support crew will carry a coffin filled with ice, a lawn chair and an inflatable palm tree, plus a square of Astroturf for the lawn.

"Be gone, demon! Back to The Pit! Be gone!"

Early the next morning, just as a cotton candy pink dawn is touching the Funeral Mountains, I get up, slip on my shorts, T-shirt and running shoes, fill a water bottle with the warm, salty water from the tap and head down the road, toward Badwater. The thermometer by the pool reads a paltry 85 degrees when I start running, but I know as soon as the sun clears the Funerals the temperature will click up faster than a New York City taxicab meter.

I run along the sandy shoulder of the road, the only sound in the desert is my sneakers, crunching sand. The heat is dry, brittle, like a long spell of fever or crumbling old parchment. I imagine the greedy atmosphere leeching the water from my pores, moisture vanishing before it even has a chance to become sweat.

The desert is still, digging itself in for the hellish day to come. The only plant I can definitely identify is the dried arms of Death Valley sage, unique to this corner of the earth. I follow the pavement until I reach a turnoff onto a gravel road. I head down the gravel, deeper into the desert. The sun is beginning to make itself felt; half its blazing diameter is visible now above the Funerals. All across the gravel road are the twisted hieroglyphics left by the sidewinder rattlesnakes in the gritty sand. An hour passes, then another half hour. I finally stop, the sun blistering on my face. I've left the road and run up a jeep trail, which eventually dead-ends into a little box canyon. The snake tracks are thick across the floor of the little canyon, as if all the rattlers on the right-hand side decided to exchange places with all the rattlers on the left-hand side. I am sincerely glad I wasn't around when the word came to change sides. It is quiet and still, and all the people in the world are gone. I sit on an already warming rock and sip my tepid water, then run back the way I came, my treaded footprints overlaying the hieroglyphics. It is like running through a microwave oven.

Before the race start, I walk down to the murky pool at Badwater. The edges of the pool are crusted with white mineral deposits, and beneath the surface of the hot, deadly water, creatures dart. Life is persistent. Above us, high on the rocks, someone has painted "282 feet below sea level," to be sure we don't forget.

Strangely, the next time I'm this far below sea level, I won't be breathing air. But that's to come.

My plan for observing the race is simple—I'll ride my bike along with the runners, run some when I can. Get as close to the race as possible, the least I can do for The List. At 6 P.M., when the runners head off, the temperature is around 120 degrees.

I ride the first 26 miles—the first marathon—on my mountain bike, keeping tabs on Marshall, who is running effortless seven-minute miles, then drifting to the back of the pack, to talk to the doctor with the coffin. At one point, I pull a water bottle off the bike's down tube and proceed to spray 160-degree water into my face. Note to myself: Carry water on person; 98.6 degrees is substantially less than 160 degrees.

Watching a running race, though, is a little like watching paint dry, and once the full chill of the desert evening sets in, I ride the two hours back to the car, with about a billion stars to light the way.

Feeling vaguely guilty, I go back to my hotel room and sleep for four or five hours.

By dawn, Marshall is through the mountains. I drop back, and eventually pick up the rodeo cowboy turned banker, who's hiking his way up the steepest inclines.

"Want company?" I ask, and he nods. I'm able to drop my bike with the lone support vehicle, cruising up and down the lonely highway, and join him.

"You know what the strangest thing about races like this is?" he asks.

Other than the very fact of their existence, I reply, I don't have a clue.

"It's the changes you go through," he begins. Then we walk along comfortably for a bit.

"In something like this, where you're being pushed to the mental and physical limits," he says. "Strange things happen to your brain. It's like every emotion you've ever had—love, hate, fear, anger, all of them—at one time or another out here, they all come out."

He talks on as we walk, steadily uphill.

The thing is, he is saying, you can't pay attention to those emotions, either the good ones or the bad ones.

"They're like thunderstorms in the desert," he says. "there's big noise and flashes and the trees shake and the wind blows like stink, but it passes. It passes. And what you've got to do is stand there and let those storms blow past."

We walk awhile in companionable silence. Then he tells me about the rodeo, about his family, about running, about the endless string of miles that have somehow come to define his life.

"I think about that a lot while I'm out here," he says. "But heck, I think about everything."

Later, I ride for hours, up and down the increasingly spread out line. I am riding uphill, singing to myself, in the full heat of midday. My body is completely covered, except for my face, which is layered with sunscreen the consistency of tar. I pull up my shirt sleeve to scratch my arm, and I notice that I have apparently been dusted with flour.

Salt, I think. The moisture is leeched away, leaving the salt.

I continue my singing and peddling until my brain belatedly engages.

I shouldn't feel so good bicycling uphill in 120-degree heat. Ergo, I am on the verge of heatstroke.

I stop peddling, lean the bike against a convenient boulder and force myself to drink a full water bottle of hot, metallic-tasting water. In no time at all, I am rewarded with a splitting headache. Since I no longer feel like singing, I get back on the bike and start riding again. The seat is hot enough to sear my butt through the layers, and the metal of the handlebars is too hot to touch.

In the evening, right about full dark, one of the sag wagons for a woman runner flags me down.

"Run with her," one of her team says. "She needs some company."

So we load my bike into the sag wagon, and they drop me alongside the Phys-Ed Teacher, then leap-frog miles ahead to the next stop.

The first few miles are what you'd expect, comparing notes on homes and families and training regimens. She and her new husband have spent hours and hours on the road, sneakers joined together in holy matrimony, and this race is his gift to her. She is very happy. But the miles wear on, and the hour is late.

Every emotion, the rodeo cowboy, now far ahead, told me. *Every one.*

"You know my husband, right?" the Phys-Ed Teacher asks, abruptly, and there's an edge on her voice. It's after midnight in Death Valley, and there are still 90 miles of running left. The temperature has finally dropped below 100 degrees.

"I hate him," she continues. "No, I want him to die. That's worse than hating him, isn't it?" I tell her I think wanting someone to die is worse than hating them.

"Well, that's what I want. I want him fucking dead."

She runs for a while in silence, and I can imagine her teeth grinding in the dark.

"I hate this," she says, and she is crying.

Time passes; the sound of sneakers; occasionally, in the distance, the cry of a night hunter.

"I have to sleep," she says.

I know, I say, soon.

The miles and the night pass.

I run into her the next day, after she'd grabbed a few hours sleep in a real bed in a place called Panamint Springs. She squints at me through eyes that have seen a little too much nuclear sunlight.

"Did we run together last night?" she asks.

"For a while."

"Anything I say that sounded stupid," she says, "was the desert talking."

"Never thought otherwise."

Later, I zoom ahead to walk alongside Marshall up Mt. Whitney. He has been running for more than 24 hours with a total of 45 minutes sleep. He is haggard, destroyed—a *haint*, my granddaddy would say, the walking dead—methodically placing one foot in front of the other, up the mountain. At one point, his support crew is worried that he doesn't have enough fuel left to make it to the top. They decide on chocolate, M&Ms, and tell him to eat. But Marshall, at least the thinking, rational, laughing Marshall, is no longer home. He continues plodding up the mountain.

One of the crew puts a handful of the brightly colored candy in his right hand and rolls it into a fist. But the fist loosens, and the M&Ms dribble onto the ground.

Finally, his main support person puts a half-dozen M&Ms in his hand.

"Marshall," she says firmly. "Put the candy in your mouth."

He does so, without taking his eyes off the road ahead of him.

"Chew it," she says.

His jaws begin to work.

"Now swallow it."

He gulps.

It is the most agonizing performance I have ever seen.

Twenty-nine hours after leaving Badwater, he arrives at the portals, accepts the congratulations and goes to sleep. A few hours later, he gets up and runs to the top of Mt. Whitney and back down, setting an unofficial record.

I won't cheat again, I think, the desert rolling beneath the rental's wheel. *I won't stand by and watch again. The only way to be fair to The List is to do, not watch. Whatever it takes.*

6

Betting Time

Up until now, I realize, I've been playing at The List. It is easier to talk about extreme sports than to do them. A part of me likes the journalists' position, being able to stay one step away, as I did in Death Valley, from The Real Thing. The problem is that experience, that fleeting, mist-like sense of *flow*, will always be just out of reach for the non-participant. "There is no easy way into another world," wrote novelist James Slater, and I am faced with the truth of that statement.

Extreme sports are all over the media, from commercials for soft drinks and sneakers to MTV Sports, dedicated solely to extremes. NBC dedicates 90 minutes to the Escape From Alcatraz triathlon, complete with its now legendary swim through one of the great shark breeding grounds in the world; Nike builds the advertising for their new bike shoe around the Markleeville Death Ride, a grueling 150-mile bicycle race through seven mountain passes in Nevada and California..."You've got 35 miles to go," the ad reads, "but at least you're still ahead of the hearse." ESPN covers the Mammoth Mountain Kamikaze Downhill mountain bike race, which, based on the sheer number of injuries, may be the most dangerous athletic event in the country.

I am confronted with the "wisdom" of Yoda, from the *Star Wars* movies. When Luke Skywalker responds to a request from Yoda by saying that he has tried his best, the little alien Zen master snorts.

"Do or do not," Yoda says. "There is no *try*."

What is holding me back is the niggling knowledge that I'll be moving into the realm of "increased consequences." A part of me enjoys the bravado of those increased consequences. But another part of me is mindful of my age, of how much longer injuries seem to linger.

I am not a natural athlete. I am not an athlete at all, by my own definition of "athlete." At times, I think my body, which I occasionally negotiate with, is engaged in an active conspiracy just outside my hearing. I spend, for example, a couple of months working with a running coach, herself an Olympic-level miler. Actually, she was the second person I'd approached for some pointers in my running. The first, after watching me run, explained that he was a serious running coach, for serious runners. I was, at best, a *jogger*, which, I gathered, was something akin to what might be scraped off the bottom of a serious runner's sneaker. He suggested I call Coach #2, who, he assured me, had time on her hands.

To her credit, she dedicates herself to making me run faster. We have numerous, meticulously monitored running sessions. I spend blistering, hot days on the University of Tampa asphalt track, methodically recording my heart rate as I run myself senseless. We keep charts and graphs, monitor my food input, tweak my shoes. I run until I am sure my brain has become unmoored from my skull and is bouncing around its cavity like a wet tennis ball.

At the end of two months, we evaluate my progress, which has been . . . minuscule.

"I've never had a student who tried as hard as you," she says, "and got less."

I occasionally wonder what pieces are missing from my genetic code, what little strand of DNA got slightly amended in translation.

Whatever, but I realize that what's in front of me is going to be harder than what's behind me; more physical, more mental commit-ment. There's more risk, I think resolutely, but there's also more reward. I hope.

Risk is inherent in life, we say. Every choice we make involves some risk, so we all are, by definition, risk-takers. *Life* is risk. And that's true—to an extent.

"Trying to find a really good definition of risk is like hunting along a sandy beach for a one-carat diamond," writes *Parade* mag-azine editor Walter Anderson. "Every grain may have the look, but none has the substance."

What we really want to talk about is better described by busi-ness writer Daniel Kehrer as *dynamic risk*: "Dynamic risks are force-ful risks; they create their own energy and motion ... These are vig-orous risks, willfully undertaken."

"Sports and physical fitness, which both usually involve some risk, are, for us, an escape from work, a recreation, a self-absorbed experience, often more a question of body vanity than anything else," says Michael Korda, the enormously successful novelist. The *flow* state, Dr. Csikszentmihalyi says, comes when we ask our body and mind to reach for the limits; our best moments occur when "a person's body or mind is stretched to its limits in a voluntary effort to accomplish something difficult and worthwhile."

It need not be sports, but sports can be the shorthand, the teacher, that shows us what an optimal experience feels like.

The single event, I think, that pushes me to the next level hap-pens in Washington D.C., where I've gone to watch a friend run the Marine Corp Marathon and spend a little time in D.C. in the autumn.

I had stationed myself at a beautiful tree-shaded spot about 20 miles into the 26.2-mile run, next to a series of steps. I was watch-ing the runners go by when one of the last of the wheelchair athletes reached my spot. He was older than most of the wheelchair racers—my age, Vietnam age—and he was obviously exhausted. Since the wheelchairs couldn't make the steps, there was a ten-foot ramp next to the stairs.

The racer started up the ramp, and his arms failed. Five more times he tried the ramp, muscles bulging, his face bright red from the exertion, and five time he failed. The crowd, myself included, had gotten quiet. Other runners and the young Marines lining the course still shouted encouragement, but the man in the wheelchair was in his own world. On the seventh try, his face was blank, his eyes focused on a universe that was ten feet long. He didn't see the Marine behind him, openly crying. He didn't hear the other runners' shouts or feel those of us in the crowd. He just went up the ramp, an agonizing inch at a time. And when he finally reached the top, he just smiled, waved and kept going.

Vigorous risks, willfully undertaken.

I return home from the marathon ready to up the ante, increase the bet. It is time to take some risks.

7

Chips, Flakes, and the Last Hard Men

Here is the first emotion I experienced as a climber: Fear. Gut-numbing, mind-bending, limb-freezing, this-is-not-an-alert fear. My palms begin to pour sweat and my breathing shallows out, until I sound like a very overheated puppy. I feel the first stirrings of vertigo, as if the butterflies in my stomach have all suddenly taken flight and are flying in some strange formation. What's worse, I'm still on the ground.

"It gets easier," says my instructor, Clark Man of Santa Fe, New Mexico. Good, I think, trying—not succeeding—to look cool in my lycra. It would *have* to get easier.

I was afraid The List was going to go stale, that I was going to go stale. I was itching to get back to the field, which had given me pause. *Why* was I itching to get back into the field? What was the particular part of the extreme experience that was so compelling? I'd actually started thinking about that subject when a member of my old pre-List aerobic class asked me out for coffee one morning. Could I explain, she asked me, why her "normally solid and sane" husband not only went skydiving and managed to sprain something,

44

but was insisting on doing it again.

"It's one of those guy things," she says, her English accent making "guy thing" into a pejorative. *"Testosterone."*

I didn't know her husband; maybe he was suffering from testosterone poisoning. He wouldn't have been the first person I'd met who was. But I figured I at least needed to give his defense a stab.

"Suppose," I say, "that one afternoon everything worked a little better. Your vision was a little clearer; your brain seemed to process a little faster; your body seem to function a couple of years younger. How would you feel?"

"You'd feel great," she says, skeptical.

"And would you want to repeat that feeling the next day?"

"You're cheating," she says. "There's no way he felt that way from just jumping out of an airplane."

"Why not?"

"Because it's so *cheap*, you know," she says. "You give the people your money; you jump out of an airplane. So where's this mystical experience you're blathering on about?"

Where indeed?

But it makes more and more sense to me. I can get an easy agreement on physical training—when we push our bodies, they adapt to the stress. We want to run faster, so the body recruits other muscle tissue to help us. Tendons become stronger; muscles become more efficient. So what if we continuing stressing both the body and the mind? Does the mind as well as the body go out and recruit other nerve tissues to help out? Do the muscles in the head become more efficient at problem solving; stronger in their ability to think clearly while struggling through the chemical soup of "flee or fight?" If we accept that premise, then doesn't it also make sense that our bodies define this "enhanced" feeling as "good?"

Whatever, but I get a cheap ticket to go to New Mexico to learn to climb. The choice of Santa Fe is two-fold. I had read that the spectacular red rock cliffs around Santa Fe were perfect places to learn to rock climb. And, secondly, Steve Ilg is living in Santa Fe, and it seemed to me about time to sit down and talk to the master.

Rock climbing—scurrying up sheer cliff faces through the grace of muscles, balance, gymnast's chalk, and funny-looking shoes—is well on its way to becoming one of the glamour sports of the 1990s. Some definitions are in order here. When we think "climbing," we usually have visions of a group of hardy Sherpas slogging toward the top of Everest, or, at least, a younger Clint Eastwood in *The Eiger Sanction*, hanging onto the "Death Wall" of Eiger by his fingernails. That's alpine climbing. Sport climbing bears the same relationship to alpine climbing as racquetball does to tennis—a smaller, more frenetic version of the original. Instead of climbing mountains, which might entail some rock climbing, sport climbers look for relatively short, difficult sections of rock cliffs to climb. And they might spend days, months—even years—figuring out how to boldly go, as one T-shirt slogan puts it, "where only small lizards have gone before."

Muscles alone won't get you up the rock, I have been told.

"You can't just do pull-ups," says Denise Jackson, one of the three or four people in Tampa who actually climb. She is also my girlfriend, and yet another person who will be drawn into the orbit of The List. "Climbing requires finesse."

More than even finesse. Climbing demands balance, even grace, a dancer's sense of where your body is and how it moves. It's a mental game as well, as you pick your way along a vertical route, searching for hand- and footholds that are as often as not made up of faith as rock. Finally, there's the undeniable element of nerve—for a species that spent much of its formative evolutionary years in trees, falling is one of the ultimate nightmares. No matter how safely anchored you are, no matter that, *intellectually*, you know you're not going to hit the ground, that you may only swing a foot from the rock, a part of you wants to gnaw into that rock with your *teeth* rather than experience the slightest fall.

I have this one other basic problem about climbing, which is that I am seriously afraid of heights. When I first mention to my parents that I'm going to New Mexico to learn to climb, the announcement is met with gales of laughter. My Mother then recounts, in painful detail, one of the family nuggets. How, as a high school student, I was unable to walk up the stairs to the top of a fire tower, because I was dizzy from the height. How I stopped, in fact, on the second level, unable to look down.

"I won't look down," I promise. Still, though, it's a question I'm afraid I'll have to address.

"Like a lot of things in life that are worth doing, climbing has a risk attached to it," Dunham Gooding, head of the prestigious American Alpine Institute guide and instruction service, tells me. At 45 years old, Gooding has been climbing 29 years. "Unlike most sports, though, in climbing, the consequences of errors are severe."

"Think instructor," he says.

"It's not all that difficult to learn the fundamentals of climbing and protection systems," says Gooding. "With good instruction, you can substantially reduce your risks and progress quickly. Without it, good luck."

Finding that good instructor, though, isn't necessarily as easy as finding the politically correct lycra tights. My first encounter with a potential guide/instructor, plucked from the Santa Fe phone book, is daunting.

"So," says Potential Guide, "what'll it be? Top-roping, figure 5.5 to maybe 5.8. Boring, huh? How about me leading, maybe four pitch, average 5.6, couple of 5.9 moves that I'll help you over. You'll flash it no problem, then we'll rap off the back. Whatdaya say?"

What I say, is "Excuse me?"

Like any sport, I discover, climbing has developed its own specialized vocabulary, and my first step is figuring out what the heck these people are talking about. Next on the list is Clark Man, who proves to be my decoder ring.

In top-roping, he explains patiently, the instructor sets an anchor at the top of a cliff, then threads the climbing rope through the anchor and comes down. Back on the ground, the student climbs while the instructor or another student reels in the other end of the rope. If the climber falls, the other person on the rope, the belayer, catches the climber. In lead climbing, the instructor climbs first, setting "protection," various kinds of anchors, in the rock as he or she climbs, and hooking the rope into those pieces. When the instructor gets to the top (or a convenient ledge), the student then climbs and removes the protection, with the instructor above providing the belay.

"For new climbers, I prefer top-roping," says Man, "because I'm able to see the student climb, point out techniques and talk them over the rough spots."

A multi-pitch climb means simply that the rope is only so long, and at some point on a long climb, you're going to have to stop and reset the anchors. Think of the cliché, "coming to the end of your rope." In climbing, that's a reality. A four-pitch climb, means you're going to have to stop on four ledges, pull the ropes up, reset your anchors and start again.

All those funny numbers (called the Yosemite Decimal System) are a shorthand way of rating the difficulty of a climb. The "5" means that the terrain is difficult (or dangerous) enough that you need a rope and some sort of protection. The number on the other side of the decimal point tells you how hard the climb is. Obviously, 5.1 climbs are pretty easy; right now, the hardest climb in the world is a 5.14. Anything above 5.10 is harder than you can presently imagine. A 5.14 is the domain of either superhumans or Spiderman.

Also obviously, ratings are totally subjective; from my own painful experience, an Arkansas 5.9 is different from a Colorado 5.9.

"There are two things you need to learn," says Gooding. "Technical skills, such as safety, technique—where to place your hands and feet—and protective systems. The other thing is judgment, and that comes from experience."

Placing your hands and feet is hard enough. My first day, standing in front of a granite wall, I couldn't understand for the life of me how anyone expected me to get off the ground. No one was more shocked than I when, following Clark's instructions, I found myself actually moving *up*.

"One of the exciting things about climbing," adds Gooding, "is that it looks spectacular. It's really easier than it looks, once you know the tricks of the trade."

Part of moving up is Clark Man's steady, low-key coaxing, like a person talking to a frightened and potentially dangerous dog. In his early 40s, Man is, by his own definition, an "old hippie." He makes silver climbing jewelry, instructs, and occasionally competes. We are near the research town of Alamagordo, climbing on a series of cliffs that look vaguely familiar.

"They should," says Clark. "They've been featured in just about every cowboy movie ever made."

The trick (okay, the *first* trick) is focusing only on the move in front of you. You're not trying to climb to the top, you're trying to climb to that little ledge about six inches from your left knee.

"Look over to your right," he says when I'm about four feet off the ground. "See that little bump on the rock? Take your right foot, right about the instep, and put it on that little bump. Now stand up on your right foot." And I move up another two feet.

"Did I mention I was afraid of heights?" I say.

"Several times," replies Clark.

Part of the boom in climbing, I discover, is a boom in climbing "technology." I am, for instance, wearing "sticky" rubber climbing shoes. The rubber isn't really sticky, but it does adhere better than it has any right to on the rock. The soles of the shoes are also very, very stiff, making them unpleasant to walk in, but able to hold their shape on the little tiny edges of rock that Clark persists in pointing out as places to stand on.

The rope is connected to a climbing harness on my waist. A harness is exactly that—a harness around my waist and upper thighs. It's made of climbing webbing, which is strong enough to lift a car. The buckle of the harness is aircraft aluminum, designed so you thread the waist strap through once, then thread it back through to tie it off. No harness, Clark tells me, has ever failed in climbing.

The most fascinating thing to me, though, is the "protection." The idea is that when you're lead climbing, you want to protect yourself as you climb. The way to do this is to hook your climbing rope, which is still being fed slowly to you by your belayer below, into various pieces of protection as you climb. Then, if you do fall, you can only fall twice the distance between you and the last piece of protection. Makes sense, right?

Originally, climbers used metal stakes, called pitons, hammered into cracks in the rock itself. The problem with pitons was that they are destructive of the rock itself and became permanent, unsightly features on the landscape. In the 1980s, as rock climbing, as opposed to alpine climbing, kept growing, it was also strongly influenced by an increased environmental awareness. The idea became not just to climb, but to climb clean, to leave nothing behind on the rock. English climbers had pioneered the use of nuts, as in nuts and bolts, for protection. A piece of climbing cord was looped through a nut. To use it for protection, the nut was slipped in a crack in the rock, and the climber's rope attached by a carabiner, a metal loop. Then, the second climber could easily remove the protection. Nuts got sophisticated. Now climbers carry multiple sets of wired nuts, steel wedges crimped and soldered to a heavy loop of wire. The nuts are all different sizes, and there are several varieties of shape, ready for any size crack. I was particularly fascinated by an even more sophisticated piece of protection, a "friend," a camming device that compresses when the trigger is pulled and expands when the trigger is released. The cams can bite into the sides of a perfectly parallel crack, where a nut could find no purchase. Like nuts, friends come in all different sizes, from tiny to outright huge.

"Of course, learning to climb has to do with a lot more than the gear," says Clark. "It's a Zen thing, you know."

Denise has a theory about instructors in high risk fields.

"There's an 'instructor' personality. They're very quiet—a good instructor never raises his or her voice," Denise says. "But when they talk, you had better listen."

"Most of the climbers I know who are good teachers don't like sticking their necks out," Clark adds. "The last thing you want in an instructor is a daredevil."

The Fear is still there as I continue climbing, but it's heavily diluted by a fascination with going *up*. There is, I think, a lot of left-over kid in most people, and that kid wants to climb stuff just for the sheer love of it. Sometimes—especially for those of us with a baseline fear of heights—that's hard to explain, just like it was tough to make Mom understand why we had to climb that tree in the front yard in the first place.

But it's not something you really have to explain to someone, is it? If anyone has any questions, talk him or her into a day of instruction. The first time your detractor finds himself or herself sitting on top of a cliff, breathing like a steam engine, soaked with sweat and covered with chalk, just taking in the view, that person will understand just fine.

Climbing is appealing precisely because it goes beyond the usual push and shove of weight-lifting or the steady rhythms of running and cycling to blend strength and motion and—I'm still working on this one—grace into a vertical ballet.

Climbing is the flip side of the hammerheaded world of triathlon, which functions under the time-honored theory that *way more* is always better. Climbing refuses to respond to the "hit it again, harder" school of exercise. You have to *think*, not just *push*. You have to follow a vertical route that, on first inspection, might seem either impossible or invisible. You have to string together a series of moves that might involve everything from the big muscle groups like the lats and quads all the way to the tiny tendons of the fingers. You have to be able to flex like a dancer. Later on that first day, Clark says to me, casually, "Take your right heel, raise it over your head, and hook it on that little outcropping of rock." Excuse me?

To climb at all, much less to climb well, also requires that elusive body sense found in dancers and martial artists—*where is my body in space; where is my center?* All those things take place while a certain rear portion of your mind, the part that remembers climbing down from the trees eons ago, is screaming: *You're going to f...a...l...l...l...l!*

I never before realized how high, exactly, 50 feet is. Fifty feet is the base of the clouds, the top of Mt. Everest, within a few feet of where Daedelus' wings began to melt. The view from the top of a 50-foot cliff, out across a "Young Guns" landscape is more than amazing. It is an impossible landscape of sweat and fear and triumph.

It is as addictive as roasted peanuts on a hot afternoon.

I finally meet the ubiquitous Ilg at an alternative bookstore in downtown Santa Fe, apparently in a parallel universe to the high-ticket galleries and jewelry shops on the square. He's too busy to talk, but we make arrangements to meet at his tiny offices in the midday heat of the following day.

Ilg is like a cross between a gnome and Arnold Schwartzenegger, small, smiling enigmatically, but seriously *ripped.*

His office is a spare room, cluttered with books, gear and a small computer. It is hot, but, without humidity, the heat has no teeth. Ilg's blonde hair is spiked up, and he has a silver loop high on one ear.

"Welcome," he says, beaming. "We have a long way to go."

The great thing about climbing, he says, is that it helps a person appreciate that extreme sports are more than strength and muscle and sweat.

"It's about dance," he says.

Dance?

"Dance," Ilg beams. Ilg beams a lot. "Our problem is that we compartmentalize our sports, our activities, our training. But that's not how we are—we're whole beings, and our fitness needs to reflect that wholeness."

It is Ilg, after all, who has said that, "Specialization is for insects."

"Part of that compartmentalization," he continues, "makes us see climbing as different from running, or snowshoeing as different from dancing. In reality, they're all part of the same process. The experience is the same, which, of course, you already know."

Strangely enough, I do—sort of.

Here is my favorite climbing story, a year after I sat in Ilg's office:

My left index finger is bleeding through the athletic tape, and a tiny chunk of my right thumb is missing, as if I'd inadvertently pulled it out and left it somewhere on this Colorado granite. Which is, of course, exactly what I did. We are in Penitente Canyon, about four hours from Santa Fe, New Mexico, and a good two hours from the closest Mexican restaurant, no small feat in Colorado.

Penitente Canyon is a premier sport climbing area. Sport climbing is pure rock climbing, usually practiced on relatively short cliffs, say 50 to 100 feet... It is hard, fast and as addicting as Raisinettes at the Saturday matinee.

In sport climbing, you're supposed to fall. That's how you discover just how good you really are, and how you get better. Say what you want, it's still harrowing to me to feel that first peel away from the rock... *Millions of years of evolution tells me I'm*... *f...a...l...l...i...n...g.*

I stand at the beginning of the next climb, looking at the gray granite. Its texture is rough, gritty sandpaper shot through with sharp quartz. The first move is a high step. I'll get off the ground by using my sticky-soled climbing shoes to hold onto the rock while I pull myself up with my fingertips in a tiny crack. I'm almost ready to start when I notice something odd. I'm not nervous, although just a second before I wasn't sure I could do the first move. Instead of a blank rock face, I see a kinetic pattern, a series of moves, step-step-step. All I have to do is move. Before I can start thinking, I start up the face. The high step comes naturally, as does each successive move. My feet are always in the right places; my hands just where I need to be. Thoughts bounce through my mind, but they don't seem to be connected to anything in particular. I am past the crux, the hardest move, and to the top before I really have time to realize it.

And just as quickly, the world refocuses around me. My finger is still bleeding. My thumb still throbs. I am, however, not the same person I was, some few minutes ago...

8

Down

*"I'm learning to fly,
But I ain't got wings.
Coming down's
The hardest thing..."*
—Tom Petty

Here is the view from the top of Mammoth Mountain:
Down, a world of down.

We are above the treeline, 12,500 feet on a knob of bald granite. Behind me, a line of Lycra-clad bicyclists snakes back to the exit
from the ski gondola, which is how we got up this granite face in the
first place. Most look like gladiators, plastic pads on the knees and
elbows, plastic chest protectors and helmets that leave only the slits
of the eyes showing, leaning against two-wheeled devices that look
like a cross between a traditional bicycle and a UFO.

They are calm, some laughing, ignoring the wind-whipped dust
devils that howl up the side of the mountain. My head is pinging
from the altitude, my mouth dry and caked from a combination of
nerves, lingering altitude sickness, and last night's tequila, a sure-fire
cure for the altitude sickness that didn't even remotely work.

Ahead of me are five more Lycra-ed warriors and steps leading
up to a red ski chute. On the other side of the ski chute is three and

a half miles of down. The Kamikaze trail. I am wearing two T-shirts and garish biking shorts, the two T-shirts being clever protection against the sharp rocks and gravel I will be sailing over at about 45 miles per hour in just a few minutes. I look at the plastic chest protectors and want very badly to throw up. But I am too scared to throw up.

"So how many times did you get to practice the course?" the bike rider behind me asks. He is in blue Lycra with contrasting elbow and knee pads. Veins pop out of his forearms. Even his mountain bike looks mean.

"Didn't get here in time," I say.

"Do a lot of downhill races?" he asks.

"First one."

He looks nonplussed for a change. His bike even quits snarling at mine.

"Where do you live, anyway?" he asks, curious as to what kind of fool would make the Mammoth Mountain Kamikaze Downhill his first mountain bike race.

"Florida."

"Oh, wow," he says. "Good luck. And you'll need it."

I carry my silver Cannondale up the red stairs and position the bike in the chute. I am trying to think of something clever, something devil-may-care, to say, but I seem to have temporarily lost the facility for speech. Ahead of me, the chute drops ten feet to the Kamikaze trail proper, which, in turn, drops away for about 100 feet to a really steep drop, steep enough to make walking it hard.

"Peddle like a mother," the guy behind me cautions. "You loose traction, you gonna be sliding down the mountain on your butt."

Although I can't see it, I know that the drop feeds into a 180-degree switchback, which I will slam into at about 800 miles-per-hour, a watermelon seed spat out of the mountain. What happens, I ask another rider earlier, if I'm going so fast I miss the switchback?

"Well," he says, "you've got about 8 seconds to learn how to fly."

"You good to go?"

The starter shakes me out of my reverie. Ahead of me, I see mountains. The sky is bright high-altitude blue. The clouds are perfect picture postcard clouds. I want to remember them just this way.

"You good to go, man?" he says again.

"Yeah," I croak. "Let's do it..."

The List, The List, The List. How much mountain biking could one expect to find in Florida? Not surprising that I got all my information (misinformation?) from magazines. And while mountain bike racing is all the rage in the bike magazines, it is, in fact, hard, involving riding a bicycle up a mountain. But the downhills, I reason, have a much better ring to them. With the downhills, gravity would be shouldering part of the load, while I just push the occasional peddle and steer. And mountain biking was born on downhills, specifically the steep hills of Mt. Tamalpais in Marin County, California, across the Golden Gate Bridge from San Francisco.

Of all the downhills—Mt. Snow in Vermont, Deer Valley in Utah—the Kamikaze, beginning at the top of central California's Mammoth Mountain, is the most feared. The reason is simple—speeds on the 3.5-mile course can hit 60 miles per hour, with big rocks on one side and a cliff on the other. Over beer in the pizza place, this seems terminally cool. At those speeds, flying over the gravel and the ground-up pumice sand of the old volcano, control is more of a hopeful illusion than a reality. Common sense is no longer your friend, just as brakes, when applied, will no longer exactly stop you, and handlebars, when turned, will no longer make the bicycle go where you want it to go.

Before I head out west to face downhills, I watch a video of a previous Kamikaze. A racer comes out of a sweeping turn at some speed approaching warp-three, and suddenly his wheel begins to wobble. In slow motion, on my television screen, he heads toward an imposing boulder, which he smacks with his front wheel. The rider is suddenly and gracelessly no longer a rider. Rather, he is a flyer, airborne, sailing over the handlebars. Or, rather, what is left of the handlebars. The bike seems to be busily returning itself to its component parts—wheels going in contradictory directions, lengths of aluminum tubing leaving the frame. It looks like one of those industrial assembly films run backwards.

The voice-over is saying solemnly saying that, based on the sheer number of injuries, the Kamikaze may be the single most dangerous sporting event in America.

"Turn it off," my friend, who's been watching with me, says. She has been one of the voices of reason as I compiled my List, pointing out in perfectly moderate language that, for example, I lived in Florida, where the highest local mountain was a seawall. Where, she asks repeatedly, do I plan to train? "I've seen all I want to see. Have a great time out there."

She stands up and leaves the room. I glance toward my Cannondale, propped against the wall across from the refrigerator, in clear view of the television set. I am sorry I haven't blindfolded it.

I bought the bike out of a newspaper ad for $100 from a guy who'd just hit the Florida lottery for big bucks. It was yellow, two frames sizes too small for me, and had been ridden on the race circuit for two seasons. In short, it looked as if it had found it's own boulder to hit and disassemble itself. It was love at first sight. "I'll need to change a few things," I tell my friends, who have a good laugh at my ability to find such a great deal. "But, basically, I think it's a good ride."

Of course, I need to replace the wobbly wheels ($250), the shredded, battered gears ($150), the bent handlebars ($85) and the cracked, yellow frame ($275 trade-in). I keep the seat, the seat post, the chain and many other small, irreplaceable parts. The result is the sleek, fat-tubed, silver Cannondale leaning against the wall in my kitchen. It is a state-of-the-art bike; at least, state-of-the-art as defined by someone who'd learned everything there is to know about mountain biking from reading bicycle magazines. It rides great on the beach. I jump it off a seawall, and it lands just fine.

My first test run is in Colorado, down the fire roads that weave around Vail Mountain. I have dutifully ridden up Vail Mountain on a shaky rental bike, a measly 10,000 feet high, and I feel like someone has scoured my lungs with a wire brush attached to an electric drill. I convince my instructor, a smiling monster named Karen, to let me lie down for a few minutes before we start back down. She smiles a happy Colorado smile, one that you automatically give to an inferior species such as myself, and lets me collapse on a warm rock like some basking out-of-state lizard. Before I can achieve REM-sleep, though, it's back-to-the-bike time.

This time, I reason, it's down. No problem at all, gravity and all that.

"Follow me," she says, then disappears down a steep gravel road. I follow, and by the second switchback I can still see the dust kicked up by her knobbies. She is waiting for me at the fourth switchback.

"You are never," she says, without preamble, barely bothering with the smile, "going to get down this mountain if you don't let go of the brakes."

I notice for the first time that my hands have locked into rigid claws, reflexively curved around the brake handles. I tentatively try to loosen a finger, but the muscles in my wrist seem to have seized up.

"See?" she says, pointing at my claws.

"What happens if I let go and can't stop?" I ask, that being a perfectly valid question in my book.

"Silly Michael," says Karen. "You go off the mountain, and you die."

"Oh."

The day before, in order to avoid the Complete Novice designation, I rent a mountain bike at the Copper Mountain Ski Resort, which is open for biking all through the summer. I choose a Haro

Extreme bike, because it looks cooler than the others and because I don't really have a clue. Besides, the "extreme" part sold me. I also buy a book of local trails, three PowerBars and a semi-waterproof jacket I tape to the top tube of the bicycle. Then I head off into the Rockies, sublime in my ignorance. Because by this time I'm a pretty good bicyclist on a road bike, I decide to skip the basic fire roads and go straight to "intermediate single track," which I have read about extensively in *Mountain Bike Action* magazine. Single track is just that—a single track that threads up, down, and through the mountains. I begin on a wide trail that winds through a mountain meadow, wildflowers still blooming. *Cakewalk*, I think. A hundred yards later, the trail narrows and heads up. I ride as far as I can, wheezing for oxygen, which seems to be in short supply. Finally, I dismount and start pushing my Haro Extreme up the mountain.

The trail turns into a 12-inch-wide groove cut into the side of the mountain. To my left is "up," steeply climbing into the clouds. To my right is "down," a long, tumbling drop I prefer not to think about. I remount the bike and try to ride, but my eyes keep glancing to the right. Perversely, the front wheel keeps trying to follow my eyes. Finally, I settle for using the Haro Extreme as a sort of scooter, peddling a little, pushing with my feet a lot.

This isn't so bad, I think.

When I reach my first downhill, I'm in pretty good spirits for someone who's been scooting a bicycle along a trail for hours. I start peddling like a crazy person down the gentle incline. It's everything I imagined, a roller coaster without rails, but with spectacular scenery—skies, mountains, rocks, trees, streams, all whipping by like an Impressionist painting. At the bottom I plow through a shallow marsh, spraying icky black mud over the bike, my legs, and the surrounding flora. I am having a ball. The next uphill isn't nearly as bad, and I hit the downhill peddling, picking up speed, aiming for the next shallow marsh. I am whooping happily as I plow into the marsh at about 25 miles per hour. The marsh is at least three feet deep.

The bike nose-dives into the muck and stops, dead. I continue on, over the handlebars, my arms extended like Superman escaping from a telephone booth. I land face-first in the muck, my screamed obscenity muffled as my mouth fills with rich, black mud. For a second, I just lay there, then quickly sit up, coughing mud from my chipmunk-expanded cheeks and trying to clear enough gunk out of my eyes to see whether I'm permanently blinded or just encased in a muddy cocoon. When I can finally see something, I look around for the Haro Extreme, which seems to have disappeared. I finally see a single peddle sticking out of the marsh.

I pull the bike, which now looks like some touring vehicle for South Pacific mudmen, out of the marsh, then just plop down and look at the thing. It's hard to tell through all the mud, but the front wheel seems to have developed a strange cant. I pick the bike up and haul it to a shallow mountain stream, where I proceed to toss it in.

Probably can't hurt it any more, I reason, then join the bike in the freezing water. *Probably can't hurt me any more, either.* The bike is still mostly covered in mud when I haul us out of the water, but at least I can see that it is actually a bicycle. Next, I take off the front wheel, and, using a handy rock, beat on it until it is back in some shape resembling round. Then I wisely (and slowly) peddle home.

"Jesus!" exclaims the guy at the bike shop when I return the Haro Extreme, the front wheel bent, the bike and me caked with mud. "What in hell did you do to it? Never mind. Leave it. It looks like a local's been riding it."

"It's all in the brakes," Karen is saying. "Don't use 'em."

I nod intelligently. What I'm actually think is, *"Riiiiight. Bag the brakes. Wait 'til I hit something solid, maybe a tree, to stop . . ."*

"It's a question of trust," she continues. "You trust the bike. The tires are gonna grip. The bike's gonna track in a straight line. All you've got to do is sit on it without falling off. You're not going to need to manhandle the thing to make it do what you want."

I think of an old Bruce Springsteen lyric, about racing cars, *"As you jockey your way through the cars ... And sit out the light, as it changes to green ... With your faith in your machine ... Off you scream into the night ... "*

I'm on a rental Bianchi that's a sort of baby-food green. I don't like it, but it did get me up the mountain. We've been doing fire road downhills all mornings, and I'm beginning to believe Karen is right. The bike knows what it's doing. It's a feedback issue as well. A road bike travels on a smooth surface, and the message it transmits back to the rider reflects that. I once cracked 60 miles per hour on a road bike downhill, and I remember straining all my senses to catch even the tiniest messages coming back from the smooth asphalt, making micro-corrections to keep the thin strip of racing rubber in a straight, straight line. The messages from the mountain bike are blunter, less subtle—big rocks, loose gravel, the fat tires chewing up the surfaces. And I recall Ralph Waldo Emerson's about skating over thin ice: "Our salvation is in our speed ... "

When in doubt, go faster. Trust the machine to keep going over pretty much anything. Let go of the brakes and your fears at the same time.

"You ready?" she asks. I nod, and we again head down the mountain.

Faith in the machine ... faith in the machine ... We are picking up speed. The bikes fly through the curves, me hanging a few feet behind her rear wheel. I ride the chemical waves sluicing through my body, adrenaline making time go all mushy and soft around the edges, so slow that I see piece of gravel, caught my by tires, slowly arc and bounce away, over the edge. *" ... And you're in love with all the wonder it brings ... And every muscle in your body sings ... As the highway ignites ... "*

We fly into a long, steep drop, and I rip past her, taking advantage of my weight and gravity. I follow a line chosen by the bike, a bump here, a shift of weight there. I am *here*, but not *here*, in the calm center of a datastorm. Sight, sound, smell, the feel of the wind against my face, the terrain through the peddles, against the sole of my shoes, to my rapidly numbing hands. The same feel of the big wind against a small sail, the curious blending of physical and mental . . .

And we are down the mountain, flatlands, the speed rush behind us. I reel the bike in to a stop and lean against a tree, waiting for my instructor. She arrives a moment later.

"You graduate," she says simply.

The whole West is mountain-bike crazy. For those of you who've been in a cave the last few years, mountain bikes are the bastard offspring of those old fat-tired paperboy bikes from the 1960s and pure 1990s motorcycle technology. In fact, the first mountain bikes were old cruisers, beefed up and raced down the steep but trendy hills of Marin County. When the first manufacturers started making mountain bikes, a strange thing happened—people bought them like crazy. Not, however, because of the mountains. Although there was definitely the allure of buying a hard-core off-road machine, what really fueled the mountain bike fires was the simple fact that the things are easier to ride than high-strung, narrow-tired road bikes. I mean, you sat upright instead of in some weird European crunched up position; you got to roll right over rocks and gravel that would have previously landed you on your face; you could jump off curbs and be cool and, finally and not insubstantially, you didn't have to wear all that drastically colored Lycra that only looks good on about three or four people worldwide.

My Cannondale, largely because of my ignorance, is a surprisingly unsophisticated mountain machine. For a start, it is "unsuspended." This means that it does not have motorcycle-styled shock absorbers front and rear. I will learn about the utility of these devices later, as I ice my glowing elbows and wonder when the feeling is going to trickle back into my fingers. The more serious downhill racers' bikes have a huge front chainring, or gear, to help them achieve escape velocity on the way down. Their bikes also tend to be over built, since a little extra weight on a downhill is a plus, and the last thing you want to happen at 60 miles per hour is for some new trick component to break. On my few, brief rides before the race, I discover that my bike doesn't like to shift *under load*, that is, when I'm peddling hard. This is probably a function, says a local bike mechanic, of the bike being assembled out of spare parts by people who had only seen mountains in Jeep ads. I agree that could possibly have something to do with the problem. We try three different front *derailleurs*, the device that pushes or lifts the chain onto different gears, and each time, the bike balks under load. Finally, the mechanic pulls out the stops.

"Be back in a minute," he says.

He returns holding a Coors Light beer can, which he proceeds to cut into little strips. he then reassembles the derailleur with beer can shims in place. The bike works like a charm.

"I wouldn't bet on this for too long, man," he says. "What are you planning to do out here?"

"The Kamikaze," I say.

"No shit?" he says. "If I'd known that, I would have used better beer."

"You good to go, man?" the starter says again.

"Yeah," I croak. "Let's do it . . . "

There's a push, and a drop as the Cannondale comes out of the chute and starts down. I am in my biggest chain wheel—the gear in the front—and the smallest gear in my rear sprocket. I want torque. If I'm accelerating, my tires are gripping. I head toward the first steep drop, peddling for torque and shifting my weight to the rear to offset the steepness. Adrenaline hits like a hammer as my body shifts into overdrive. My vision narrows—*flee or fight*, I think absently, *focus on the threat*—my hearing is keener, my palms are sweating through the thick gloves. In seconds I am through the steep drop— steeper than I've ever been down—heading into the first switchback.

Faith in the machine . . . Faith in the machine . . .

Time no longer exactly means anything. People on bikes fly past me, 60 miles an hour to my piddling 45 . . . *45 miles an hour . . . I'm*

driving along at 45 miles an hour, open the car door, and step out .
. . Is the ground hard? My arms are numb to my shoulders from the
pounding coming up through the forks, to the handlebars. I force
my eyes to look far ahead, checking the terrain I'm sailing toward,
resisting the temptation to look directly in front of me. If the rock is
that close, I'm already over it. I've either fallen or I haven't. Bruce
Springsteen and Ralph Emerson alternate in my head, a sound track
running in some closed off compartment in my mind. *Salvation in
speed . . . Faith in the machine . . . Salvation in speed . . .* I realize I
am peddling as hard as I can, breathing like a bellows, welded to the
bike as we hurdle through another switchback.

I turn on to a wider road, and I realize, absently, that I am
almost down. I pick up my cadence, urging the bike onward. One
more turn, and I see the finish line ahead of me. I have been riding
forever, hours, days, months, and, suddenly, it's over. Nine and a
half minutes have passed since I was pushed out of the red chute at
the top of the mountain. My legs are wobbly as I steer the bike off
the course. I stop by a grassy spot and lay the Cannondale down,
then plop down next to it. I feel like a friction toy rolled off the end
of a table, mental wheels frantically spinning, adrenaline sloshing
around, winding down. My vision and hearing are returning to normal. My muscles quiver, and I realize my thumbs and most of my
other fingers are completely numb. I am barely able to take off my
helmet and wipe the muddy mixture of sweat and dirt off my face.
I am completely alone. I know no one in Mammoth. I lean back on
the warm grass, my ears buzzing from the altitude and the impend-
ing adrenaline crash.

I've dodged a bullet, I think. *I screwed up, didn't take the sport
as seriously as I should have.* When I close my eyes, I see the switch-
backs sailing past, flashes of blue sky and a red gravel road. I jolt
fully awake, as if I'd fallen into a *f . . . a . . . l . . . l . . . i . . . n . . . g*
dream. *Lucked out,* I think. Exhilaration tempered with fear. I think
about the rest of The List, watching the white clouds swirl above the
old volcano. *It won't happen again,* I vow. *I won't die for The List.*

I won't. It is an hour before I wearily stand and push the Cannondale back to the car. I go back down the mountain, go to my room and go to sleep. The next morning I get up early, ride back up the mountain and ride the Kamikaze course a half-dozen times, pushing harder, faster, each time down.

9

Between the Rock
and a Hard Place

Let me tell you about a bad day:

I am in San Francisco Bay, and I am swimming. Alone. The water is bitterly cold, the wind-whipped chop and swirling fog making it seem even worse. I have come to this freezing bay to train for the Alcatraz triathlon, with its infamous autumn mile-and-a-half shark-infested swim from Alcatraz to the mainland, but on this particular day it's too choppy and foggy to even make out the outlines of the old prison from my sea-level vantage point.

I realize I shouldn't be out in San Francisco Bay alone, that I have moved beyond acceptable risk into just plain stupid. I am, however, slightly lost. I have only barely started The List, and it has begun twisting my life around. I've run in Death Valley, done the Kamikaze, learned to rock climb. The general consensus among my best friends is that, having completed my "mid-life crisis," it was now time to get back to the real world.

"Look how far you've gone," says one friend, over pizza at the very same place where The List was created. "The joke's on everybody else. Not so long ago, there was a fat guy sitting in this room, and now there's not. You're strong; you're fast. What are you trying to prove?"

That refrain has suddenly become very common.

What are you trying to prove?

I think I would be doing better if I had the correct answer, which is, I think, something like: *I am trying to prove . . . my manhood . . . that I'm not as old as the calendar says . . . that I'm cool . . . that I'm attractive to members of the opposite sex . . . that I'm a baaadddddddoooggg . . .*

Instead, I say the truth, which is that I'm not trying to prove anything. I want, I say, to find out where the edge really is; see what it's like out there; taste it; feel it; smell it; touch it. I want that, you know, feeling of . . . well, that *feeling*. I want my brain to work better. I want to be caught up in that data stream, feel the bits and bytes flooding through my eyes and ears and mouth . . .

"You want the rush," my friends say flatly.

I'm not saying I don't want the rush, I reply, but I am saying the rush is only a tiny part of what's there, the experience.

Heads nod knowingly.

"I want you to meet a woman I'm dating," a close friend of mine says one night. "She's a shrink, and she's fascinated by people with death wishes."

"I do not," I say emphatically, "have a death wish."

"Have some more pizza," he says.

Later, I am at a party at a friend's advertising agency. I am cornered by a young woman in a basic black dress, long blonde hair hanging down her back. She steers me out of the herd, into an eddy, sits me down in a desk chair and pulls up a bench across from me. She leans forward on her elbows, and I notice her eyes are a muddy blue. I am, I think, trapped in a Calvin Klein commercial.

"Tell me what it's like," she says, stopping just short of licking her red lips, "when you think you're going to die."

I can't help myself. I break out laughing.

"I wouldn't know," I say.

She is clearly offended.

"Wouldn't know, or won't say?"

I take her hands in mine. They are slightly sweaty.

"I am not crazy," I say. "And I intend to live forever."

I stand up. She jots her number on a piece of paper.

"Call me when you're ready to talk," she says, tossing her hair.

On the way out of the office, I toss the paper in the garbage.

A couple of days before I'm scheduled to leave for San Francisco, my beloved Chow Chow dies unexpectedly. I pack for Alcatraz in a bleak, gray mood, dumping my clothes in a bag, spending a strained evening at the bike shop watching the mechanic go over my bike.

"You might want to pay attention here, Michael," says Bear, the mechanic, who keeps reassembling the Cannondale as I keep wearing the parts out. "I believe you're going to have to put this bike back together when you get to San Francisco."

I watch him spin the wheels, listen to the clicking of the gears. The next morning, I get up early and fly across the country. I doze off, and I dream of struggling in bottle-green cold water, losing my breath, thrashing and sinking and . . . I wake up with a start. We are landing in San Francisco.

I check in to my hotel, make a stab at reassembling the bike, then grab my wetsuit and a couple of towels. I hike down through the party time of Fisherman's Wharf, down to the Aquatic Basin—a small boat basin at the end of the Wharf, slip out of my jeans and sweatshirt and wrestle my way into the wetsuit. I stuff my street clothes in my backpack, then cram the backpack up underneath an old boathouse.

Without so much as a stretch, I hit the freezing water in a low, flat dive.

The cold seeps through my wetsuit; my shoulders ache; my mind rattles, focus lost, caught up in the motion of the bottle-green water.

There's something underneath me.

My stroke falters, my rhythm broken. I swallow dirty bottle-green water. I splash like a child in a kiddie pool. This is not a joke—they're under there, in that bottle-green water. The deep ocean killers, the tigers, the whites. Stupid, stupid, stupid.

Nothing. Nothing there but my imagination.

I begin stroking again, trying to get my breath under control, *Mikey blow bubbles*, I think, somewhat desperately. *Mikey blow bubbles.* But my stroke is all over the place. Instead of pulling water, the flat edge of my hand slips though the cold, dirty water of the Bay. I falter again. The fog seems thicker. I can just make out the entrance to the Aquatic Basin. I look around me, feeling the animal, my animal, in my head, throwing all its force into the bars of its cage. In my head, I see the bars bending and straining under the onslaught. I look around me for a boat, for another swimmer, for a log, for heavens sake.

But I am alone in the cold bay, trapped between The Rock and the hard place of my mind. The animal screams in my head. I tack back into the yacht basin, breathing shallowly, sweat pouring off my forehead into the cold, green water. It is maybe a quarter mile to shore, but my strokes are sloppy and my kick has fallen apart. The shore gets no closer. My arms and shoulders are aching now; my legs and feet are numb. I thrash, and, somehow, a hundred years later, I stagger onto the sand. I am burning up. I peel off the top of my wetsuit, sucking in huge quantities of the foggy air. Finally, unable to stand any longer, I collapse onto the sand and hug my knees, shivering and sweating at the same time. I bite my lip, and still a tear rolls down my cheek.

The next time I look up, I am surrounded by about a dozen foreign tourists, their cameras clicking away. Some laugh and point and talk in a language I don't understand. I put my head back on my knees, and, eventually, they go away . . .

Once you're on the Rock, goes the old country song, *there's no escape from Alcatraz . . .*

I don't even remember the first time I heard of the Escape From

Alcatraz triathlon, but there's no doubt how it ended up on The List: the swim. The legendary swim.

There are lots of harder triathlons. The Ironman in Hawaii, for instance, or the Earth Journey—three days of living hell—in Vermont. But only one features a swim that was—and is—widely thought of as, if not impossible, at least stone cold crazy. To me, that *mile and a quarter of treacherous water* between the old prison of Alcatraz and the Aquatic Basin in San Francisco is so lodged in the national consciousness that I couldn't pass it up.

"Think about it this way," a race organizer tells me over the telephone, "We tell everybody to stop half way across and take a good look, 'cause you're in a place damn few people have been and survived to talk about it." Hyperbole, to be sure. But, hey, even Clint Eastwood had trouble escaping from Alcatraz.

When I push the race organizers about why anyone would come up with such a race, now in its ninth year, they are blunt:

"Because," one of them tells me, "it's hard as shit. It's scary out there in the bay. It works on your head. The currents can be vicious. We've seen whirlpools develop. We've seen powerful—Olympic—swimmers dragged off course. And say whatever you want about how unlikely a shark attack would be, but they're down there. You know it. I know it. Everybody swimming in the race knows it. Let me tell you, that fact will never be out of your head, until you're too hypothermic to think any more."

To enter the race, I've signed the most comprehensive liability release I've ever seen. First is a general release, then paragraph after paragraph of what can go wrong—"drowning, struck by a boat or ship, animal attack, etc."—which I must initial. When I get to San Francisco, before I can pick up my race packet with my official race number, I have to sign yet another liability release. Finally, at the mandatory prerace meeting, I must *recite* a liability release into a microphone. You cannot, one of the race officials tells the crowd at the meeting, claim ignorance.

The swim, billed as 1.5 miles, is only one third of the race.

There's a 25-mile bike leg that weaves through the Presidio, past Seal Rock and out the Great Highway along the beach, looping back, crossing the Golden Gate Bridge, and finishing at the military base in the Marin Headlands. From there, you get at 13.5-mile run along the trails and roads of the Headlands, considered one of the tougher trail runs in the country.

The way it works is, just before dawn, we'll all get up and hike down to Fisherman's Wharf. Then, a bagpipe honor guard will lead all 250 of us plucky souls onto a ferry for the ride out to Alcatraz, where we'll all jump off the ferry into the freezing cold bay (actually, I exaggerate, the water temperature will probably be 50 degrees, easy), swim to the mainland, jump on our bikes, etc.

There are two things I've learned getting ready for Alcatraz. The first I've come to think of as the Second Law of The List: Escalation. Which reads, roughly, that the closer you get to an item on The List, the more it seems that you should have picked something harder. Instead of swimming from Alcatraz to the mainland, what you should be doing is swimming the English Channel, or maybe the Bering Strait. The Law of Escalation makes sense. The List grew from Ground Zero, a nonathletic-type person peeking through the keyhole at a distance world. The further I get into it, however, the more my view becomes that of a participant, surrounded by other participants. Some of those other participants, a very few, have done things that I couldn't have imagined when I started The List.

I discover, however, that even among elite participants, Alcatraz has an almost mystical feel to it. My informal poll on why people are here is usually answered, "Because this scares the hell out of me."

The second thing I discover is that no one actually knows anything. Everyone has an opinion on Alcatraz, but no one I know has ever done the race. Even the race organizers have their own weird spin on training: "Spend a lot of time in real cold water." Finally, at a local post-race party, I get the lecture that everyone has been waiting to give me.

"You're doing Alcatraz?" says a local triathlon champion, someone better on his worst day than I can aspire to be. I'm surprised he knows who I am, much less what I'm doing.

"Where do you think you are?" he starts winding up. "You live in *Florida*. The water temperature here is the same as a hot shower. Where do you plan to *train* for a freezing cold swim? Your refrigerator?"

I try to turn the lecture into a joke, but he's having no part of it.

"Seriously, Michael, you can drown out there," he says. "Alcatraz can hurt you."

I start to say that I know that, but he turns away and heads out the door.

"Have a good swim," he says, disgusted.

Granted, my training regimen seems a bit strange. I swim regularly with a masters swim group for my technique. Since my first triathlon, I've actually gotten to be an acceptable swimmer—in the pool. I decide that I need two additional items of training—cold water, and a long open-water swim. The first is easy. I will spend large amounts of time standing in cold showers.

"You're kidding," says my occasional training partner John Rodolf.

"Any better ideas?"

"Well, just don't expect me to stand in there with you," he says.

Secondly, as I live in Tampa, I will swim across Tampa Bay, which amounts to about two and a quarter miles.

"Remember when we were out sailing in the bay," says Karen Luzier, who owns a wonderful sailboat. "Remember that big tarpon with the huge bite taken out of its middle? What do you suppose is out there that can snack on a 100-pound tarpon, and do you really want to swim with it? Besides, that's not really water in Tampa Bay—it's number-three diesel fuel."

I finally talk my friend Louie into joining me for the swim on the basis that I've never heard of a shark in Tampa Bay, and, besides, if there were, the Bay is so polluted that the sharks would be too mutated to bite. John grudgingly agrees to paddle a surfboard along-side us, to keep the thundering cigarette boats from turning Louie and me into chowder.

The swim goes off without a hitch. The water does, in fact, taste like diesel and has the consistency of warm chicken noodle soup, and the last 25 yards to the pier is, unfortunately, through a school of jellyfish. We emerge unscathed, except for John's sunburn. As we're walking away, the owner of the little pier's bait shop runs out and stops us.

"Did you two just swim across the Bay?" he asks. Louie and I beam like proud fathers. "You morons. We've been chumming for sharks all summer off this pier. The place is alive with 'em."

Louie looks stricken.

"But you said . . . " he starts.

"Louie," I say brightly, "were we eaten?"

"You're not just crazy," he says darkly. "You're nuts."

Sleep's pretty much out the night before the race. I tried calling people on the phone, but, all too soon, people remind me of the time zone difference between the West and East coasts. Around 4 A.M. I give up any premise of spending any more time in bed, get up, and methodically recheck my gear. My bike is already racked in an old warehouse, about a mile from the Aquatic Basin. After we exit the water, we run a mile to the bike, which will give us a chance to get the feeling back in our extremities before we ride. I wish the bike was still here, so I could go over it one more time.

At 5 A.M., in the dark, I take my wetsuit, running shoes, a can of Exceed Sports Meal—a chocolate energy drink so buffered that it will barely come out of the can, much less the drinker—a towel that I swipe from the hotel bathroom, a giant, economy-sized container of Vaseline and an enameled pin of a great white shark, which I will clip inside my wetsuit for luck and head out.

My head is clear. The thinking is over. The worrying is over. I am in the quiet place, where there is nothing left in the world but the task in front of me. Somewhere in the back of my head, a green light that reads, "Waiting For Data Input" is blinking. The animal of doubt and fear and pain rests, quiet in its cage.

I walk down the quiet streets of Fisherman's Wharf, past the crab sandwich shops, the photo-processing kiosks, expresso bars, nautical-themed souvenir shops. The Wharf smells of old food and the fog; from the direction of the water, a sea lion, disturbed, barks loudly. At the Aquatic Basin, there's the usual prerace hubbub, but it's subdued, muted in the fog. The sharp, piercing lights of television cameras stab through the foggy dark, touching the real athletes, the people for whom Alcatraz is simply another race. For the rest of us, outside the circle of lights, the race is something more than that. A test, surely; a validation, maybe. We are scared—I am scared—but the fear has no strength; I am scared the way you might feel a breeze on your face walking to the office. The breeze might be cool or hot, comfortable or uncomfortable, but it doesn't change anything. You note its touch and keep on walking.

I look out across the dark water, toward where the old prison will materialize, solidify out of the fog.

"There's not a lot of point in talking about it," a racer tells me the day before. "We all know why we're here, don't we?"

I set up my gear on the beach, put on my wetsuit, and mill around until I hear the first strains of bagpipe music. Then the whole ragged bunch of us hikes down Fisherman's Wharf to a waiting ferry, for the ride out to Alcatraz. First, of course, we get a pep talk:

"Just keep in mind," says an organizer over a loudspeaker, "that swimmers in wetsuits look like seals, which are the primary food for sharks...Swimmers, like seals, swim in a pack...Remember, sharks pick off the stragglers...Have a nice swim."

In no time at all, we are at the prison—Rocky Beach, which is usually under water—beneath the crumbling guard towers. I've covered most of my exposed skin with Vaseline. My wetsuit is cut away around my shoulders to give my arms full freedom; this also compromises its warmth. The Vaseline won't offer a lot of protection from the biting cold, but it will, I hope, buy me a few more minutes before hypothermia sets in.

And hypothermia will set in. Despite the wetsuit, the 50-whatever-degree water, which conducts heat far more efficiently than air, will begin sucking the heat out of my body as soon as I hit the water. As the temperature of the core of my body begins dropping, the rest of my body will begin taking heroic efforts to preserve the organism—me. First, we'll shiver, as the body tries desperately to keep the machine warm. The swimming motions of my arms and legs will help, but it won't be enough. Somewhere out in the bay, when my core temperature has dropped around five degrees from its usual 98.6, my body will begin shutting down "nonessential" systems, among them the one that thinks. At various times in the swim, kayaks will approach me and ask me my name. If I can't answer, the plan is to pull me out of the water and get me to the medical boat, hovering on the edges of the swim.

Good plan!

"It's time, campers!" and the doors of the ferry open. It's about a ten-foot drop to the water, and I get in line as quickly as I can. *Don't think . . . Jump in water . . .*

I do. When I hit the water, it's like diving head-first into a concrete block. The cold takes my breath away, and as I sink into the bottle green water, all I see are stars. A few feet below the surface, the stars clear and I struggle back up, dog-paddling to Rocky Beach. About 100 yards out is the "rabbit boat," it's bright orange flag practically glowing in the fog. I sink chin-deep in the cold water, letting the cold soak through me, letting my breathing drift down, down, down. Then I dip my face in the water and hold it there. The salt water tastes briny, dirty. I raise my face and look up the sheer cliffs, to the old prison, then start swimming toward the start.

When the gunshot comes, it's anticlimactic. I take one more sight of the orange flag, put my head in the water, stroke. *Mikey blow bubbles,* I think absently. This phrase, I realize, has been hardwired into my head. I have a simple plan—watch my stroke to make sure my hand is pulling water, and raise my head every 6 strokes to watch the orange flag. Somewhere out there I know is a huge orange buoy, set this morning based on the latest information on the current. The overall plan is to swim toward the buoy, which is in the wrong direction for the Aquatic Basin, and the current will pull us home. I will also think calming thoughts for whatever companions I have Down Below. *I am not a seal . . . I taste like an old tire . . . If you're hungry, eat the woman in the nice blue wet suit next to me . . .*

After about 20 minutes, the tops of my feet feel as if they're tangled in seaweed, a strange effect of the cold I've noticed before. This lasts for about another ten minutes, by which time my feet, along with my hands, are numb. I would like to say I noticed my mental facilities slowing down, but it's not something you notice. Instead, thoughts just slip away. In the middle of the shipping channel, there are steady, oceanic swells. The water tastes like Tampa Bay, and the fog has cleared enough for me to see the ghostly outline of San Francisco. It's real deep here, I think, more or less. I raise my head and see the orange buoy and the brightly colored kayaks, moving in and out of the swimmers.

"Hi!" someone says to me, frightening me.

Talking sharks!

But it's a paddler in a kayak.

"What's your name?" he says.

Name?

"Michael," I say slowly. "Bane."

"You okay?"

"Sure." *Why wouldn't I be okay?*

"Good luck," and the paddler is gone.

I round the buoy. I don't *have* to round the buoy, but I want to round the buoy. I like rounding the buoy. The current is at my back. I am going faster. I have to watch my hands, though. For some reason, I forget to watch my hands, and I stop moving. I am lying there paddling, but I don't seem to be going anywhere. When I remember to look at my hands, I see they are flat under, the edge cutting smoothly through the water. *Flat hand*, I think, and I start moving again. I like moving again. When I raise my head to sight again, I see the entrance to the Aquatic Basin.

Hot damn!

I swim through the entrance and, ahead, I see the beach.

The beach!

I like the beach.

I swim until my knees hit the bottom, the sand; then I struggle up. The timing clock says 43 minutes. I like the timing clock.

The wetsuit practically pops off when I unzip it. I stomp out of the suit and see my running shoes, right where I have left them. I slip my feet in the sneakers—elastic laces—and they pull right on. "Hurry!" people around me are saying. I am hurrying. I pick up my tank top, then come to a dead stop. There are four holes in it—one for my head, one for my right arm, one for my left arm, one for my whole body. But which is which? I look around me and see others struggling with this question. I try one hole, and it's too small—my head won't fit. I take the shirt off and stare at it. I've done this before . . . On the third try, my head slips right in, just like that. People around me applaud.

"Run!" someone else is saying, and they show me the way. On the mile run to the bike, I can feel my brain coming back to life . . . swimming back to the surface from whatever storage bin it had been relegated to by the survival tyranny of the body.

I couldn't get my T-shirt on?

At the bike, I chug down some more Exceed, as much to dilute the dirty water of the bay sloshing around in my stomach as anything. Then I am riding. I race under Alcatraz rules, which means that I have to come to a complete stop at every stop sign and stop light. The road is wet with drizzle, and I am flying through the hills. The Cannondale rolls smoothly, comfortably, familiarly. I sweep down the steep drop, past Seal Rock, to the Great Highway. I envision my feet spinning in perfect circles, to the rhythm of old rock songs. To my right, in the ocean, a single surfer catches a small break and carves toward shore.

A 180-degree turn at the zoo, and I'm on my way back. I pass the same places, climb the steep hill at Seal Rock and, huffing and puffing like a steam engine, head toward the Golden Gate Bridge. The bridge is slick and windy. I grab a drink of water, then miss the holder when replacing the bottle. I see the bottle bounce once on the steel-grated roadway, then fall the long, long way into the cold bay.

As I start out on the run, I see the "real" athletes coming in. They are racing the clock, drawn completely now into their own quiet places. They are away from pain, away from fear, lost in the rhythm of their own shoes on the wet pavement. I salute them, then turn off the road, into the woods.

The fog settles in for the run through the pristine Headlands. The trail is damp, and, at times slick. Occasionally, a beam of sunlight finds its way through the fog, and the ground steams. The trail is a nightmare of shifting terrain. We might feed from a dirt road to a narrow trail along a ridge line, then do a steep, rutted descent to a sandy beach on a secluded cove. We have a choice, then, of soft sand or water. I take the harder packed sand and the water. The trail follows an old road back up, the steepest climb of the race. I run when I can; walk when I have to. With each turn in the road, it climbs higher.

I hear huffing, and, for a time, a woman racer with an English accent jogs alongside me.

"Every hill has a top," she says. "Every one."

I hope she is not the woman in the blue wetsuit, whom I offered up to the Shark Gods at the beginning of the race.

The race turns off the road at its peak and heads along another ridge line. This trail is the narrowest yet, and, in the deepening fog, it seems a gray tunnel. I can hear my cross-country shoes smacking the rocks, feel the pain in my knees and hips from the bike and the trail so far. But I seem to be completely alone, following a course that seems destined to go nowhere. There is a sharp pain in the middle of my back, and I realize, for the first time apparently, that my neck is bleeding, chaffed raw by the collar of my wetsuit. I wonder how high these ridges are...I wonder what I could see if the fog would miraculously lift...I wonder if there's anybody else here except me...

"The mind wanders," the banker, running 146 miles across Death Valley, told me. "It seeks its own place. Just let it go. It doesn't matter."

Each step increases the toll on my body. The cross-country shoes, while they grip the damp ground, have no support, no cushioning. The ridge line is all rock, and each step seems to reverberate up my legs, through my aching knees, into my head. The cool and the damp take their toll as well. I think I'm rusting...The trail weaves and bobs, off the ridge line, back into the woods. Later, the woman with the accent, will ask me, "When you were on the ridge line, did you think you were in Hell?"

Now let me tell you about a good day:

I've been running now for a couple of hours, along the twisting trails of the course.

I run absently, aware of the sound of my cross-country shoes on the trail and little else. I am aware that my right shoulder now aches from the swim, that both my feet are blistered, that I've probably pulled a muscle in my thigh on one of the descents, but the thoughts are far away, untroubling. I run a steep, stair-step decline, and suddenly I step out of the woods, onto the last mile of pavement. Race volunteers hand me a cup of water and shake my hands, and I jog off for the final mile. I run smoothly, my stride straight and true, my arms pumping effortlessly; if only for this moment, the athlete I never was.

As if on cue, the fog lifts for the first time that day. I see Alcatraz and the bridge and sailboats on a bay that is bright Caribbean blue.

10

The Ethnic Platoon
Skates Again

Perhaps I am not born to skate.

This thought occurs to me while I'm lying on my back in the middle of a crumbling, broken-glass-covered parking lot, watching blood dribble from my arm onto my t-shirt. So far, I have skated approximately, give or take a few feet, just under two yards. My skates, new black and florescent green Rollerblades, however, have gone on without me. The net result of this tricky piece of work is that my skate-shod feet fly into the air, my butt smacks down on the asphalt and lots of unsanitary-looking grit embeds itself in my elbows.

Item 9: Skate Marathon.

The skate marathon turns out to be the annual Athens-to-Atlanta Road Skating Marathon, a decade-old, 85-mile jaunt from the college town of Athens, Georgia, into metropolitan Atlanta. That means the race precedes the trendy ascendancy of in-line skates by about nine years—I have this vision of a hundred refugees from a roller rink rolling through the Georgia hills. *All skate! All skate!* The race will roll along the backroads, which will also be open to more conventional traffic as well as the Lycra brigade. *Ought to be fun . . .*

There is also a 38-mile leg, which is all rolling hills and none of urban Atlanta. I decide that The List does not require me to skate in urban Atlanta traffic—I may be, as my friends now claim, crazy, but I am not a complete lunatic.

It takes about three days to regularly remain upright on the new skates. I have to keep telling myself to lower my center, get my center of balance as close to the ground as possible. I have a long time until the race, however, and I figure all I have to do is keep skating. I also practice complex (read: impossible) techniques, like braking. I do this by skating up to the top of a parking garage, then turning around and skating down. If I fail to brake properly, I will leave my signature, in bright red, on the wall of the parking garage. This technique is taught to me by a woman skater named Barbara Lane, who, one particularly memorable afternoon, leaves a 12-foot swath of red along the parking garage wall.

Denise and I have worked our way up to six-mile skates, signing up for all the short skate races we can find, when I realize that the race is only a couple of months away. *This won't do.* We go out one afternoon and grind our way through a boring, hot 20 miles.

"Well, she says, "if we can skate 20 miles, we ought to be able to skate 40 miles."

I rub my aching back and worry about her logic.

Denise and I get into Athens on a drizzling Saturday afternoon in October and check into the race-central Ramada Inn. All sorts of strange people are milling around the lobby, as if several odd groups are having separate conventions at the hotel. Our first challenge is to figure out just how we're going to get home from the Dacula—no "r," no vampires in Georgia—Elementary School, where the 38-miler ends.

When I ask one of the race volunteers about transportation back to Athens, she says, "Beats me."

We decide to rent a second car, drive it to Dacula tonight, park it and use it to get back to Athens, which is a perfectly good plan until we discover that apparently, without our knowledge, every place in Athens that rents cars has decided to close at noon. I finally decide to take a long shot and call the used car dealers. Somewhere fairly far down the list, I find someone who says, "Come on down!"

And we do, to a 1950s prefab building and a flickering neon sign that says, "Buy Here! Pay Here!" Inside, there are a couple of Army surplus metal desks and cracked paneling faded the color of old spilt coffee. "Howdy!" says a big man behind one of the desks. "You folks is in luck."

I have an overwhelming urge to buy a car, which I sublimate.

Eventually, after more cash than paperwork trades hands, we end up with an '80s vintage, oil-burning, smoking Ford for the day.

"We closed tomorrow," our benefactor says. "When you bring it back, just throw the keys through that busted window."

We decide not to overly tax the Ford by shutting it off, so we pick up the other rental car and head to Dacula. The first thing I notice about the course we'll be skating tomorrow morning is that apparently Georgians have a different definition of "a few little hills."

The highway roller-coasters up and down, long climbs alternating with, to my eyes, terrifying downhills. Even training in parking garages hasn't gotten me used to cannonballing down a steep hill. The difference between a bicycle and a skate is that a bicycle has real brakes, while in-line skates only pretend to have brakes. For every hill I drive up and down, my mood gets a little sourer. And, secondly, 38 miles on twisting backroads in rural Georgia is a *long way.* If it is a long way in the car—albeit, the Ford—how long must it be on skates?

When we finally get to the metropolis of Dacula (past Winder, through Carl and Auburn) and find the appropriate place to leave the rental, Denise hops in the Ford with a question on her lips.

"I thought you said the hills weren't bad," she says.

"They grew."

Back in Athens, we arrive in time to pick up our race packet, sign yet another liability release ("I know that skating on open roads is a potentially hazardous activity . . . ") and attend the mandatory prerace meeting. The crowded meeting room of the hotel is filled with what looks like a collection of warring tribes. There are street skaters from New York City, looking like only extras in that great urban drama can look; lean and mean professional skate racers from somewhere out west, in matching jerseys and matching rail-thin bodies; a large collection of bearded, tie-dyed folks who look as much like vendors at Grateful Dead concerts as skaters; a smattering of nattily dressed yuppies, some foreign entrants with (honest) their own photos on collectable trading cards; California Venice Beach blondes, male and female, and a scattering of people who just look lost—my and Denise's category. To me, the room looks exactly like those old movies about World War II, where every platoon has the exactly correct ethnic mix. I keep expecting Lee Marvin to step forward and explain how he's going to whip us all into shape.

Instead, Henry Zuver steps forward and tells us where we can expect the big hostile dogs on the course.

With that information, we head back to our room, to replace our everyday street-skating wheels with rock-hard racing wheels. Every sport has its gadgets, and in-line skating is no exception. Denise and I will be skating in "recreational" skates, in-line skates that you can just buy over the counter. Her skates have four wheels; mine five, the theory being that the more wheels you have, the faster you can go, your rolling resistance being spread over a greater surface. The somewhere-out-west people will be using slickly designed, dreadfully expensive, equally dreadfully uncomfortable racing skates. These little monsters consist of a hard boot, molded to fit your foot (or the other way around, to hear some of the racers talk) bolted to a frame made of some mysterious space-age material. The frame holds five wheels, which spin on precision German bearings. The racing skates are as light as feathers, with the rolling resistance of a marble on a polished glass floor. Our concession to the race is to change to a harder skate wheel. The softer the wheel is, the greater adhesion it has to the road. While adhesion can translate into more stability, it also means more rolling resistance, so you have to push harder to roll the same distance.

Our new wheels are as hard as stones, with about the same amount of adhesion. This will enable us to fly through the Georgia countryside like Wile E. Coyote and his Acme Rocket Backpack, we figure.

Unfortunately, I have yet to learn the military truism that the battle plan seldom survives the first encounter with the enemy.

At dawn Sunday morning, we wolf down a quick breakfast, don our skates with the rock-hard wheels, and join the rest of the Ethnic Platoon in front of the hotel. Not only is it dark, but it is still drizzling rain. The highway is glazed with water and the shimmery rainbows of oil.

"This," announces Denise, "is not going to be fun."

The Platoon skates uphill in mass to the formal starting line. One person falls on her butt on the slick street.

We mill around for a few minutes at the start line, then, unceremoniously, someone says, "Go!" So we go. Actually, the people in front of me go. The somewhere-out-west racing contingent lower their bodies onto an impossibly low, bent-over racing crouch and sprints for Atlanta, ignoring the fact that the road is like an ice skating rink. The rest of the Platoon, 250 or so skaters, start spreading out. We have opted to start in the rear. I have visions of working my way forward. I am reminded of the old Southern comedian, Dave Gardner, who always said that, "A man's reach can sure as hell exceed his grasp."

The slick highway is a major challenge. Unlike bicycles, skates don't have a lot of glide in them—you stop pushing, they stop rolling. To maximize the push and the glide, the skater assumes an unnatural position—bent-over at the waist, the back parallel to the road, knees flexed. The driving leg then pushes *out*, not back, to make the skater roll forward. The longer that outward push is, the longer you glide and the faster you go. The longer you glide, the less energy you're going to use. The endurance side of extreme sports is all an energy/output equation, I am learning. How long to do you need to go, and how much energy are you going to spend to go that far? The more efficient you are, the farther you can go on less. Efficiency, though, is one of those trick questions on the test. It is a factor, made up of technique, equipment and, for lack of better words, body sense, the ability to do the same task using smaller muscle groups instead of those big haulers like the quadriceps of the legs. Like in rock climbing—if you constantly pull yourself up with the big muscles of the arm, those muscles will burn out sooner than later, even if you're Sylvester Stallone (well, maybe not Sly).

The problem with all the wet asphalt in front of us is that it raises pure hell with efficiency. Instead of long, graceful strokes propelling us along, I'm taking short, clipped strokes to keep those stones I'm skating on from slipping and dumping my butt on the ground. The short strokes don't propel me as far or as fast, so I've got to take lots more of them. The short strokes also alter my body position—I can't bend as low to the ground, because I'm pulling my leg up short.

Yeech.

We skate through Athens, and after a few twists and turns, we're out on the highway proper. It's dark, and I concentrate on the flashing red lights of the skaters who were smart enough to remember to bring lights. Denise and I take the first hill in the dark, which, given my druthers, is perfect. I half brake, half slalom down the hill and arrive at the bottom in one piece. I may yet survive.

The sun eventually makes a grudging appearance through the clouds, gray tinged with a pale orange, as I am skating past a field with horses. The horses shake their manes and run to the fence with a stiff, prancing gait.

"I realize how stupid this looks," I say to the horses.

They nod in total agreement.

I wish I could tell you about how scintillating, how stimulating the race is, but, in fact, 38 miles on skates is . . . 38 miles on skates. There is a sort of brain death that sets in. I settle into a stroke rhythm, ignore the fact that my lower back feels like it has been smacked with a stick and try to get my brain to completely shut down. I stutter my way down hills, then catch the people who passed me on the way up the next hill. Real skaters, racers, will barrel down the hills at speeds approaching 60 miles per hour; rationally, I know this isn't a bit different than barreling down the same hill at the same speed on a bicycle. If anything, skaters are closer to the ground, which will ease the impact a bit. I have, however, hit the ground too many times on skates to ever feel comfortable when the speed creeps above 25 miles per hour or so. Ground is hard, my climbing instructors have told me. Indeed it is.

The first 15 miles are as uneventful as anything I've done. Stroke, glide; stroke, glide. Watch the fields roll past; wave to folks on the way to church.

The next 15 miles are tougher, but mostly because the road is nasty, wet, and bumpy. The skates vibrate so bad I'm afraid fillings are going to fall out of my teeth, and pretty soon my ankles are numb. This doesn't make that much difference, because I'm using a pair of off-the-shelf Rollerblades with a thick plastic boot, like a ski boot. I lose flexibility in my legs, which costs me efficiency points, but I'm able to lace the boots tight enough to allow me to ignore the fact that I can't feel my ankles. Kind of like having them in casts.

There are a couple of steep climbs, steep enough that at a few points, I feel like no matter how hard I push, I'm rolling backwards. One doomsday drop culminates in a two-inch concrete lip on a little bridge. More than one person hits this tiny lip at about 40 miles per hour. It's a physics quiz. The lowest two inches of your body, in this case your skate wheels, go from 40 miles per hour to zero miles per hour in less than a quarter of an inch. The remainder of your body continues on, gaining speed, the remaining distance to the asphalt. How far will you continue to slide, assuming concrete has the abrasive factor of, say, heavy grit sandpaper?

It's a quiz Denise and I thankfully fail to participate in.

Mostly, after a few hours, I am tired. We bend over as much as possible to stretch our abused backs, stretch our shins whenever we stop. As the morning wears on and traffic increases, there is the indescribable experience of being passed by a fully loaded 18-wheeler doing 70 miles per hour. There is a huge, momentary s...u...c...k...i...n...g feeling as the truck pulls you into its draft, followed by a moment of nausea as you imagine yourself smeared along the Georgia countryside. Also, strangely, the highway gets much scarier as church lets out. Carloads of Sunday-go-to-meeting dressed people whiz by, shaking their fists and often shouting curses. A couple of times, rearview mirrors fly by inches from my face. I look up once to see a small child in a dark suit, shooting me the bird through the back window of a car.

"Do you suppose," I ask Denise, "that this Sunday's sermon was 'Devil Worshipers On Wheels?'"

"I think I saw that movie," she says.

Along about mile 35, three and a half hours in, I'm counting strokes, then trying to calculate how much longer I'm going to be out here. Various places on my feet have, despite my best efforts, blistered and are now somewhere beyond pain. My lower back feels as if someone has been driving self-tapping metal screws into it, and I can no longer remember all the lyrics to Elvis Presley's first ten hits.

Somewhere in the middle of this reverie, I look up and realize that I'm at the top of a long, steep hill.

The hell with it, I think.

I knot myself into a little ball, like Robert Redford in "Downhill Racer," my clenched fists in front of my face, and just cannonball the hill. The skates pick up speed like crazy, like, somehow, I have inherited the Acme Rocket Backpack. I feel time go soft as adrenaline slams into my system. My vision narrows, my eyes locking on the bumpy highway. With my increased perception, I realize that I don't have a snowball's chance in Georgia of making it to the bottom of the hill on my feet. I am vibrating like crazy, and the more rigid my body becomes, the harder it is for me to remain in control. I unflex my screaming legs every so slightly, raising my center a few inches—and I am on the ground, my tailbone slamming into the asphalt at about 35 miles an hour.

I see a universe of stars and a flash of pure, blue-white pain that makes consciousness flicker like a match in the wind. The match flickers, then glows again, and I remember to spread-eagle out on the highway, giving me as much sliding surface area as I can. Old guys heal slow, and I'd prefer not to break something—or have the Georgia asphalt belt sand its way to the bone. After what seems like a couple of miles and a very, very long time, I slide to a stop, exactly straddling the double white line in the middle of the highway.

"Oh god! Oh god!" Denise says as she skates back uphill to me. "Are you hurt?"

I, in fact, can't seem to move. I lie there like road kill, waiting for the pain level to drop from the hellishly agonizing level, waves of searing heat rolling off my tailbone. I finally perform some sort of limp fish flop maneuver and roll onto my belly.

"We've got to get you out of the road," Denise says. There is traffic, and if I don't move soon I will become literal as well as figurative road kill. I begin crawling to the side of the highway, with assists from Denise. A carload of people stop.

"Can we do something?" they ask Denise. She shakes her head. Kill me, I think. Make it quick.

"Are you sure we can't do something?" they say.

I make the side of the road and actually manage to sit up. The pain has gone from hellish to simply awful.

"I'm okay," I say. "Thank you very much for stopping."

They drive on.

"Is anything broken?" says Denise. She seems so calm and efficient that I figure she must be scared to death.

"Just a lot of blood," I says. "Nothing feels broken."

"Can you stand up?" she says.

"Not yet, but give me a minute."

We clean off the blood, and I eventually creak to my feet. Everything is swaying slightly, but I appear to be relatively functional. In a lot of pain, but working.

"What do you want to do?" she asks.

"Finish," I say.

So we skate on. I now skate like Pinochio, rigidly upright, my legs barely moving. The remaining two miles takes us a little over an hour to finish. I gingerly sit down on the curb next to the finish line, unlace and unbuckle my skates and pull them off. My socks are stained blood red in places.

"How are you really?" Denise, herself no worse for the wear, asks.

"I feel," I start to say, "like Item 9 is scratched off The List."

What I actually say is, "Like crap."

11

Carbon Fiber and
the Lords of the Air

Nowhere is the boundary between "extreme" sports and "regular" sports as clearly defined as in windsurfing. It was windsurfing, after all, that got me started, that gave birth to The List. Yet, for most of its participants, the sport of windsurfing is as benign as a day on the beach, sunburned people on boards with brightly colored sails, puttering across yacht basins in gentle breezes. Still, the first item on The List is "Windsurf Big Wind."

Tom James, presently the editor of the largest windsurfing magazine in the country, once told me that he majored in philosophy in college because it was something he could practice at the beach. I find myself thinking of his words at the beach myself, where I'm waiting for wind and trying to sort out this "extreme" thing. I am starting to ride the crest of what looks to be a big wave. Extreme sports a year or so ago barely registered on the media radar; now they seem to be everywhere. MTV has led the way with *MTV Sports*, which seems to be about dudes doing dudish things. Every commercial for a 4-wheel-drive vehicle involves young, healthy people attempting something life-threatening, then driving home.

I get a call one day from a sports magazine editor.

"Let me see," she says. I can hear papers shuffling over the telephone. "You're a . . . risk specialist, right?"

I wonder if there's a government rating, RS-1 maybe.

It causes me to question the whole concept of "extreme." The first uses of the word in connection with sports that I could find was the linking of extreme and skiing, which took place probably ten years ago.

"As near as I can remember," says extreme skier Rob Deloria, "it was the North Face apparel company who started using the term in the '70s. Then it was *everywhere.*"

The simplest definition of extreme skiing was skiing where the consequences of failure were high. This is a nice way of saying that if you fall, you die. In fact, extreme was so used—or overused—in skiing that by the time the word started being applied to other sports, the mere whisper of it would cause skiers to wince.

It is still, I think, a valid word.

Extremes are the frontiers, places of both mind and body, where monsters still lurk behind the trees and trails end in sheer drops. Extreme sports are different from adventure sports because of that "consequence" factor. You can have a wonderful adventure, for example, mountain biking some of the trails in the North Carolina mountains, but your actual risk, versus your perceived risk, is very low. The consequences of your falling or being unable to complete the ride are small—bruises and road rash. Compare that to the Kamikaze or any "extreme" mountain bike downhill. The bruises become broken bones; the road rash more like the flaying of skin.

By working backwards from "extreme," I am starting to develop a working definition of "risk." Risk is higher when the consequences of failure increase. While this may seem like a perfect intellectual exercise, it's very important to anyone out there treading the edges. As I learned from the Kamikaze, the first step in getting through these things in one functioning piece is to really understand what the risks are.

Secondly, sports language, like most of the rest of the English language, is going through its own escalation. To read the ads or watch the television commercials, everything is death-defying, extreme, on the edge, spooky, or crazy.

This is slightly askew, since, as a society we have become increasingly ambivalent about risk-taking. On the one hand, we have traditionally venerated risk-takers, especially in sports; on the other, we have defined product liability so strictly that we have closed playgrounds rather than risk falling out of a swing. The opening ritual for anything on The List is the Signing Of The Liability Releases.

The urge for risks in sports, writes sports philosopher and martial artist George Leonard, runs counter to the tendency in modern industrial society to reduce or eliminate risks from every aspect of life. "The arena of sports," he writes, "has provided a place for people to take calculated risks without breaking the law."

Nowhere is this urge as blatantly visible—or the language hyperbole as clear—as in bungee jumping, a onetime outlawed "sport" turned national mania. The idea's pretty simple—tie a rubber band around your legs and jump off a high place, sort of like committing suicide without consummating the relationship with the ground. What began with a group of self-acknowledged crazies lobbing themselves off bridges and from balloons has become a steady stream of college students, accountants, secretaries, and executives jumping off cranes suspended over parking lots, bouncing on the tethered ends of their bungee cords like dysfunctional human yo-yos. Hundreds of thousands of people have now "gone ahead and jumped."

"It was the best experience of my life," a woman friend tells me after her first bungee jump. "A lot better than sex. And probably a lot safer, too."

While a bungee jumper might feel a certain rush of immortality ("The only thing you've truly accomplished," sniffs the politically correct *Utne Reader*, "is not dying."), in fact, bungee jumping is very safe, as safe as riding a roller coaster. On my scale, that comes out to *high perceived risks + low actual risk = big thrill + low medical bills*. And that's good.

"Adventure," writes Walt Burnett, "is a human need. We recognize it as the daring thing which makes us bigger than our usual selves. Adventure is the curiosity of man to see the other side of the mountain, the impulse in him that makes him break his bonds with lesser things and frees him for greater possibilities."

I am starting to see each item on The List on that scale.

I also see, though, that what's missing in bungee jumping is the element of skill. Go up top; jump off. You get the rush, but not the experience, Mihaly Csikszentmihalyi's *flow*.

With windsurfing big wind, you not only get the flow, but the literal *flow*, sailing a piece of high-tech plastic over bucking seas. Technically, I suppose, I've windsurfed big winds, but I decide that it's only fair that I sail them again for The List. At first, I chase the big wind everywhere. I hit a long stretch of business travel researching magazine articles, so I pack a wetsuit and a windsurfing harness with me wherever I go, then rent the rest of the equipment when I get to where I'm going.

From the very beginning, there was a simplicity to windsurfing that appealed to me. Windsurfing is a new sport, barely a decade old. That means not only does it not have a history, but it lacks traditions as well. With other forms of sailing, there always seems to be guys in white jackets and jaunty blue nautical caps, who stand ready to tell you the rules. And there are lots of rules. Me, I couldn't even speak the language. After I'd been windsurfing a while, I was drafted onto a "real" boat as crew by a captain who reasoned that since I was a good sailor on little skinny pieces of carbon fiber, I'd be a good sailor anywhere. How was I to know that "the lines to port" meant "the ropes on the left?"

Windsurfing is simple—no lines to port or convoluted "Hold to, me hardies!" mysteries to master. Instead, there's a board and a sail. The sail is threaded onto a mast, which is attached by a flexible foot to the board. There is also a boom, which is attached at a 90-degree angle to the mast. The idea is too stand up on the board on the water, hold onto the mast and let the wind push you along. A lot of people find this a little like trying to chew gum and do handstands at the same time, but it's possible to master in a few weeks.

Big wind, though, changes the whole equation. The boards get shorter and shorter, with less and less flotation. In fact, if you stand on a high-wind board and there's no wind to drive it, it will sink. Like a water ski, a high wind board is only happy when it's driven by high wind, planing over the surface of the water. The equation gets even dicier when you add in the tipsiness factor: smaller boards are less stable than larger boards. Unless they're going fast, high-wind boards have all the intrinsic stability of a greased log. The final variable in the big-wind equation is the fact that you can't just stand on one of these boards and sail—you have to participate, and participate very specifically. You have to *fly* them, your body hooked into the boom through a harness and your feet pushing the nose of the little board off the wind. The board will respond like a carbon fiber rocket, only inches of it remaining in the water, while it sizzles across the waves like a drop of water on a hot cast-iron frying pan.

It's that sensation of speed, of being able to launch this little board into the air off the platform of the waves, that gives the sport its edge.

The first time I do actually launch a board off a wave, I perform a complex, sophisticated maneuver called an "endo," which involves sticking the board nose first into the water, then cleverly following the board with the rest of my body. This maneuver is made even more hilarious by the fact that I am still attached to the boom by my harness. The result is a Rube Goldberg-like contraption made up of carbon fiber, aluminum, and flesh, pivoting around a mythical point where the nose of the board touches the water. I also get an excellent demonstration of the time dilation effects of adrenaline. My endo takes me at least an hour from the time I lost control of the board until the time my head resurfaces.

The problem with catch as catch can in the wind department is that I am not catching much. Wind is . . . wind, by its nature fickle. The closest I come to really big wind is on a glacier-carved lake several hours north of Toronto. The water is clear and cold, just above freezing. All around the lake, the leaves are turning. While I'm suiting up, I watch a long, sleek mink steal a fish from a lethargic fisherman. The mink, stealthy as cat burglar, first drags the line with the fish on it out of the water, an inch at a time, the mink's eyes never leaving the dozing fisherman. When the fish is finally beached, sharp little mink teeth disconnect the thrashing fish from the line. The fisherman wakes up just as the mink heads into the woods with its prize.

"Heh!" the fisherman yells at me. "Did something just steal my fish?"

There's about a 35-mile-per-hour wind—nothing compared to the big winds in Florida. But the six-foot wind-driven waves stand to make the afternoon interesting. Ocean waves come in sets of three; if you can count, you can usually get out on even a big day. But the wind-driven waves on the lake just keep pounding. I angle my rental board—I would have preferred my own, shorter, board— off the wind, and run smack into a neck-high wave, which sends me and the board back into the rocks. On second thought, I'm glad I don't have my own equipment. After about three tries, and three trips back to the rocks, I get the hang of it, which involves sort of jumping about three waves to really get under way.

What follows is a great afternoon, jumping waves and making long carving runs across the lake. The wind is steady and cold, but practically the only uncovered part of my body is my eyes and nose. When I crash and burn, I can feel the cold of the water gnawing at me, a huge mink with a tiny black-suited fish.

It is a wonderful afternoon, but it's not . . . extreme.

Toweling off, looking for the mink, I make a decision.

I'm going to have to go to the Gorge.

The Columbia River thunders through the gash between Washington and Oregon, its roar echoing along the Victorian logging towns that line its sides. About an hour and a half from Portland, on the Oregon side of the mighty Columbia, is the town of Hood River, stapled up the sides of the mountains leading to stately Mt. Hood. Once Hood River's livelihood was linked to the trees, the huge forests of the Pacific Northwest. But the logging industry died, and Hood River seemed destined to die along with it.

But miracles, as Willie Nelson once noted, occur in the strangest of places. In addition to the huge volumes of water passing through, the Columbia River Gorge creates a huge volume of wind, a giant machine fueled by the imbalance of temperature between the waters of the Pacific and the miles of green forests. Throughout the summer, into the early fall, the wind screams down the river at anywhere from 25 to 65 miles per hour, every day, without fail. In the early 1980s, as the sport of windsurfing was being born, a few hardy pioneers discovered the wind machine of the Gorge and the quaint— and cheap—Victorians on Hood River's hills. By the time I come to Hood River, it is the windsurfing equivalent of a ski town. Every car has roof racks, a stack of boards and a bumper sticker that reads "Pray For Wind," or "Welcome To Oregon. Now Go Home."

It is autumn, the wind machine less reliable. But as I drive along the riverside highway, I stop high above the river over a sailing spot. Far below me, in the gold-washed autumn light, the sails move like prehistoric dragonflies, darting along the water, then soaring on the gust, hanging motionless over the river. Sometimes a half dozen boards launch at the same instance, at different angles, a complex chemical equation of molecules and force. I feel the wind against my face and imagine the marshmallow shove of the wind, the lift as the board begins its run. The wind and the water has the jagged rhythm of good rock and roll, the sharp edges and the reprises, the steady back beat that blends with the pounding of your heart. I can close my eyes now and still see those sails dance, mylar leaves in the autumn sun.

In Hood River, I hole up in a cheap no-tell-motel, pressboard paneling and a lumpy mattress. It is, however, $22 a night, which I figure will leave me enough to rent about five days' worth of gear. The morning dawns sunny, cool and still as a tomb. The flags hang listless against their poles.

Uh oh.

More on faith than anything else, I rent equipment and take it down to the Marina to set up. All around me, other people in wet-suits are rigging gear, taking no notice of the fact that there is no wind. I decide that everyone else knows best, so I hurry to get every-thing rigged. Then I sit on a picnic table, and wait. Around 9 A.M. everyone begins checking their watches and looking west toward Portland, as if waiting for a train to arrive. And from the west, up the Gorge, something is coming—wind.

"Show time," someone says.

The river lists and quivers. The flags flutter, then snap. And the wind hits like a fist. Trees bend, leaves swirl and blast away. From the shore, a dozen boards launch into the river, dancing quickly into the mile-wide current. The morning sun holds the mylar sails in sharp relief, Kodacolor sharp. I wrestle my own gear to the water, wade into the cold river, then step onto my board.

And we are gone, away, flashing into the channel. I raise up, do a little hip curl, and hook my harness onto the lines trailing from the boom. Then I settle back, my butt a foot off the water, and let the board run. I am sailing sloppy now, the little board bouncing off the tops of the waves. Ahead of me, and to my left, I watch a board launch high into the air, the rider just missing a complete 360-degree loop and splashing into the water. Then I blow past.

The wind is gusty that first morning, the sail a living thing in my hands. It fights to escape, and suddenly I am snatched forward by the invisible hand of the wind. I miss my turn, and fall into the cold water. I lie on my back and maneuver the sail so the leading edge is into the wind. The lift is there, waiting. I push up and kick with my back foot, and with a snap I am back on the board, flying again.

I only leave the water long enough to eat and rest. Like everyone else, I finally go home when the great wind machine powers down in the afternoon.

For the next four days, I sail. I catch the big wind, and, for a moment, am weightless, formless over the river. I race the sluggish barges, filled with logs destined for Japan. In the evenings, I drink brown ale, eat grilled trout and talk about sailing big wind with people I don't know. Many of them have walked away from the "real world," rebuilt their lives, to stay close to the great throbbing wind machine of the Gorge. It is as if the concept of *flow* lies on the town like a benevolent tide. I talk to Eric Stanford, a photographer, mountain climber and world traveler whose house on the Washington side overlooks the river.

"Where else would I want to be?" he says. He came to windsurfing after years out on the edge. One ride across the river, and he was hooked. I talk about the feeling, the fleeting sense of *flow*, and he just smiles.

12

Waterlogged

"T A-DA!" SAYS JONATHAN DERKSEN, MY INSTRUCTOR, PROUDLY. "This is your duckie!"

My duckie doesn't have web feet or quack, although it does float. Duckie is slang for an inflatable kayak. When you think kayak, you usually think of those garishly colored one-person plastic boats usually seen tearing down rivers on Mountain Dew commercials. Inflatable kayaks came by their moniker during low water years on the East Coast, claims Eugene Buchanan of *Paddler* magazine, when rafting wasn't feasible.

"Instead, a guide would paddle out in an inflatable, and all the clients would follow behind him," he says. "Everyone thought it looked like baby ducks following the mommy, and the name stuck."

In the last few years, duckies have gone from the status of pool toys to high-performance water craft, largely because of their shorter learning curve.

Kayaking is not a skill to be learned overnight, because of a little maneuver called the "Eskimo Roll." Kayaks, not being the most stable of all water craft, occasionally roll over. Experienced kayakers can easily right themselves with an Eskimo roll, a move that involves twitching the hips like Elvis Run Amok while shoving *just right* with the paddle. Inexperienced kayakers who fail to master this maneuver get to stare at fish and contemplate drowning, a situation made worse by the inescapable fact that you're more likely to roll over in high-speed, whitewater sections of the river than when the boat is sitting at the dock. Exactly the kind of sections where your head is most likely to become an unfortunate 12-pound keel.

Actually, I prefer paddler Jeff Bennett's definition of duckies— "[Inflatables are] to hard-shelled whitewater kayaks what mountain bikes are to road cycles; they provide access to thrills that might otherwise be impossible to gain without years of practice."

In other words, perfect for someone pursuing The List.

I'd sort of left the whitewater List item on the back-burner, mostly because it seemed if not easy to do, at least easy to find. I figured when the opportunity presented itself—a waterfall and a kayak—I'd take the next obvious step. As it happened, I landed a whitewater raft trip to Central America, to Honduras.

Ah ha, I thought. *Opportunity knocks.*

The exact point when I knew I wasn't in Kansas anymore came New Year's Eve at the airport in San Pedro Sula, just a hop, skip, and a jump from Miami International and the main point of entry for the aging banana republic of Honduras.

The plane landed uneventfully enough, but where a traveler might expect to find immigration or customs, there was a salsa band, playing at heavy metal volumes for the hordes of baggage handlers and, apparently, their assorted significant others. The walls of the tiny room shook with the music, and some of the yellow-shirted baggage handlers swayed to the rhythms.

Every baggage handler knew exactly two words of English: "No problem," which was the universal answer to any question.

"Where can we catch the plane to La Ceiba?"

"No problem."

"Does anybody need to stamp these papers?"

"No problem."

"I seem to have misplaced my Uzi."

"No problem."

No problem indeed. Of course, I've come to Honduras not so much for the ambiance as for the whitewater, a crashing torrent that flows down from the 8,000-foot peaks of the Nombre de Dios Mountains only eight miles from the Gulf coast.

San Pedro Sula is a shock for deplaning Americans, unless, of course, said Americans are fond of salsa music and speak fluent Spanish. The trick to finding the connecting airplane is to wander out of the airport, past men with guns, past assorted black market money changers who can turn your dollars into lemperas—known locally as "lemps"—to a different entrance. What looks like a darkened, deserted terminal is actually where you find your connecting flight to La Ceiba.

I have to tell you the truth here—La Ceiba is not, perhaps, the garden spot of Central America. One of the rare Honduran guidebooks we were able to find put it this way: "La Ceiba is not a particularly attractive town, and there's not much to see in the town itself...It's difficult to find postcards anywhere on the North Coast..."

Luckily, postcards weren't a critical issue. Early on in the history of The List, I'd met Dick Eustis. Eustis was a well-known and well-respected river guide in Colorado when he just got sick of being cold and decided to head south—far south. Eustis and several of his cohorts from the Rocky Mountain Outdoor Center in Colorado had stumbled into Honduras while looking around for challenging new rivers to run.

"We'd been hearing a lot about Costa Rica when we met a Honduran, who kept talking about these great rivers," Eustis says. "It was getting to be winter in Colorado, so we loaded up and headed south."

After a nine-day trek across the southern United States through Mexico in rickety trucks with kayaks strapped to the top, the crew arrived in La Ceiba.

They immediately headed up a narrow dirt "highway" dubbed "La Culebra," the snake, by the locals, along the Rio Cangrejal, the place of crabs, which feeds into the Gulf at the northern end of town.

Eustis was amazed.

"It was one set of rapids after another," he says. "The farther up the road we went, the tougher the rapids got."

Also the more spectacular the scenery and wildlife—wild parrots, iguanas, even jaguars make their home in the Honduran rain forests. Just to keep the unwary traveler jumping, there's also six-foot-long fer de lances, one of the deadliest snakes in the world. "Locally," adds Dick, "they call them 'two-minute snakes,' 'cause that's how long you have if you get bitten." There's plenty of antivenom, though. Unfortunately, it's all in Costa Rica.

"The short story is, avoid snakes," Dick concludes. "Especially ones that look like they have a purple beard."

No problem.

First thing the next morning, we load the rafts and head up La Culebra. Since I was there for the rafting, I figured rafting the rivers would be a pretty good idea, but I'd already filled Dick in on The List and my need for kayak instructions, and he'd laughingly agreed.

The road, La Culebra, was originally a banana road, carved out of the jungle to allow shipping fruit between port and interior railhead. The farther into the interior we go, the more the road comes to resemble a donkey path. In sections, huge chunks of fallen hardwood trees have been cut away to allow the passing of a vehicle by the narrowest margin. A vicious flood several months before has scoured away the rain forest—along with hundreds of hapless villagers—from the sides of the Cangrejal. The waters ran so fast that even the granite boulders that line the river have been scrubbed free of decades of moss, some shining as white as skulls.

The river is fast, as billed, one set of drops after another. After a certain point, rafts can't put in, and the upper reaches of the river, including some spectacular drops, belong to the kayaks.

The river, though, is rock and roll from the start. Unlike a lot of American rivers, where sections of rapids are punctuated by long, calm floats, the Cangrejal is in a big hurry to get to the Gulf. The sets of rapids are close together, the breaks short. The river offers whatever your fancy, from mild Class 2 to unrunnable Class 6. The raftable section of the river is like an hour-long roller coaster, with bumps.

I decide it is probably a good idea to mention to Dick that I've never been in big whitewater before.

"Oh," he says.

Actually, I've never been in a raft before. Denise has assured me that Dick wouldn't think of letting me row down a big river, given this fact.

"That's okay," says Dick. "We'll just give you a crash course in rowing. Do exactly what I say, and you won't drown. That's a joke."

No problem.

"Okay," Dick shouts over the river, "we're just going to blow over the boulder . . . Whoops!" The raft teeters on a boulder until we rock it back into the currents. Waves crash over our heads, and we seem to be permanently on the verge of getting tossed out of the boat. Dick's instructions are crisp, explicit and, unlike some sailboat captains, not delivered with the threat of a keelhauling. Of course, given that at any point we seem to be headed for certain disaster against a rock face, there's a spectacular incentive to pay attention and do exactly what Dick says.

The water boils, and we slam, bang and buck. The river is warm, 80 degrees or so, and, over our shoulders, we see clouds building at the top of the Nombre de Dios range. Parrots fly in circles above us. We pass Hondurans on the banks of the river, celebrating the new year. The night before, we'd drunk Salva Vida beer and listened to automatic weapons fire. Happy New Year. No problem.

We pass iguana hunters on the way up La Culebra, stalking and shooting the big lizards out of the huge rain forest hardwoods. A charcoal smuggler drifts past us on a raft made of lashed-together logs. He steals wood from the forest, a national preserve, then cooks it to charcoal and sells it for a few pennies for cooking. He stands and polls his raft across the river, studiously ignoring us. The logo on his shorts reads, "Nike."

There is that jarring conjunction, our high-tech rafts and kayaks mirrored against wash day on the Cangrejal, where the city's women come to the broad delta to wash their clothes in the river and drape them over the stones to dry. New Firebirds and horse-drawn carts. The open thunder of the river and the mysterious darkness of the rain forest.

"I think we can get you up to speed in a duckie," Dick Eustis tells me the morning after our first raft run. "I don't want to try it in a hardshelled kayak, since you'd probably drown."

I agree that drowning seems like a bad idea.

"Any idiot," Dick says, "ought to be able to learn how to boat in a duckie."

No problem, any idiot says.

My plan is simple: I will spend the morning in the impossibly blue waters of the Gulf of Mexico paddling around in my duckie, learning the four main strokes, discovering the secrets of climbing back into the thing and, in general, playing around like a kid in a very big bathtub. In the afternoon, we'll haul the duckie up the mountain, and I'll run as much of the Rio Cangrejal as Jonathan thinks is prudent, or however much I can convince him to let me do—whichever comes first.

It is a flawless Caribbean day. Men lounge aimlessly in the thatch-roofed bar on the beach, watching us with a certain amount of humor as we unload the light blue duckie from the back of one of Rios Honduras' battered Toyota trucks. An old man with a horse-pulled cart made of a truck transaxle and cracking gray timbers, loaded to the brim with green bananas, stops to watch. We shove the duckie into the water, and Jonathan wades in for the lesson as I ungraciously crawl into the rocking kayak.

"This is really simple," he is saying. "There are a total of four strokes—forward, backwards, sweep front, sweep back. That's it—all you have to remember. Anybody can remember that much."

I keep my opinions to myself, as I have a history of forgetting my address. The duckie, though, is great fun, much like sitting on a rubber raft in a pool. The Gulf water is warm, and the swells are slight—we'd actually hoped for surf, but nature refused to cooperate. The strokes are self-explanatory. Using a double-bladed kayak oar, forward is forward, backward is backward. The sweeping strokes are like reaching to the side with a broom and sweeping, forward and backward. In little time I was puttering around the Gulf like a veteran, much to the amusement of the men on the shore, starting into their second (or third, or fourth) Salva Vida—life saver—beer.

The only other critical maneuver was "self-rescue," or, how to get back in the boat when you've fallen out. That's another plus for duckies—if you do fall out, you have a nice, fully inflated salva vita, life saver, of your own. Rule One is stay with the boat. I find I can easily stay with the boat, but getting from the water back into the duckie is a little like climbing a rope ladder—harder than it looks. After about 15 minutes of watching me struggle back into the boat like an injured walrus, Jonathan has his own suggestion—"Try not to fall out."

We're ready to head for the river. As we were towing the duckie in, some of the local fishermen in brightly painted wooden *cayugas*—one of the origins of the word *kayak*—cruises by.

"Give me 30 minutes and I could improve that guy's stroke," muses my teacher. "On the other hand, I don't have to paddle out on the ocean for ten hours a day. More I think about it, maybe he could teach me something.

"The thing about duckies," Jonathan is saying as we bounce along the rutted dirt road paralleling the Cangrejal, "is that they're not sexy. People use duckies instead of kayaks on first descents of wild rivers, because you can pack them in. But to say you've done a first descent in a duckie, well, it just doesn't have that ring to it. Maybe we should start calling them 'shredders' or something."

We put in at the edge of what amounts to a private park, a few scattered tables in a clearing carved in the rain forest, where the owner of the closest shack charges a few pennies to visit. Jonathan picked this particular spot because of its calm eddies, a place to give me a crash river orientation before lobbing me downstream.

"The other thing about a duck, as opposed to a kayak, is that it's slow," says Jonathan, "so you've got to compensate by paddling like a crazy person."

The river in a kayak is a very different creature from the river in a raft. For a start, you're lower in the water, so even small rapids loom larger. The boat is less forgiving than a raft, more able to magnify your small errors into major screw-ups. Jonathan explains the proper way to enter the current, at 45 degrees, and I make a few tentative passes from the quiet eddy into the main stream of the river. I quickly retreat. Unlike the warm womb of the Gulf, it's quickly obvious that the river means business.

"You're supposed to be having fun," says Jonathan.

"I always look like this," I reply, and we head out into the baby rapids.

I'm stiff as a board, sloppy with my forwards and backwards and sweeps, but the duckie—I've begun thinking of it as my duckie—is surprisingly responsive. We fly through the rippling Class 2 rapids like an out-of-control amusement park ride.

"First rapids!" shouts Jonathan over the sounds of the Cangrejal. "Now are you having fun?"

In fact, I was—huge fun. Around the bend, though, was the next set of rapids, short, but a steep drop, with waves cresting over my head. From my vantage point at river level, it looked like trying to sail a inflatable raft into a washing machine.

"Don't think," Jonathan says. "Just follow me through."

The amusement park ride suddenly turns into a hairy roller coaster as the duckie noses over the edge of the drop, then sails into the river as waves crash over my head. My butt hits something hard as the hydraulic pressure of the water forces the duckie away from the looming rocks, shoving it off another small cliff. And, suddenly, I'm through, back in the calm, large amounts of the Cangrejal running out of my mouth and nose.

"You got off line a little there," Jonathan says, "But you made the right moves. When in doubt, paddle like hell!"

He strokes his kayak over and looks at me closely.

"Honest," I say, "I'm having fun."

"Relax," he says. "The worst that can happen is you can drown. Ha ha."

The next set of rapids come up quickly. These are bigger, with multiple drops studded with huge granite boulders, and much longer, requiring something that passes for skill. The waves blasting off the rocks look like a big day at a surfing beach. Branches hang down from the rain forest, obscuring part of the right side of the river. I follow Jonathan into the first set of rapids.

Within seconds, I'm sucked toward the overhanging branches. The duckie is bucking wildly, and it's all I can do to keep my butt anchored and keep paddling like hell. We skate along the right-hand bend, me ducking desperately around chunks of the rain forest the size of my leg. Most of the time, all I see is water, the waves over my head obscuring my vision. And then, as before, I'm through, equal parts adrenaline and river water draining out of my body.

"You recover well," says my teacher. "I'm surprised, though, that you decided to take such a harder line down."

Ha ha.

We beach the kayaks and walk up ahead to scout the last set of rapids, a long steep section called "Lava." I am uncomfortable with rapids that have their own names. It seems ominous to me.

"This is a significant section of rapids," Jonathan says as we climb up over the boulders. It was scary as hell in the raft. At the beginning of Lava, the Cangrejal begins funneling into a narrow granite gorge. In places, the rocks overhang the river. There are car-sized boulders, boiling holes in the water, and a steady pounding of huge waves. From the top of a nearby boulder, the rapids seem to go on forever.

Jonathan sits down on the rock and starts pointing out landmarks.

"Start where you want to end up," he says, pointing at the calm water far downstream. "See that black rock sticking up just before you get to the pool?"

I nod knowingly.

"You want to be just to the right of that rock when you go past it. You're going to be traveling pretty fast, so try to fix a picture of what it will look like in your mind."

He methodically works his way back up the rapids, reading the water like some Apache reading the prairie. To him, the line through the rapids is perfectly obvious. To me, it's an obscure vision, lost in the thunder of waves, the boiling haze thrown up by the churning waters. I need, he stresses, to see that invisible line that stretches from the top to the bottom of the rapids. I need to hold that line in my head and make sure the duckie tracks along that line—right of this rock, hard left around the hole, swing to right to avoid the suction under the rock. I think about that string as we hike back down to the boats.

"You don't have to do this," he says. "I've taught good kayakers who've taken a pass on this one."

I shrug it off. A duck's gotta do whatever it is a duck's gotta do.

"Well, don't worry about falling out," he says optimistically. "One way or the other, we're all going to end up in the same place."

With that Zen thought in mind, we head into the river.

The current snatches the duckie out of the eddy, and I'm into the first drop before I have time to really finish worrying. From then on, it's crazy time, my shoulders screaming as I fight to keep the duckie on the invisible line. Rocks loom up out of the spray like glistening white ghosts, appearing hugely, then disappearing, before my mind grasps what has happened. I pass the first marker to my left as a solid wall of river water passes over my head. The nose of the duck edges right, to the overhanging rocks with their vicious suction. *Paddle like hell . . . paddle like hell.* And we're back on the line. Time seems frozen as my body pumps chemistry into my bloodstream—flee or fight time. We nose into a huge hole, and I seem to be looking at the bottom of the river for a second. *The line . . . hold the line.* I'm paddling, but my left paddle is pulling air, since that whole side of the boat is no longer connected to the river. I pass the next marker slightly to the right, dead on the line. The funnel narrows now; the holes are deeper; the waves higher. The duckie sloes to the left, but I manage to coax it back to center. I drop into one last wall of water, and I'm through, into a calm pond overhung by rock. The duckie bounces off the rock wall and is still. I am, I discover, shaking.

Jonathan, on the other hand, is grinning.

"So," he says. "Want to do it again?"

Amazingly, before I can stop myself, I say yes.

The question, though, is, *have I fulfilled the whitewater-off-a-waterfall item on The List?* Denise says yes; I say maybe.

"You've done big water in a kayak," she says. "That ought to count, don't you think?"

I agree, but there's still a nagging feeling that I haven't given it my best shot. After all, I did write *waterfall*, not *big water*. Maybe, I also think, I'm taking this a bit too seriously.

Six months later, though, another assignment takes me to New Zealand. One of my activities there is something called "river surfing," which involves pitching one's self into whitewater on a Styrofoam "boogie" board, the type happy children might use for body surfing at a day on the beach.

It is when I stand 200 feet over the snapping, clawing rapids of the Karawaga River outside of Queenstown, New Zealand, that I am struck with how far I've gone, both literally, in miles, and spiritually, in my head. *When,* I find myself wondering as the dark, bitterly cold water torrents beneath me, *did The List take over my life? When did I first notice a normal, everyday existence giving way to some mad dash around the world, chasing . . . what? And did it even matter?*

"Feel like doing it, mate?" my guide, 20 years my junior, asks with an inflection that says, "If, that is, you're able to stumble your old bones down this cliff."

"No problem," I say.

Imagine being caught in a cosmic washing machine in the "agitate" cycle. Imagine being lifted out of your bed and shaken hard while somebody turns the full force of a firehose on your body. Make that an icy firehose—the water temperature is just above freezing; my wetsuit feels more like a T-shirt.

You cannot "fight" the river. You are in it, a part of it, being acted on by not just what you can see on the surface, but surging, racing currents below the surface. They pull you in contradictory directions, shove your legs apart and together; it is so unimaginably strong, and you are so very, very small.

The boulders, when they appear, are monstrous, house-sized. You see rounded curves and jagged edges. You distantly feel the impact on your lower body. You ride the waves, crash over the edge, feel the pressure drawing you down, down, down; shaking you hard; turning you loose. And then you can breath again; your legs cramp as you kick your way into an eddy, hunched onto the cold rocks, staring back into the living, breathing lair of the River Gods.

The river draws us on, the cold working its insidious way into my very bones. There are other rapids, strange swirly things that suck you into holes, spin you, spit you out. To borrow an old cliché, we are caught in the coils of a massive snake, tossed by the rippling muscles while hypnotized by the beauty of its scales.

Here is where I finally get it, where, I think, The List finally hits home:

I am sitting in a restaurant, staring at a plate of smoked salmon pasta. I am holding a glass of red wine in my left hand. I sip it; it's a dark, smoky merlot. I don't know where I am. I don't recognize the people around me. It is as if I have just been born, on the edge of a plate of pasta, holding a glass of wine. Pieces come back, but with agonizing slowness. I hold the wine, look at the people, remember the river. Part of the river. I don't remember, for instance, the last set of rapids. I don't remember how I got out of the river. I don't remember climbing the steep cliffs to the car, shucking my wet suit, drying off, riding to a nearby winery. Talking. Carrying on a conversation. I don't remember ordering the wine, but it is one of my favorites.

My god, I think, chills dancing up and down my spine. *What have I lost?*

The Lake Taupo district of the North Island is unquestionably beautiful, but it chafes at Queenstown's smug title as the adventure capital of New Zealand.

You can do anything in the Lake Taupo district, we're told, so we immediately go looking for anything to do. That's how we came to be, once again, donning wetsuits and climbing helmets, only a couple of miles from the thermal boles of Tokaanu Thermal Park, in the shadow of the old cone of the Ngaurahoe volcano. Dave Stott of Plateau Outdoor Adventure Guides meets us with a bevy of guides-to-be, unemployed city youth the government is paying to learn a trade—river rafting.

Today, though, we aren't rafting. We're going to take an inflatable kayak off a seven-meter waterfall ("Actually," says Stott, who, up until two years ago, used to be a bicycle messenger, "it's closer to eight meters. I measured."). Let's put this in perspective—it's sort of like paddling off the roof of a two-story building. *That,* I think, *is definitely a waterfall.* I resolve not to think about it.

"You don't have to do this," Denise says. She's been especially worried since the Karawaga rapids. I have been at times distant, rattled, worrying the lost minutes like a cracked tooth, trying to find what's missing in my head.

I shrug off her concern. It's not that bad, I say.

Suited up, we haul the specially built duckie down a narrow trail. The duckie has been reinforced to take the impact, and there's a flat plywood bulkhead for me to set my feet firmly on, and there are added airbags for extra floatation in the nose, the idea being that you might want to get back to the surface as quickly as possible.

It's a cold and crisp morning, and in the distance we can see a ski resort perched on an old volcano cone. We turn a corner and are confronted by the torrents of water, crashing a long way down into a pool.

"Oh, shit. No way!" says one of the guides-to-be.

"The water's a little up," says Dave diplomatically.

I take one look at the waterfall and decide I'd better get myself together. *Mikey blow bubbles*, I think.

We hike the boat to a beautiful spot just above the waterfall. It's so pristine that I keep expecting Bambi to step to the edge of the stream for a sip. I stick my hand into the water, and my fingers go instantly numb.

"Well," says Dave, "time for a safety briefing."

Which is, make sure your feet are flat on the kayak's bulkhead ("So your ankles don't break on impact, don't you know?") paddle hard, so you've got some speed when you go sailing off the edge of the world, get your oar over your head so you won't eat it on impact, and down you go.

"You know this is at your own risk," says Jason, one of the guides-to-be.

"Isn't everything?" I reply. Before I have time to really think about it, I slide into the kayak, splash a little of the ice-cold water on my face to, hopefully, take some of the edge off and get shoved into the fast current.

"Arms up! Arms up!" shouts Dave as I rocket toward the edge. I raise my arms, and time begins slowing down. The nose of the kayak is thrusting into air, not water. The nose of the kayak begins pointing downward, and we are falling, falling, falling. It takes about two forevers—my old friend adrenaline, twisting reality—to hit the impact zone, I see stars from the shock of the cold, and then we are *sinking, sinking, sinking* toward what Dave calls the Green Room, the cold, calm water deep underneath the waterfall. From the Green Room, I look up and see the kayak is between me and the surface.

"Time to bail," an alarm goes off in my head, and I'm out of the boat. The hell with the duckie. The pool isn't that big, and I don't want to get blown down the next set of falls, which don't look all that—how to phrase this, *survivable*. And then I'm back on the surface, in a world of light and air, swimming for the shore, my kayak following along behind me like a wet puppy dog.

Whitewater off a waterfall.

No problem.

13

Claustrophobia Check

THE FEELING IS BUTTERFLIES—DEFINITELY BUTTERFLIES.

Butterflies that flutter around my stomach and threaten to make a permanent home in the back of my head as I slowly circle the crystal-glass-clear, 72-degree year-round, water of north Florida's Ginnie Springs, looking down. There's a hole in the bottom of Ginnie Springs, and in a few moments, I'm going to glide into it, through the looking glass, down into a dark, dark world of smoothly sculpted limestone walls and ceilings, where cold currents rush out of tiny openings and air pockets shimmer silver, puddles of mercury trapped on the low ceilings, caught in my lights.

Time for a reality check:

In the palmetto scrub flatlands of north central Florida, below the grazing pastures of the gray Brahma cattle, not that far from the Disney-spawned suburbs, is an awesome underground world—a collection of springs and rivers and caves to challenge even the broadest imagination. The "doors" to the labyrinth are the springs, where the underground water has erupted through to the surface, and the sinks, where the ground has literally fallen away. I've traveled to Ginnie Springs to come to grips with that proverbial hole in the ground, because the springs sit smack over the heart of underground Florida, Mecca for cavern and cave divers from around the world.

In all honesty, of the 13 items on The List, cave diving is proving to be the hardest nut to crack. Unlike most of the other items on The List, SCUBA is primarily an intellectual, rather than a physical, exercise. The intellectual challenge is driven by the fact that even basic SCUBA is insanely equipment intensive; the challenge is to become knowledgeable in and comfortable with a self-contained underwater life support system.

The other challenge is that SCUBA itself is fairly rigidly structured. In order to be issued a "C-card," a certification that allows you to fill SCUBA tanks with air, a person has to complete a course offered by one of several certifying agencies. The courses aren't particularly hard, but they are time-consuming and, once the equipment is factored in, expensive. I sail through the basic SCUBA course, then move quickly onto the more advanced offerings.

After a series of classes that includes diving to below 100 feet, underwater navigation, exploring wrecks, rescue and other specialties, my instructor asks me what I really want to do.

"I want to dive caves," I told him.

"Idiot," he says.

Like most people in Florida, I first heard about cave diving from newspaper headlines announcing another death in the caves. Eventually, I run down John Orlowski, who, with his wife, Shelley, are two of the top cave-diving instructors in the world.

"It's like this," says the ultra-low-key Orlowski, who moved to rural north Florida to be close to the caves he loves, "underwater caves are the most unforgiving environment on this planet. It's like being in space—the consequence of a systems' failure or a mistake in judgment is swift and brutal. You die, and you die hard."

For years, cave diving was nearly invisible, a sport that kept itself out of the limelight. It has recently, though, come out of the closet.

"When the diver is properly trained and using the proper equipment, cave diving is probably one of the safest forms of diving," says

Orlowski. He and Shelley exchanged their wedding vows in a legendary underwater cave system in Mexico. "When the diver isn't trained, it's probably the most dangerous."

Orlowski himself helped to boost the visibility of cave diving when he and partner Steve Gerrard raced to Venezuela to rescue a diver trapped deep in a cave, an event chronicled on television's Rescue 911 show and in the pages of *Reader's Digest*.

"Actually, we thought we were going in to retrieve a body," says Orlowski. "The diver was lucky enough to find a large air pocket, and he was waiting for us after 36 hours."

It's easier to talk about cave diving than it is to do it. For a species that spent many of its formative years climbing trees to escape animals with big teeth, the idea of going down in the dark sets off all kinds of alarms. I've managed to arrange a "tour" of some of the systems, all that's possible for a non-cave-certified diver, and even that's pushing the envelope. Finally, however, I'm in the water.

"Not me," I think, hovering over the entrance to a small cave in Florida's Ginnie Springs, one of the gateways to the huge underground world not that far from Mickey Mouse. A voice—my voice?—keeps repeating, "Not me." The hole in the bottom of the springs seems like some kind of item from a particularly grim Grimm tale, just waiting to snap me up. I talk calmly to myself as my partner gestures downward. Then, my heartbeat more or less under control, I drift through the entrance.

Once inside, there is the inescapable knowledge that the clock is running—every exhaled air bubble that becomes pooled mercury in the ceiling crevices is another minute gone. The logic of the air bottles on your back is simple and absolute: you don't want to still be underwater when the air runs out.

Divers began penetrating Florida's underground world almost as soon as Jacques Cousteau and partner perfected the Aqua-Lung in the early 1950s. With the earliest penetrations came the first deaths. More so than their dry-land counterparts, underwater caves are totally unforgiving. A simple equipment problem that might be an inconvenience in open water, where the diver has a clear shot to the surface, can be a death warrant in a cave. The floors of many underwater caves are covered with the silt of ages, a silt so fine that, when stirred up by an unwary diver's fins, can completely obscure the way out. More than one diver has spent the last air in the bottle looking for the now-hidden way home.

After grim years in the 1970s, with more deaths and more and more caves being closed off to protect uneducated divers, the statistics began to turn. The secret was, not surprisingly, in knowledge. Caves could be dived safely, but only through the rigorous application of painfully learned techniques. Divers developed a training procedure, taking an open-water SCUBA diver through a four-step process to full cave-diver certification.

"First and foremost, there has to be a certain attitude and mental preparedness," says Orlowski. "Cave diving may not be more physically demanding than open-water diving, but it is mentally much more strenuous ... With open-water diving, the theory is that if you have a problem, you can always go to the surface. Cave divers don't have that option. You have to handle the problem right there, on the bottom."

And the problems can be many—equipment failures, rocks taking their toll on fragile gear, the occasional cramp or numbing cold. Or The Fear, the simple knowledge that there are tons and tons of rock and water between you and the World Above. Your pupils dilate; your breathing becomes rapid and shallow; you are sweating inside your wet suit which, up until a moment ago, was barely keeping you warm. Your brains says, simply, one word, "Out!"

There's a question I hear welling up out there, and it boils down to, "Why?"

With cave diving, that's a tough question to answer. Orlowski talks about how beautiful, peaceful, and relaxing the caves are. I speak with Michael Madden, another top cave diver. He's camped out in the jungles in Mexico, getting ready for another expedition into the Nohoch cave system, the longest cave system in the world.

"I've got 20 divers in there now, and I'm heading back as soon as I finish some computer mapping here," Madden says through a crackling phone connection. "I mean, the classic description for cave diving is 'The Star Trek Syndrome,' to boldly go where no person has gone before. I think that's what stimulates most of us."

Madden first began cave diving after instructing for a couple of years in Mexico.

"I'd take my students for their training dives in these fresh-water sinks, and I'd see these black holes leading back into caves," he remembers. "I'd just be staring at these holes, thinking, 'I wonder where that goes?'"

They're both right, I think, but that hardly captures the haunting beauty of the smoothly twisted stone walls, the rooms, the narrow passages. I remember one diver talking about "flying" through a cave system, as close as you can get to visiting another world and still be on Earth. It is, I think, that other-worldly quality that resonates with some people; the closest I can come to describing the feeling of cave diving is as a space walk, extravehicular activity in a hostile environment.

I float through the easiest cave system, entranced. The fear that seemed so strong when I followed the fixed line into the cave has vanished, replaced by wonder. As a preplanned experiment, we shut off our lights for a moment, and it is dark beyond imagining, womb-dark, a world without a word for light. We flick back on the big cave floods, and in the crevices see small fish—there are many denizens in the cave; the deeper you go, the less use for unnecessary appendages like eyes. We move downward, the passage narrowing until my tanks touch the ceiling, my body inches above the floor. The first time my tanks touch, a shock wave ripples through my body—narrow, so very narrow. The animal in my head, which, up until this point has been silent—largely, I think, out of shock—starts rattling the bars.

And this cave is practically huge, by cave standards.

I decide then and there that a "tour" doesn't fulfill the cave-diving entry on The List. I will have to learn how to cave dive on my own.

This proves to be harder than I originally anticipate. The first instructors I talk to listen patiently, study my log of dives and suggest I, "come back in a couple of years."

Eventually, I turn to Shelley Orlowski. I figure anybody who gets married in an underwater cave might be sympathetic to my pleas.

"We can work something out," she says.

What working something out means is that I continue to take dive classes, one after another, whenever I can scrape up the money and the time. What I'm leading up to is John's Full Cave course, eight or nine days of intensive training in the north Florida cave systems. Before I can be certified as a cave diver, I have to have a minimum of 15 cave dives, in at least five different cave systems. And, of course, I'll need to have my own equipment, which is totally different from recreational SCUBA equipment. Of course.

I finally meet the Orlowski's standards for training and head down to Live Oak, Florida, and two weeks at the No-Tell Motel, $22.95 a night; $25 for the "deluxe" room with a remote control for the television. I pull out all the stops and pop for the deluxe.

After a long drive into the country, I turn left down a sand road to the Orlowski's trailer. There are horses, dogs, cats, a vegetable garden, a fountain, fish, and dive equipment all over the place. There are also, in the middle of the menagerie, the Orlowskis. John is tall, with the emaciated rock star look; Shelley short and dark, but also with the rock star look. Pierce their noses, and they could pass easily on Melrose Avenue in L.A. While Shelley heads out to teach another class, John and I talk. Rather, I talk; John coaxes. What he's looking for, I finally decide, is motivation—am I here on a whim, or am I really committed. This is actually a pretty good question, so I answer honestly.

"I don't know," I say. "We'll see later."

As it gets later and later, I figure we're not going to do any diving. But just before sunset, John abruptly stands.

"Let's go do a little diving," he says.

We load up his cluttered dive van and drive to Peacock #2, a hole in the limestone strata with an entrance into the underground world. This time, however, we're not going to be entering that world. We're just going to drop down around 18 feet in the cool lake and let me practice following a line.

In the caves, lines are life. They're your umbilical cord to the outside world, the way home. Famous caves, like the north Florida system, have permanently attached mainlines, laid by explorers like the Orlowskis. The lines are color-coded and intricately mapped. Where there aren't any fixed lines, I'll lay my own, using one of a number of reels that I'll have to get used to carrying. That's Rule Two of cave diving: Always have a continuous line to the surface. Rule One, by the way, is: Always be trained.

We drop into the cool water as the sun sets, and John runs a long circle of nylon cord off his main reel around the bottom of the little lake. First, I get to follow the line with my eyes open. The next lap, I follow by feel, with my eyes closed. Not that it matters; with the sun down and the lights off, the little lake is as dark as a tomb. Finally, I take off my mask, stow it, and follow the line by feel again. Masks have a way of becoming diver safety blankets, a little piece of dry land to hang onto. A surprisingly large number of divers will panic when their masks are knocked off or lost.

When we surface, the north Florida sky is alive with stars.

The first days are easy. I follow John through the cave systems at Peacock #1 and Telford Sink. As before, The Fear quickly gives way to almost an enchantment, caught in the lure of a totally alien environment. It is like, I think, entering a Giant's Lair, stealing through some part of a Great Game, played out in the flooded labyrinths below some long-dead castle.

John works patiently on my skills—learning to kick without stirring up silt, adjusting my buoyancy to compensate for the almost

200 pounds of dive gear I'm carrying. Telford is silty, with visibility reduced to a few feet. I feel my heart rate increase, the animal in my head pounding on the walls.

The line! The line!

But the line is there, just within my reach. I stifle an almost overwhelming urge to grab the thing.

"You'll want to hang onto the line, but you're going to resist that impulse," John has told me. "Panic is a strange thing. It affects different people different ways. One of those ways is to clamp down on the mainline and not move. You sort of freeze up. Of course, it makes your body easy to find."

It is amazingly hard not to grab the line. The world is reduced to a soft brownish-gray ball, around two feet in diameter, centered around my nuclear-powered cave lights. The mainline drifts in and out of that glowing sphere, like a dream, an image caught in a fading, too grainy photograph. I become better acquainted with the animal in my head, always on the verge of emerging in its screaming, mind-numbing glory.

"Of course I'm scared," John tells me before the dive. "Anybody who's not scared is a complete fool. But fear doesn't have anything to do with how you act. Even if you're going to die, you might as well die doing the right thing, which is trying to get out."

The mythology of cave diving is full of such stories, the lost diver methodically searching for a way out, until all the air is gone. One of the most experienced cave divers, hopelessly trapped in an underground avalanche, continued digging until the very end. He died, but his partner was able to make it to safety. "When faced with dying or achieving the impossible," writes Orlowski in his manual for cave diving, "some people choose to live."

Of course, there is one tunnel that John doesn't like to go into, since a woman cave diver became separated from her fiancee—and the mainline—and panicked and just kept swimming down a long dead-end tunnel. Her frantic claw marks are etched into the silt of the currentless tunnel, maybe into the limestone itself. Finally, John says, the claw marks stop.

At first, I am put off by this macabre talk. Then it finally dawns on me what is happening. Cave diving is a deadly sport, with no margin for error. The people who train new cave divers want that point driven home so deeply that there can be no question of misunderstanding, no question of, "Why didn't you tell me . . . " Every cave diver I meet can name someone—a friend, an acquaintance, a spouse, an instructor, a student—who has gone in, but not come out of, the caves.

Every one.

The next morning we drive to another cave system, Madison, the entrance to which is in a beautifully landscaped private park for cave divers. It is bright and sunny, and the sink itself is a clear crystalline blue. There are two entrances to the cave system, John says in our extensive predive briefing. Because there's a substantial flow of water out of the cave, we'll go in the smaller, off-to-the-side entrance to avoid the big flow.

And, oh yes, the "smaller" entrance is a lot smaller. Just big enough to shove yourself through, tanks scraping on the rocks, chest in the silt.

"It's not far," John says. "Ten or 15 feet. I'll go through first, and you follow my light."

Another test, I think as my stomach knots and the animal in my head goes stark raving crazy.

Once underwater, John slips through the little hole in the wall like an eel. I peer in, and see his light beckoning. *It's not far,* I think. *Ten or 15 feet.* I put my head somewhere else, bury my chest in the muck, and start pushing my way through. What seems to work best is crawling on my fingertips. I can feel my tanks scrape on the rocks above me—*the rocks above me . . . tons and tons of rocks above me . . . crushing me crushing me crushing me*—I move like an inchworm, until 15 feet are up. I pop out of the tunnel. John signals "okay?" I signal "okay" back.

We do endless drills—take off mask, put mask on; shut off the right tank, shut off the left tank; turn lights off, and do it all in the dark. The purpose of the drills is to, as John puts it, make sure my brain keeps working, no matter what.

"The one piece of equipment that can't fail is your brain," he says. "As long as your brain is working, you have a chance."

The Madison cave is, for me, what cave diving is all about. I feel like I'm flying, through the tunnels, into the rooms. We fly along the top of the caves, through upside-down valleys and mountain ranges in miniature. When my gauges read that I've used up a third of my air (Rule #3: One-third going in, one-third coming out, one-third in reserve), I turn sorrowfully. I can't wait to come back.

Mid-week, we pick up another student, and the training gets progressively tougher. We practice following mainlines out of caves with our lights off, moving along the lines as they twist and turn from the caves, only the lightest touch connecting us to the way home. First above ground, then underwater, in the dark, we practice finding a lost line:

In a dark that is darker than dark, the pure absence of light, I disconnect my reel, loosen the tension knob, and tie off the end to a knob of rock I have located by touch. Now, I know where I am, and I can get back to my reference point. I feel the rock wall behind me, and in my mind, I visualize a straight line away from that wall. Crawling along the rock bottom of the cave, I follow that line, until I reach the far wall. I add a bit of air to my buoyancy wings, and begin climbing up the wall. Without light, with no visual clues at all, up and down have no meaning. I add more air and start climbing back across the ceiling, reeling out line. When I get back to my reference point, I have "captured" the mainline in my loop. I now know the way home again.

In one drill, John drops behind us, and, suddenly, he is gone. The other student and I frantically search the dark surface of the sink, but no John. As we prepare to resubmerge, Shelley walks to the water's edge.

"Where's John?" she asks.

"I don't know," I say.

"Great," she says casually. "You guys killed my husband. He's not much of a husband, but he's all I got."

At that moment, John's head pops to the surface.

"Anybody want to explain how I got dead?" he says. My face burns crimson in the dark.

The drills get harder. We practice out-of-air drills, moving with the lights out and only touch contact between divers. We practice swimming through "restrictions," narrowings in the tunnel, without our regulators, holding our breaths. A swim of 25 feet—not even an effort swimming along the bottom of the pool—is a lifetime of anxiety. Most of our drills are in Cow Sink, a small, beautiful jewel-like cave. There are numerous rock formations, strange shapes, perfect little rooms; when I think of cave diving now, I think of little Cow. Now John is actively trying to trick us. Once, John and another instructor jump from the mainline to a side tunnel with its own line. The other student follows, but I refuse. I stay on the mainline and use my light to signal down the other tunnel. After a few minutes, the other three divers turn around and return to the mainline.

When we get out, John asks, "What would you have done if we hadn't come back?"

"I would have left you a message on the mainline with my writing slate, then I would have exited," I say nervously.

"That's correct," he says. "It's easier to get a new partner than a new life."

"But you're the instructor," the other student blurts. "I followed you because you're supposed to know what you're doing."

"What did I tell you on the first day?" John replies calmly. "Following anyone blindly can get you killed, along with whomever you're following."

"But . . . "

"There aren't any 'buts . . .'" John says, again mildly. "You'll only get one mistake. This is the hardest dive training you'll ever do, and we have a reason for making it that hard."

I have been in the caves for nine days, diving two, three sometimes four times a day. The fear doesn't really go away, but I find myself looking forward to each new cave system. Technically, John says one morning, I've completed the course, but if I'd like to hang around and dive awhile, feel free. I jump at the invitation.

We do one last set of drills, lights out. I pretend I am out of air, and the other student hands me his "octopus," a separate breathing regulator on a seven-foot-long hose. We then begin the long, dark swim out of the cave. Most of the mainlines have some sort of surveyors marks or tags, and I have counted marks going in, so I'll have some kind of reference coming out. We move slowly, me in the lead, breathing off the long hose attached to my partner's tanks. I have an "okay," a very light touch on the mainline, but my fingers are locked tightly together, so the line won't slip away. My partner is touching my leg and maintaining his own light hold on the mainline. Every minute or so, I see a brief flash of light as John monitors our position. John picked this cave because the mainline goes through all sorts of contortions, around, over, down, and through. At several points, the mainline runs through narrow constrictions, blocking forward movement. Several times, I am stuck briefly. *I got in*, I think (the animal screams and shouts and beats the bars of the cage) *I can back out*. About halfway home, there is thrashing behind me. My partner has lost his hold on the mainline. He still has my leg, but he's thrashing, feeling for the lost line. With each thrash, he jerks the regulator in my mouth. I am like a hooked bass. I decide to give him 30 seconds, then I'm turning on my lights and going back to my own regulator. I start counting... *lollipop one... lollipop two... lollipop three...* let the air out of my wings and sink a foot to the stone floor of the cave. Keeping a solid hand on the mainline, I make sure my own regulator is handy and that I can easily reach the light switch. Then I wait. At lollipop 25, I feel my partner's hand groping up my leg. *Good*, I think. *He's connected to me; I'm connected to the line. Follow my arm, and pretty soon, he'll have the line back...*

Which is exactly what he does.

When we emerge, the Florida night is cool. There is just enough of a breeze to keep the mosquitoes at bay. We shuck the tons of equipment, and sit in the night.

"You like this, don't you?" John asks me.

"Yep," I say.

"Like it enough to keep doing it?"

"Yep."

"Good."

14

Air

I AM HANGING, SECURELY WRAPPED IN A CANVAS COCOON, above and behind the bed of a bright red Japanese truck. I am wearing a blue helmet and swaying in the wind. To my left, which I can see out of the corner of my eye when the wind weathervanes me around, is a county prison; to my right is a windsock, which is sticking straight out and looking like it wants to rip free of its moorings. Above me is a brightly colored kite; ahead of me is a runway. It ends in a stand of trees.

"Comfortable?" asks Dave Glover, my companion sausage creature and pilot of the aforementioned kite.

I nod. Trussed up as I am, as long as I don't see Sharon Stone with an icepick, I'm as good as I'm likely to get.

"You know, there's never been a fatality involving tandem hang-gliding," Dave says, as if this is supposed to be comforting. He has the bedside manor of one of those family doctors in Norman Rockwell paintings. We hang together under the single dragonfly wing of the kit, and he runs through the basic instructions. Push the bottom bar forward to slow down, pull back to speed up; hips to either side to turn.

"Gentle, small motions," he cautions. "No need for a death grip.

And when in doubt, let go. The kite wants to fly. Really."

I nod and attempt to look happy. I am actually practicing deep-breathing exercises, which I continue while Dave runs through his preflight check.

We are hooked in, all set, the kite ready for the sky.

"Ready?" he asks.

I nod, jauntily, I think.

"Hey, this is going to be great!" he says. "One other thing—if you feel like you're going to hurl, don't turn your head toward me to tell me, okay?"

I nod. And we are rolling down the runway, the red truck gathering speed down the runway.

"It's going to be a little bumpy going up," Dave says, his helmeted head next to mind. "Nothing to worry about."

I nod. Bumpy. That's always good.

There is a tiny *ping* as Dave frees the hang glider from the embrace of the speeding truck. And then . . .

. . . I am falling . . . up.

I am in an elevator, cut loose from it's cables and falling wildly toward the 33rd story. I am trapped in a reverse bungee jump . . . a "Nightmare on Elm Street movie," where undead Freddy snatches you up through the ceiling . . .

Suddenly, below us, the red truck has gotten very, very small, a scuttling red beetle to which we're attached by a reinforced cord. The beetle careens off the runway, heading toward the stand of trees. Tugged by the inexorable cord, we keep climbing.

"Whew!" shouts Dave. "I love it every time!"

I attempt to nod, but am unable to complete the maneuver, due to my heart, which is apparently lodged in my throat.

I have these ambivalent feelings about flying. Part of me feels the pull that the Wright Brothers must have felt, that reverse gravity that causes one to stare longingly and lovingly at birds in flight, to feel the pull of a kite in the wind and think, "Why not?"

Balanced against that longing is the pure rat-scrabble fear of a species that evolved out of the trees—that of taking the long fall, arms flailing, clutching at nothing but pure air, an endless primeval scream ripped from an unwilling throat. Okay, maybe it's too many bad movies, but I am honestly afraid of heights—although my co-sausage, Dave, has a theory that no one is actually afraid of heights; what we're all really afraid of is the loss of control that falling brings. Ironically, as I will later learn in the mountains, he will prove to be exactly correct.

John Harris—the person responsible for strapping me to this particular kite— got all of the first part—the longing for the air—without the downside fear of the long fall. He grew up on a farm in Missouri, watching kites drift in the winds of hot midwestern summers. He even managed to get a degree in engineering and head for a career as an oceanographer before he stumbled on a grainy wire service photograph in the local Winston-Salem, North Carolina, newspaper. The picture was of a fledgling hangglider. That was in 1973.

"Your own personal wing," he says today, still with an element of awe. "No airport. No engine. No launching strip."

He began an almost frantic search for information on the hangglider and finally traced the maker down through the newspaper. Once he found the kitemaker, he did the only thing that made any sense—Harris bought one, and, armed with a poorly made eight-millimeter film of "How To Fly" and a tremendous amount of faith, carted the flimsy thing to the high dunes of Kitty Hawk, where the Wright Brothers found their wings, and jumped off.

"It flew, more or less," he says. By the end of the first hike back up the dunes, he was "hooked on the idea of a personal, portable flying machine. I thought everybody ought to be able to fly one of these things."

Exit John Harris the Engineer; enter John Harris the Hang-Gliding Evangelist. Since then, Harris and his Kitty Hawk Kites, located across the highway and slightly south of his first flight, have put 170,000 people on kites and lobbed them off the same dunes. The dunes, as the Wright Brothers figured out in 1903, are an ideal place to fly. Stand on any of the dunes along North Carolina's Outer Banks, that impossibly thin stretch of sand that barriers the mainland from the Atlantic, and watch a brown pelican just hanging in the sea breeze and you'll see the first reason why. The usually steady easterly wind and the dune's gently sloping launching ramps make launching incredibly easy. You can start low, learn the basics, and gradually move to higher dunes. And, speaking from experience, there's a lot more "give" to soft sand than to, say, concrete. Plus, there's something undeniably cool about Jockey's Ridge State Park, which is probably the only park that's headed south. The sand dunes are migrating to the south. They're threatening homes and roads, and the mobile sand has already swallowed a miniature golf course, which possibly proves that even a dune can have a sense of humor. On our way to the launching spot, we hike uphill past a pointed concrete cone, the top of the golf course's castle, an artifact for future archeologists.

My first experiences in launching off the dunes, last summer in a fluky, gusty southwest wind, helped me learn the origin of the phrase "lawn dart," a tricky maneuver that involves cramming the nose of the kite—and my nose as well—into the soft sand.

"Uh-oh," said my instructor. "Lawn dart time."

Sand and all, though, hanggliding retains that sense of adolescent fantasy, of stepping off a cliff and, miraculously, going up instead of down. Flight, breaking free from gravity for the tiniest part of a second, is a powerful drug, one that is not easily forgotten.

Training fledgling flyers, however, is more prosaic.

Hanggliders appear amazingly simple. Imagine a large kite with an aluminum trapeze slung underneath it. That's all, folks. Of course, today's gliders represent more than 20 years of evolution, sleek flying machines that share few handling characteristics with the first clumsy kites.

"We say that gliders will fly themselves," Harris adds, "and that's the literal truth. Part of learning to fly now is learning a light touch, so you don't disturb the glider."

Controls, learned in ground school, are simplicity in themselves. The pilot hangs suspended ("Like a sack of potatoes," says chief instructor Bruce Weaver) underneath the center of the wing in a harness. Hands rest on the control bar, the lower leg of the aluminum triangle under the wing. Pushing forward on the control bar noses the glider up into the wind, which slows it down. Pulling back on the control bar has the opposite effect, pulling the nose down and increasing speed. To turn the glider, shift your weight in the direction you wish to turn, which involves a sort of push-pull movement on the bar to get your hips going the right way.

"That's it," says Weaver.

To land, you push the bar all the way forward—this is called flaring. To get an idea of how it works, watch any bird. Wings flair; birds (and good hang-glider pilots) land gracefully on their feet.

The next steps involve the Sisyphusian task of walking up the dune, which will remind you that you're not in nearly as good shape as you think you are, hooking in and performing a "hang check" to make sure your precious sack of potatoes is securely attached to the glider. Then, standing, with the control bar held securely to your thighs and the glider nosed into the wind, you start running toward the edge of the dune. If there's any sort of wind at all, within about three steps you'll notice an interesting phenomenon—you're running, but your feet are no longer touching the ground. With your instructor running alongside shouting instructions—"Shift your weight right! No, your *other* right!"—you sled through the air down the face of the dune. You fly. "Flare! Flare! Flare!" And, ideally, seconds later, you land on your feet.

"It's not hard," says Bruce Weaver as we wrestle the ungainly butterfly back up the face of the dune. "You just have to dial the movements into your body. You might also want to consider not having a death grip on the control bar. The kite'll fly itself."

To prove his point, one of the other instructors takes a pink-winged Eaglette, the training gliders Kitty Hawk Kites use, runs to the edge of the dune and keeps on flying. His hands don't touch the control bar until it's time to flare.

"See?" says Bruce. "Overcontrol—not undercontrol—is the problem."

The most recent training wrinkle is tandem training—the student and an instructor fly together on an oversized kite launched from a truck or a boat, or even pulled aloft with an ultralite aircraft, basically a powered hangglider.

"Think of flying as a sandwich," says Dave, one of Kitty Hawk's top tandem instructors. "The bread of the sandwich is training on the dunes, learning takeoffs and landings. But you don't really get to fly much while you're learning. The baloney of the sandwich is tandem instruction, where you really get to fly."

Item 8 on The List: *Skydive, and whatever those kite and parachute thingies are . . .*

Item 8, as might be obvious, came after the first pitcher of beer had been consumed. Afterwards, I decided that, on the balance, skydiving might be the easiest thing on The List to accomplish, since it seemed to be a case of "You pays your money, you jumps out of your airplane." Still in Tampa, I also figured the proximity to the Zephyrhills Sport Parachute Center, north of the city, wouldn't hurt. In fact, the telephone book is full of skydiving academies.

The only drawback to quickly knocking off Item 8 is that just the thought of jumping out of an airplane makes me sick to my stomach. I have this persistent vision of being scraped off the field, the drop zone, with a spatula, my mortal remains crammed into a sandwich-sized baggy. Everyone shakes their head sadly: "Chute didn't open, but he died like a man . . . we guess."

I finally hit on a strategy that I think will work. I will give my buddy Denise a gift certificate to a skydiving academy for her birthday, since she has at least evidenced a passing interest in jumping. Then, out of humiliation and fear of being drummed out of the Guy

Corps, I will jump with her.

Before I can think of the thousands of reasons as to why this is a stupid plan—after all, "stupid plan" has been my theme song—I start making phone calls.

The first calls aren't very promising.

"This week only," the female voice on the telephone, probably belonging to someone in the, say, 16-year-old range, "we're offering discount skydives."

Discount skydives? Is this smart?

"For example," she continues relentlessly, "if you sign up no later than Friday, which is tomorrow, I can offer you $50 off your first jump . . . Can I have your credit card number?"

I say I'll call her right back.

The next academy is only a phone call away.

"Your good luck, man," the operator (an instructor himself, he informs me) says. "We're in the middle of a price war. Our war is your good fortune . . . "

Price war?

I make another call to speak to a friend of mine who writes books about skydiving. As a rule, he says, price breaks aren't really important in a sport where they can scrape you off the drop zone with a spatula.

"Ask them whether their instructors are on salary and how long the instructor you get has been working there," my friend says. "Ask how many jumps your instructor has. Since you're probably going to be doing a tandem jump, that is, you'll be attached to the instructor, ask how long the instructor has been tandem rated and how many tandem jumps he or she has. Other than that, just have a good time."

Sure.

About the fourth phone call, I get the First Right Answer:

"We don't do sales," the person says. "And we don't offer discounts. In fact, we're about the most expensive school around."

I sign up before I lose my nerve.

The next weekend, Denise and I are on the way to Zephyrhills. I don't know what I expected. I guess I had some sort of television vision of guys and girls in Air Force khakis, starched and creased, running around neat, immaculate classrooms with clipboards while powerful airplanes roared overhead.

"This is it?" asks Denise incredulously when we pull up to the Zephyrhills—Z-Hills—drop zone.

It looks like a Grateful Dead concert, only without the stage. The drop zone itself, a couple of football fields worth of treeless Florida cow pasture, is surrounded by a motley collection of aging, paint-flaking school buses, campers, pick-up trucks, beat-up cars, brightly colored tents, lean-tos made of military surplus canvas, quilts scattered on the ground, cookfires, long-hairs in tie-dye holding babies of indiscriminate sex, wandering dogs, loud music and, incongruously, people falling out of the sky on brightly colored parachutes, all under the blaze of a Florida sun that would melt lead.

"Do we have backstage passes?" Denise asks innocently.

Instead of the neat, immaculate classrooms of my imagination, there are a series of prefab, partially constructed buildings, raw plywood and torn strips of tarpaper, plus the occasional trailer. A number of people of all ages, and judging by the languages being shouted all over the place, from a variety of nations wander from building to building. Or, shielding their eyes from the brutal Florida sun, staring into the sky, watching parachutes open.

And the plane . . .

Suffice it to say if an aging Volkswagen bus could be morphed into an airplane, that vehicle is sitting in front of us. It looks like a 1952 Airstream travel trailer with wings. All it needs is a Ford Fairlane station wagon with fake wood paneling to pull it around.

"I am not filled with confidence," Denise says.

"It's not as bad as it looks," I say confidently—a confidence I don't, by the way, even remotely feel. "But if I hear 'Dueling Banjos' from *Deliverance*, we're out of here."

Eventually, we find our "academy," which is a wooden building with most of its walls, a roof and a VCR.

"You guys gotta watch the film first," the receptionist says, wiping sweat from her face. "Then sign all the liability releases."

I like the film.

"No parachute is 100 percent safe . . . No airplane is 100 percent safe . . . You could be killed . . . "

The video itself shows an ambulance and a bunch of people, presumably with spatulas, clustered around an nondescript lump on a drop zone.

After about 10 minutes of video explaining that anyone who would willingly jump out of an airplane didn't have the sense of a can of peaches, we were presented with liability releases, which say the same thing—the DEATH part in upper-case letters—to sign.

"You know," says Denise, who is, additionally, a lawyer, "I believe these things will hold up in court. Not that it would matter to us . . . "

After signing away our lives, we start "ground school," which is primarily fitting a parachute harness and meeting our instructors, the guys who are going to be strapped to our backs for the duration.

"The plane is leaving in a few minutes," says a woman who sticks her head in through a missing wall. "You guys gotta go."

We're quickly fitted, then hustled to the "jump simulator," which is a shed about two feet off the ground, with an open door built to simulate our airplane's door—in other words, a large hole covered by a blanket. We hurry in through the side door, connect to our instructors and duck walk to the faux airplane door. Outside, we can hear the "Volksplane" cranking up. It sounds as if one of its rubber bands needs rewinding. Arching our backs, we jump gracefully two feet to the ground.

"Perfect," my instructor says. "Let's get on the plane."

I look back and see Denise grinning a grin usually reserved for particularly bad situations. I wave, and we race toward the Volksplane.

"I don't mean to sound stupid," I say as we wait to clamber in the empty belly of the beast. "But what about landing?"

"I'll explain on the way down," my instructor says.

"Oh."

As the plane lumbers down the grass runway, we get the short history of Z-Hills, which is, in fact one of the premier drop zones in the world. For most of the year, skydiving gypsies from all over make their temporary homes in the trailers and tents around the Z-Hills drop zone, living off savings or working around the academies for enough to scrounge flights up. The camp is called The Dark Side Of The Moon. Pink Floyd, I suspect, would approve. Some of the gypsies never leave, staying to become instructors or settling into the shaky central Florida economy with the other refugees.

I make the mistake of looking out the window.

Oh, shit.

As Denise will say later, the very worst part is taking off in a plane you know you won't be landing in.

The plane grinds like a Volkswagen bus heading up a steep incline, and I wonder if there's any chance I can talk my way out of this. I am sick to my stomach, sweating and rank with pure animal fear. The animal in my head is comatose with shock.

"You're doing great," says my instructor, which is good, since I'm still sitting on the floor of the plane. Denise waves. She looks green.

And then we're at 13,500 feet, our destination above the cow pastures. There are fleecy clouds around us. The sliding door in the rear of the Volksplane is slid up by a bunch of happy jumpers, who, laughing and talking, throw themselves out the door into the whipping wind.

"Okay!" my instructor yells over the wind. "Let's go!"

In a daze, I assume the waddling duck position, with my instructor clipped to my back. I check and recheck the clips. After all, he has the parachute. I have him. We waddle back to the door of the Volksplane, and for the first time, I look *down, down, down,* right into the pit of my nightmares. What, I think, am I doing here?

"Okay, Michael!" shouts my instructor as we crouch in the doorway, the wind blasting around us. "Take your left hand, and grab the right side of your harness!"

Moving slowly, like a Volkswagen through molasses, I accede to his request.

What does he really want?

"Okay, Michael!" He is so damned enthusiastic. "Now grab the left side with your *right* hand! That means you're going to have to let go of the door, Michael!"

Let go of the door?

Slowly, with a great act of will, my fingers come away from the worm metal of the Volksplane's sliding door frame. As soon as my hand clears the frame, my instructor falls left . . . and down.

He shouts something enthusiastic, and for one instant, I see the doorframe and the Volksplane falling away from me and the ground out of the corner of my eye. I am falling, free falling.

Months later, Nick diGiovanni, a 20-year skydiving veteran who specializes in jumping off buildings, will give me the best definition of free fall I have ever heard. It is like, he says, your mind is an index card file. Every one of those index cards contains an appropriate response to various outside stimuli, from current ones—like your boss is mad at you—to older, darker ones—you are being chased by a hungry saber-toothed tiger. When faced with a situation, your mind rapidly flips through the card file, looking for the appropriate response. But there is no appropriate response for falling at more than 100 miles per hour from a couple of miles in the air, and there's no way for you to "create" that card on the ground.

"You gotta do it," Nick says.

In the first few hundred feet, my mind goes stark raving crazy flipping through the card file, looking for something that matches *brain numbing noise, incredible speed, and the ground rising below you.* Not surprisingly, it can't find the card, so it takes the only other option available to it—it throws its little mental arms up in the air and shuts down.

"Is this great, or what!" my instructor, who I notice is still attached to my back, shouts above the roar of the wind.

He's asking me?

I manage to engage enough brain cells to arch my back and assume the flight position, my arms out and slightly ahead, like Rocky the Flying Squirrel. A few feet away, I see Denise, whose face is frozen by the speed and the wind into a rictus of a grin. She appears to have achieved a hamster-like flight position. She waves, and I think I wave back.

We fall from 13,500 feet to 4,500 feet in approximately 55 seconds. It is, even today, the longest minute of my life. At 4,500 feet, there is a slight bump, and, all of a sudden, the noise and the speed are gone. We rock gently below the parachute.

"Let's talk about landing," says my instructor.

"Good idea," I think I say.

A couple of minutes later, we land on our butts in a Florida cow pasture. A few feet away, Denise and her instructor turn a half-gainer, then skid to a stop. I wonder if kissing the ground would be appropriate.

But the kite thingies are better, or maybe free fall has given me a different perspective, a new set of index cards.

We are really flying, about 1,000 feet above the runway about 45 minutes north of the dunes. From underneath our glider, I can see far out into the Atlantic to the east; south all the way to the dunes themselves. We make lazy circles, searching for thermals—columns of heated air spiraling up. We catch a small one, and the kite climbs another couple of hundred feet.

"Look at that hawk over there," says Dave, pointing downward to a huge red-tailed hawk making lazy circles in his own thermal.

"His thermal is better than our thermal," Dave says. "Birds know these things. Next rotation, we're going to slide over to his thermal."

With a slight shift of weight, the kite slips across the sky into the neighboring column of air. We rise again, but not nearly as fast as we were rising. A quick glance show us the hawk has now faked us out and grabbed our thermal, where he's headed for the stratosphere.

"Okay," Dave says. "Maybe birds are smarter than people."

The flight is hypnotic, everything you might have imagined flying to be in those summer afternoon daydreams. The glider responds quickly to gentle movements—and, as billed, we take our hands off the control bar, and the glider flies on. But the wind is dying, and the miniature cyclones of the thermals vanish, leaving us back in the thrall of gravity. We slowly spiral down toward the runway.

I would like to report that we landed as gracefully as the aforementioned hawk touching down. Actually, thanks to the last gasps of a small thermal and my own innate clumsiness, we landed like Bruce Weaver's proverbial sack of potatoes, breaking pilot Glover's winning streak of perfect landings. Then we quickly reload the kite back on the truck, and it's reverse bungee time again.

Months later, I will actually become certified as a paragliding pilot, flying the soft wings, as opposed to the hard wings of the hanggliders, off the gentle hills around Boulder.

I will crash only once, smacking Wile E. Coyote-like into a cactus.

Ouch! the imaginary cartoon balloon over my head will say.

15

The Zen of Ice

T HE PLASTIC BOOTS—DOUBLE PLASTIC MOUNTAIN BOOTS, white, like oversized Mickey Mouse feet—crunch in the old snow, the sound muted by the wind. My instructor came to New Hampshire seven years ago with a newly minted degree in political science, intent on spending a summer away from the books before she started work. Any day now, she shrugs.

"There are two things to remember about ice," she is saying. "One, ice is not a solid, like rock. It's a liquid, a thick liquid. The second important thing flows, so to speak, from that first, and this is, *don't fall.*"

The ice we are talking about doesn't reside in cubes in glasses. Instead, it is the curtains of ice that stretch along this cliff face in New Hampshire, just outside the little town of North Conway, nestled in the White Mountains. North Conway is best known for its apparently endless string of factory outlets, drawing shoppers even on a bitterly cold afternoon in January from as far away as Boston. But North Conway's attraction for me has nothing to do with discounted Calvin Kleins or Bass Weejuns. It has everything to do with these frozen cliffs, the Frankenstein cliffs, one of the legendary ice climbing areas in America, and, for me, the best place to cross Item 7 from The List.

I arguably know less about ice climbing than I do about rock climbing, which is little indeed. But ice, with its hidden flaws and traceries of fault lines, carries with it something that rock does not—the true and ineradicable stench of danger, of risk. In rock climbing, protection is pretty, as they say, bombproof. A steel nut slipped into a crack, or a mechanical camming device with its hardened teeth dug into the rock, or even a bolt driven into the wall, offers a relatively secure place to attach your rope. Fall, and, in all likelihood, the protection will hold you.

On a frozen waterfall, though, the protection is usually an ice screw, a giant, almost foot-long screw with a hollow core. Where the pointed end of the screw would be is a ring of jagged teeth, which look sort of like the mouths of mutant leeches in old science fiction movies. The teeth chew away at the ice until the threads can catch. Then the climber finishes screwing the screw into the ice, the excess ice driven out through the hollow core, and clips the rope into the screw's head.

So far, so good. But ice, remember, isn't really a solid. Cranking a screw into a frozen waterfall is not the same as screwing a lag bolt into a 4 × 4 pine post. Pine is . . . pine, but the nature of ice is hidden, cloaked. Ice can be hard as steel or as soft and mushy as a snow cone. It can be as brittle as old glass or as malleable as a plastic sheet. Its hard surface can hide an even harder interior, or it can hide a spider's web of tiny fault lines, waiting to splinter at the slightest tap of a hammer. It's a safe bet that a pine post is likely to be a pine post for its entire length. But even the smallest frozen waterfall is a topographical map of different ice states, each with their own characteristics, their own natural laws.

Tomorrow, pine will still be pine, but ice may be something different. Ice is crystals in flux, growing, shrinking, changing states, melting, driven by pressures from within and without, by subtle shifts in temperature and humidity, by gravities we can never completely understand. Even the word "ice" isn't enough—climbers might refer to snow ice, granular ice, glacier ice, soft white ice, rotten ice, rime ice, hoarfrost, *neve*, *firnspiegel*, water ice, brittle ice, green ice, blue ice, black ice, *verglas* . . . live ice. Ice is a mysterious animal, in a lair we can only approach at our own risk.

On my way to New Hampshire, I had stopped in a climbing shop in Nashville to buy a pair of "expedition quality" climbing gloves for the ice. The clerk takes my money and stares at the bright blue gloves.

"Going on an expedition?" he asks.

"Ice climbing," I say, shrugging it off.

"Been climbing 20 years," the clerk replies, bagging my purchase. "Only fools climb ice."

Before my trip, I run into a serious rock climber, a professional on the indoor climbing circuit. I ask him whether he's excited about climbing this winter. He looks at me as if I was a not-very-intelligent bug.

"I buried three friends last winter," he says. "I want nothing to do with ice."

"Teaching ice is different from teaching rock," my instructor is saying as we hike along the cliffs. "We can take pretty much anyone and get them up the rock. But ice is so much more physically demanding, that we insist the student be in very good shape before we'll teach them."

"Why is ice more physically demanding than rock?" I ask.

"You'll see," she says.

It is seriously cold, below zero, a nasty, wet New England cold, with a wind whipping through the valley to add insult to injury. I am stuffed into borrowed ski clothes; I'm warm, but I have the mobility of an eight year old bundled up for the first snow of winter. We have spent most of the morning introducing me to the concept of self-arrest, that is, using my ice ax to arrest my slide, should I fall on a shallow ice slope.

I first have to meet My Friend The Ice Ax. Imagine a long-handled pick with a long, curving nose, serrations on the underside of the curve. The long nose of the ax will be driven into the ice, and the under serrations will grip tightly. The other side of the pick can be either a hammer or an adze. I'll climb with two axes, one with an adze, the other a hammer. But whenever I'm on an ice or snow slope, I'll always have an ax in the uphill hand, using the spike on the end of the handle as a walking stick, or using the long nose for self-arrest.

We practice arresting on an iced-over gravel road, frozen hard and as slick as those oil-soaked test pads in television car commercials. My first fall, I quickly slide all the way to the bottom.

"That is," she says, "what happens when you *don't* self-arrest."

For the next hour, I practice falling, then rolling over and jamming the nose of the ax into the ice. I fall face forward, I fall backwards, I fall feet first, and each time, I practice twisting, rolling and jamming my body weight onto the ax.

"Self-arrest has to be a reflex," she says. "Below the conscious level. If you fall out of your bed at night, you should automatically self-arrest."

"Will it work?" I ask. "Will it stop a really bad slide?"

"Depends on how steep it is and how hard the ice is," she says. "Even if it doesn't work, it gives you something useful to do in those closing seconds of your life."

The first frozen waterfall we approach hardly qualifies as a cliff. It's more of a gentle slope, coated with a meringue of hard bluish-green ice.

"It's harder than it looks," she says.

I don climbing harness and crampons—spikes that clip onto the bottom of my Mickey Mouse boots—while she talks about the dance of ice.

"You're going to find this hard to believe at first, but ice is about elegance," she says. "Guys especially like to slam that ax into the wall, kick those crampons in like a rampaging bull. But ice is about using a minimum effort to move up the wall. You'll catch on soon enough."

Ice climbing is the ultimate Spiderman fantasy. At its most extreme, your axes are tethered to your hands, and you step up using only the two forward-facing spikes—the front points—of your crampons. Set the axes, step up, set the axes, step up. You are a spider on a windowpane, moving up.

Ice climbing has always been a part of mountain—alpine—climbing. Obviously, much of the great mountains are ice and snow. But sport ice climbing, climbing frozen waterfalls, is relatively new, dating back to the late '60s and early '70s and driven by Yvon Chouinard, dubbed by *Outside* magazine as "the godfather of ice-climbing." Chouinard refined the alpine techniques and modified the mountain climber's equipment for waterfall ice.

We practice the beginner techniques, the flat-footed French technique, *pied a plat*, which involves twisting the ankles into all sorts of strange contortions to get the crampons flat against the ice, and front-pointing, facing the ice wall. We practice using only our hands, then one ax, then both axes.

Finally, we're ready for the first short climb. First, my instructor is going to climb to the top of the cliff and set her anchor for the top rope. Along the way, she'll protect herself with ice screws, and I'll be belaying her from the ground. As she gets ready to climb, she stops and moves her face close to mine.

"You are the most important person in the world," she says. "And I love you very much. Don't drop me."

We both laugh, but the point is made.

Once the anchor and the rope are set, she rappels down. We exchange places, and she picks an easy, short waterfall a couple of feet to our right as my first climb.

It is, in short, incredibly hard.

What looks so simple, so easy, when an accomplished ice climber makes the moves becomes a clumsy nightmare for me. For a start, my ax seems determined to not catch on the brittle ice. I pick my impact point, drive the ax into it, and, presto, ice cubes.

"Gently, Michael, gently."

I move up, but slowly, raggedly. My worst sin (which haunts me throughout The List) is an urge to move before I'm in balance. I need three points anchored in the ice to be in balance. I set one ax solidly (well, more or less solidly), then, leaning my weight against the ax, I step up on my crampons. Once I move my full body weight up, I adjust my feet to give me a solid platform to move from. When this works, it is an amazing feeling; when it doesn't, the primary feeling is an urge to throw up.

This is compounded by the fact that *ice is cold*!

It is below zero and windy, but I am already sweating profusely, a combination of fear and the fact that ice climbing engages major muscle groups of the arms and legs, generating heat. The combination of sweat and ice quickly seems to soak everything; my gloves soon squish.

I finish the first short climb and am deemed ready to climb to the top of the cliff.

"Remove the ice screws on your way up," my instructor says.

This route is steeper, and I quickly feel the heat in my triceps from the steady hammering with the axes—it's like hammering nails in as high above your head as you can reach. We have not trained our bodies to work this way. The more I front-point, the more my calves, which have the unpleasant duty of holding up my body while the points are attached to the ice, start lighting up. I imagine my calves looking like some sort of cartoon container, rapidly filling up with lactic acid and fatigue poisons.

"Is it supposed to hurt this much?" I shout down.

"Imagine," she shouts back, "wearing high heels all your life! Ice climbing is revenge!"

But I finally make the top, and it is one of the most sublime experiences I remember having, about the most fun you can have while freezing.

Over the next couple of days, we move to harder and harder routes. I am beginning to understand that concept of elegance. The cold, the wet, the fear, the effort suck strength at an incredible rate. In rock climbing, when arm muscles start flaming out, you can usually find a place to rest, to recover your strength. You can find a place to rest on the ice walls, but that doesn't make the cold go away. In fact, it makes it worse. As soon as you stop moving, you stop generating heat. Instead of a net heat gain, there's a net heat loss. One minute, you're thinking how hot you are; the next, your teeth are chattering.

Our climbs get longer, from one pitch—length of the rope—to two pitches—two lengths of the rope.

"Again," she says, "unlike rock climbing, on ice, we don't want to fall. We don't want to test our protection unless we absolutely have to. Most of the time, the screws will hold. Most of the time."

The fear is that if the ice screw pulls out, the added momentum of the longer fall will "zipper" all the other screws out of the ice. There are other equally good reasons for not falling. For starters, there are the 12 sharpened steel points on each of your feet, plus the two ice axes tethered to your hands. That means in even the smallest fall, there are a total of 26 knives flailing around, looking for something to stick into. Sort of advanced, psychotic juggling.

My instructor climbs the first pitch while I stay on a shivering belay. She sets three screws into the waterfall, just above a tiny ledge about 60 feet above the ground, anchors herself, then places me on belay. The climb is easy at first, becoming increasingly steep. As the "second," the second climber up, I also have to pull the ice screws that my instructor used to protect herself on the way up. The first screw practically pops out—had she fallen against it, the screw probably wouldn't have held. The second screw, though, about 20 feet higher, has apparently been screwed into aircraft grade titanium, then welded into place. My calves are quivering—"sewing machine legs"—as I find a balanced spot on the nearly vertical wall to wrestle with the frozen screw. I find a little chip of ice that lets me place my left foot almost flat against the waterfall, then I set the front points of my right boot. I stand up, hammer my left ax into the wall, then loosen the tether and slide my left arm through to the elbow. This gives me the stance of a quick-frozen subway rider and allows me to use the ice ax in my right hand to chip away the ice around the screw. Then, as with any self-respecting male when faced with a recalcitrant physical object, I use the butt of the ax to pound the screw head until it starts turning.

I have gotten the screw to back out a couple of turns, but there are clearly ice trolls underneath the waterfall holding onto the other side of the screw. I am looking down over the screw, and I can't figure out where the water is coming from that keeps pooling, then refreezing, around my screw. I realize, finally, that it is my sweat.

"Oh Michael," my instructor shouts. "It's getting cold up here. How long to you plan to stay there at that screw?"

Just then, I crank the last turn, grab the screw with wet gloves and attach it to my climbing harness. Then I hold my glove up to let the sweat trickle out.

Once I make the ledge, we perform the same maneuver—she climbs; I belay. She belays; I climb. On the second pitch, though, my non-athlete's body finally makes a few connections. The face is steep, and I front point my way along easily. The screws act like screws ought to. The axes tap gently into the ice and catch solidly. At one point, I tap gently, and about 75 pounds of ice sheers away from the waterfall next to me and falls into the valley, shattering into a million crystal pieces.

I pause then and look out across the White Mountains. They are, indeed, white, with the afternoon sun fracturing off the occasional frozen waterfall across the valley. The wind is sharp, almost metallic and tastes of ice crystals. When I exhale, I can feel not only my calves, but my triceps in my arms and the muscles in my neck quiver with exhaustion. The only sound is the wind. *What an odd place*, I think, *to feel so peaceful.*

As long as you remember ice is thick liquid, my guide is saying as we trudge along the cliff face, you'll be okay. She points out different ice formations, different kinds of ice, different strategies for each icefall, but she keeps coming back to The List.

She is a *parasailer*, as well as a rock and ice climber.

"Those are the parachute thingees?" I ask.

"Yep."

What she is wrestling with herself is life after the frozen waterfalls, the "real world," always scratching on the edge of her consciousness.

"When I'm climbing," she begins, "when I'm flying . . . it's so hard, but there's this feeling of, I don't know, accomplishment? But it's not accomplishment exactly. It just feels good, you know, like magic or something."

I nod.

"I'm familiar with that feeling," I say.

"So the question is, if I quit doing this stuff, does the feeling go away forever?"

"I don't know."

We walk along for a while longer; the sun is setting, the wind rising out of the valley.

"So, I think I know where you're going, Michael" she says, unstrapping crampons and clipping her ice axes to the day pack. "But how do you plan on getting back?"

Ice, I think, haunts me. Since I walked along the Frankenstein cliffs, I have climbed ice in fairyland box canyons in Colorado, on towering icicles above ski towns, in piles of frozen froth in Alaska, where you have to beat away the meringue to get to the solid ice underneath. I have been scared—no, make that terrified—and cold and wet, sworn to myself at least five times that all the fires in hell couldn't get me, miserable ice climber that I am, to set foot on another frozen waterfall. Yet, somehow, Item 7 never seems to get completely crossed off.

16

Over the Edge

THE WORLD CHANGES, BUT THE LIST IS THE SAME. After much agonizing. I have left Florida for the foothills of the Rockies—Boulder, Colorado. I have told myself that the move is based on sound business judgment, but underlying that judgment is the simple fact that it will be easier to train for the remaining items on The List in the thin air of the mountains than in Florida's muggy winters.

I lay out a training schedule for the last three items: the Iditabike, the deep dive, and Denali. The logistics are simple—for the next six months, I'll be traveling every two weeks, doing something life-threatening. It doesn't look so bad, written down in black and white. At least, I think with more than just a touch of gallows humor, it's a different life-threatening event each time. To have one's life threatened by the same thing every two weeks would get, I suspect, boring. Instead, many things will have the opportunity to kill me—avalanches, rock falls, drowning, moose stompings, freezing, simple exhaustion. What more could I ask for?

"I hope you're happy," says my best friend. "You managed to really get yourself out there this time."

I agree that I've finally gotten over the edge a bit.

"You understand, don't you?" he persists. He is a SCUBA diving instructor and an expert on the cold, dark wrecks of the north Atlantic. When he talks about risks, he is not talking hypothetically.

Understand what?

"Understand that you can't fuck up at all," he says. "You've used up all your margins. If your head isn't together, if your focus wavers just once, you're going to die out there. One of these things is going to kill you."

I have this reflexive urge to minimize The List, to explain that it's not as bad—or as spooky—as it looks. My friend, though, is having none of it.

"You almost died in that river in New Zealand," he continues. "By your own admission, you're lucky you weren't scraped off the mountain in that mountain bike race. That's the problem, buddy. You got lucky once or twice. But you can't keep getting lucky. I *know* what I'm talking about."

My friend is not the only person who's worried. I start getting calls from other folks I've met along the way. More than a few of these calls contain the phrase, "Do you understand that you can die? Do you understand how far you've pushed this?"

Frankly, I am weary of being told I can die. I know I can die, and I know it on a level they can't imagine, a gut level, a cellular level. Some nights I wake with a lurch, covered in sweat, grabbing for an ice ax or a breathing regulator that isn't there. I dream of losing the mainline, my hand slipping off the line as my cave lights flicker and die. I feel the dark in the back of my throat, and, suddenly, it is swirling snow, and I am stumbling, lost, lost, lost . . .

I am afraid of the cold and the dark and the heights and the depths, but I have come too far, given up too much.

"A step at a time," Denise counsels me. "Concentrate on what comes next, just like rock climbing. Take each move as it comes."

I talk to John Orlowski, my cave instructor. One of the absolute rules of cave diving is that any dive can be called by any of the divers at any time, and caver etiquette demands that no questions be asked. He proved that to me one day as we were descending into a deep cave system. The dive had been going perfectly, and there were no problems that I could perceive when John called the dive and signaled a return to the surface.

When we got out, I didn't ask, but John offered an explanation anyway.

"The deeper we went," he said, "the more certain I became that someone was going to die. So I called the dive."

"If you feel bad about anything," John says, "you've got to be man enough to walk away from it. Out here on the edge, if it feels bad, we can't risk doing it."

Just nerves, I say. Too much, too quick.

"Well," he says, "when I call a dive, I figure those caves will be here tomorrow. The same goes for mountains."

I get another call from my best friend.

"I've been asking around," he says. "And I can't find anybody who has gone up as far as you're going up or as far down as you're going down. I think you're out there on your own on this one; sort of George Plimpton From Hell."

Thanks, I say.

17

The Intensive

"I THINK YOU NEED TO COME FOR AN INTENSIVE," Steve Ilg tells me over the telephone one night.

"An intensive what?"

"An Intensive," he reiterates. "A one-on-one training session with me. Frankly, I'm worried about you, Michael. The time frame for this 'Big Finish' isn't realistic. Your body doesn't have time to get ready."

Frankly, I'm worried about me, too. It's all very well and good to announce you're planning on doing three major events in six-months time; something else again to do them. The key problem is the prerequisites. Neither Denali nor the deep dive are walk-ons; both require an extensive series of prerequisites to get on with any reputable guide. The truth is I have neither the mountaineering nor the diving prerequisites, which means I'm going to be hustling back and forth between up and down for several months.

My first bump against those prerequisites comes while I'm searching for a guided group on Mt. McKinley. There are many ways to climb a mountain. You can, if you so elect, pick a mountain and start up by yourself, which, if you happen to be a world-class climber like Alex Lowe, works just fine. I'll later run into Alex in

Talkeetna, the little town at the base of Denali, and he'll talk about taking his skis, grabbing a plane up to Base Camp, and seeing if he can make the summit while he's waiting for his climbing partner for a much more "serious" climb to arrive.

"It would be," he tells me, "sort of fun."

If you don't happen to be among the top ten climbers of your generation, another way of getting up a big mountain is to form a climbing team and create your own expedition. On a mountain like McKinley, where there's a constant danger of falling to deep, bottomless crevasses, a team roped together makes much more sense. If you fall into a crevasse, there's someone to help you get out. But a team implies that all the team members knew what they were doing, and, in all honesty, I didn't.

Up until McKinley, everything on The List had been an individual activity—I was the sole person at risk. But mountaineering is a team endeavor, something I really hadn't given a lot of thought to when I wrote The List. Heck, so far, the *Eiger Sanction* movie is still my mountaineering Bible. Manly men, driving spikes into the Death Wall of the Eiger, hauling themselves up by thin ropes and sheer force of will.

Of course, I knew that was nonsense. I also knew that with my lack of experience, putting together my own team seemed pretty far-fetched.

"Finding people to go to McKinley with you is no problem," said Nancy Prichard. "Do you know what to do when you get there?"

The answer to that question was a resounding, "No!"

Which meant that I was a major liability.

That left only the third option, a guided climb. A guided climb is, essentially, a package trip. The guide company provides an experienced guide or two, team climbing equipment such as ropes and sleds, food, and a measure of security. You pays your money, and away you go.

Not hardly.

Guiding on Denali began in the mid-1960s with the legendary Ray "Pirate" Genet, a brilliant, driven climber who saw his fortune in guided climbs to the windswept summit. And who could pass up a wildly bearded, Hemmingwayesque adventurer whose motto was "To The Summit!"? But Genet himself died on Mt. Everest in 1979, and the National Park Service, chaffing for cash, decided to open up the mountain to other groups. They awarded seven franchises, which have become increasingly hard to retain as the Park Service tightened standards. No more than nine clients can be taken up at one time, and the client to guide ratio can be no more than four to one.

I poured over the six remaining franchisees. Ironically, Genet's operation lost their franchise for several reasons, not the least of which was the death of a client. I didn't like that, "death of a client."

No matter how you approach it, Denali is daunting. Despite the number of climbers who come to the mountain, despite the stunts—the youngest, the oldest, the first blind climber to summit—Denali kills roughly 1 out of every 100 climbers who try for its summit.

One in 100.

If the New York Marathon, with 15,000 runners, ran those risks, there would be 150 dead people at the end of every race. Even a modest local race, with 500 participants, could expect five deaths. No other endeavor carries those kind of risks, and the guide services are deadly serious about what they do.

I decide to go with the American Alpine Institute of Bellingham, Washington, a small company dedicated to alpine climbing. Their wordy brochures cover climbs around the world—they don't do "tourist" trips, or "adventure travel." They exist to climb. AAI also has a reputation for flawless instruction in mountaineering techniques, and the best record of any company for getting clients to the top.

AAI has also never lost a client, which I find very promising.

I call Dunham Gooding, the founder of the company, in Bellingham, explain what I'm trying to do and ask about his four

McKinley trips.

"No," he says.

"No, what?" I reply.

"No, we won't take you up the mountain," he says. "You're not qualified."

Keep him talking, I think. I blather about climbing, about risk sports, whatever. Dunham listens. Finally, I pop the question.

"What do I have to do to be qualified?" I ask. "You tell me what I have to do, and I'll do it."

"Let me think about it a few days," Dunham says. "I'll get back to you.

In the meantime, I call Steve Ilg in Durango. What I need, I tell him, is a training program aimed at riding the Iditabike, climbing Mt. McKinley, and pulling off a deep dive.

"Let me see," says Ilg. "That's long-distance biking, steady high-altitude hiking, carrying a heavy load and, I'm just guessing here, but a little swimming thrown in so you'll be comfortable in the water."

I say that sounds right.

"The problem here is that these things are mutually exclusive, exercise-wise," Ilg says. "I think you need to come to Durango."

Durango sits nestled in the San Juan Mountains, a former mining community reeling under the impact of a flood of sudden imports drawn by a flawless outdoor lifestyle. Ilg, though, is an original Durango boy, come home to make his mark. And he is calmer than when we first met in Santa Fe—which, given how laid back he was then, is pretty scary. His fax has outlined a three-day "intensive," a one-on-one workshop designed to keep me moving in the right direction.

The problem, he has outlined by telephone, is the old bugaboo of specificity of training. The best training for hiking up a mountain is hiking up a mountain. The best training for riding a bicycle long distance is riding a bicycle long distance. If you want to do many sports, you're going to have to do some complex juggling. If you want to do many sports in a short span of time, something has got to give.

On paper, Ilg's plan is simple—he'll put me through the paces of weight-lifting, stretching, bicycling, and "other cardiovascular activities," then spend some time using his own special body work to make sure I'm "aligned." All the usual things a person might do to a '56 Chevy truck to keep it running.

Ilg, as usual, beaming like he knows some universal secret, meets me at a small health club in downtown Durango. As is also usual with Ilg, the workout is as much talk as lifting.

We have, he says, come through the physical to the kingdom of the mental.

I nod.

Ilg frowns. I'm not getting it. He can shift gears faster than I can.

"I can train you for the physical, despite the problems," he says. "But the physical is only the very tip of the iceberg. The question is, are you going to be ready in your head?"

I shrug, irritated. The hardest thing about approaching the mental aspects of extreme sports is not standing up and shouting, "Bullshit!" So much easier to run or bike or climb, to spend hours in the gym watching cast iron weights go up and down, feeling the stretch and flex of muscles, the dripping of sweat and the burn of the lactic acid. Weight-lifting for the head is too solitary, too lonely, too . . . *nonempirical.* I've learned too well about adrenaline and beta-endorphins and the rush-rush-rush of blood through my heart. I know how to create charts and graphs, measure the steady strengthening of my muscles or the second-by-second improvements of my running. I crave the feel of the burn, of hanging on the very edge of athletic performance. I hurt, and recover, and hurt again.

And what Ilg is telling me, really, is that these hard fought gains are easy, are the ante of the game.

We are back to martial arts, to the dance Ilg talked about so eloquently when we first met. I think again of Bruce Lee, who once commented that *kata*, the ritualized, dance-like marital arts motions taught to every student, don't matter. Unfortunately, that insight is only available after years of learning *kata*.

"Turn into a doll made of wood," Lee wrote. It has no ego; it thinks nothing; it is not grasping or sticky. Let the body and limbs work themselves out in accordance with the discipline they have undergone."

A wooden doll it is, then. What, I ask Ilg, do you have in mind? He smiles.

It's already after dark when Ilg picks me up in his truck. It's around 10 degrees, and clouds race across the moon and stars listlessly spit hard, icy snowflakes. I'd already been told to dress for exertion—tights, sneakers and a heavy shell—so I'm basically freezing. "Don't worry," Ilg says, "You'll warm right up when we start running."

He drives out of Durango to the base of a tiny ski area, not yet open for skiing, where he parks alongside the road and hands me a pair of snowshoes.

"Ever run in snowshoes?" he asks.

This is, I say, the first pair of snowshoes I've even seen up close.

"Great!" he says. No one should be that upbeat. "This will be fun!"

We put the snowshoes on over our sneakers and start out walking.

This isn't so bad, I think as we walk up the first slope, probably an easy green. Pretty soon I am huffing from the altitude, but Ilg sets a brisk pace. The snow is falling lightly and steadily now, muting an already silent landscape. The night has the brightness of an old sepia photo, the ambient light reflecting off the snow fields. We walk for about half an hour, until we reach the ridge line, where, in just a few more days, the lifts will be disgorging hordes of Colorado skiers.

"Are you warm?" Ilg asks.

Very, I reply. Not so bad at all . . .

"Good!" he says. "Let's run."

Awkwardly at first, I follow Ilg, running along the ridge line. The snowshoes, trick aluminum and plastic things that don't bear the slightest resemblance to those boats Sergeant Preston of the Mounties used, barely offer any more resistance than running shoes. We jog slowly, Ilg letting me get the hang of the snowshoes.

"Now sprint!" and he's off like a horse out of the gate, little white rooster tails of snow flying off each snowshoe. I chase as best I can. In a couple of hundred yards, my lungs are on fire. Just when I'm seriously considering passing out, Ilg slows to a jog.

"Catch your breath," he says happily.

We slow to a walk, then go back to a jog, after a couple of minutes, he's off again, me right behind him. We sprint, jog, walk across the top of the mountain. I remember how, just a few hours ago, I was pretty smug about the shape I was in.

Wooden doll, I think.

We come to a steep slope down, steep enough that I would have to pause a few minutes before launching myself off on skis.

"Come on," Ilg shouts, and races down the slope. He takes huge, bounding steps, moving straight off the hill, then dropping down the slope. "Come on!"

I head down and am immediately waist deep in fresh powder, my snowshoes making me wallow like some great mastodon trapped in a snow white tar pit.

"Bound, Michael," Ilg shouts from below. "Bound *up!*"

I bound up, and a second later am on my face, rolling down the slope.

"Get up and run!" I hear from a distance, my head buried in the snow.

I struggle up, covered with powder, and run down the slope. I make it three steps before I'm on my face again.

"Bound! Graceful! Light!"

I half run, half fall down the slope, leaving a trail like a deranged garden slug through the pristine snow. When I reach the bottom, I look like some wheezing snow apparition, cold and wet.

"Good," says Ilg. "Now jog."

Jog, walk, jog, sprint, jog, walk, jog, sprint, jog, walk, jog, sprint, jog, walk . . .

We come to another slope, steeper than the first one we went up.

"Up," Ilg says. He has become increasingly more focused, less New Age as we run through the snow. His commands become brusker, the speed a little faster. I start jogging up the slope. Within a few feet I hear the blood pounding in my ears, my heart hammering so hard it threatens to rip away my shell. I focus on putting one foot in front of the other, breathing, simple things, as the slope gets steeper.

"Run," Ilg, effortlessly ahead of me, says.

And I stumble, walk.

"Run, Michael," he says.

My face is flush, and my breathing is coming in short, painful gasps. I imagine the snow hitting my flushed, burning face, then sizzling away into water vapor.

And then we are at the top. I bend double, gasping massive amounts of the cold air.

"Good, Michael," Ilg says. "Now jog."

Not good, I think, jogging at a barely moving pace along the ridge line.

"Sprint."

"Now jog."

"Walk."

"Sprint."

I am lying on my face on another steep slope, struggling back up, running, stumbling, sliding down.

"Good. Now jog."

And it goes on and on, until, what subjectively seems like hours and hours later, we come to the steepest slope of them all. We pause at the bottom, and I take every second I can. I am soaking wet, from sweat, from melting snow, alternately burning up and freezing to death. I am having, I think absently, an out of body—or perhaps out of life—experience.

"I'm going to need you to run up this hill, Michael," Ilg says almost sadly, as if he knows how much this is going to hurt me. "How do you feel?"

"Great," I say. Let the irony just lie there, like a melted snowman.

"Good," Ilg says, and starts running up the ski slope.

I want to get this exactly right here—to say I hurt is not fair to the actual feelings running through my legs and arms and chest and lungs. Ilg had taken me to a place beyond hurt, beyond any rational concept of exercise, and there was one more hill left to climb.

Every step is in slow motion. From a distance, I see my quadriceps contract, the smaller muscles in my hips helping to lift the leg. The leg moves forward and splashes down in the powder, and the quad begins lifting the rest of me up as the next leg cycles. My lungs are beyond laboring, the cold air sucked through clenched teeth. There are bright flashes behind my eyes, as if something important upstairs is short-circuiting. I hear a waterfall in each ear, and the snow looks like white fire.

And then we are at the top.

"Catch your breath," my tormentor says. "Now jog."

We jog—or, in my case, hobble—a few yards to a steep drop.

Oh God! I think, panic welling up, *do I have to jump off a cliff?*

But Ilg stops suddenly. The listless snow has given up, and, to the north, stars glow like hard, cold stones in the bitter air.

"Feel it," Ilg says, low and intense. The New Age exercise guru is gone now, and I look in the eyes of a man on fire. "*Denali.* Feel it. *FEEL IT!* It's out there."

And I feel it. I feel the cold and the wind and the pain.

"And the depths and the cold. Feel it," Ilg is saying.

My eyes close, and I feel my body sway to invisible currents, pulled by tides of blood and chemistry.

"If you make a mistake," Ilg says, low and hypnotic, his words boring into my head, "you are going to die."

A wooden doll, I think, caught in the winds and the tides, between the roof of the world and the abyss, driven by a list written on a paper napkin in a pizza joint. The moment, caught in some elastic putty of time, stretches. I open my eyes, and the moon has come out, chasing the last of the clouds from the winter sky. I can make out the North Star, a fire in the sky. I look over my shoulder, to the south, then back to the north. *I'm coming*, I think. *It's time to finish this.*

"Well!" says the old Ilg, smiling. "It's about time to go down now, don't you think?"

18

The Deeps

ALL I HAVE TO DO NOW IS KEEP TO THE GOSPEL according to Ilg, which involves around 20 hours a week of lifting weights, snowshoeing, running, biking, while, at the same time building up some real skills. I do immediately discover a basic truth, which is that no one wants to go out bicycling or running with you when it's 8 degrees and snowing.

People will, in fact, avoid your phone calls, or give you some obvious ruse like, "I want to sit in front of the fire and have dinner."

The plus side of the Ilg Treatment, though, is that the mountains in the winter are magic places. The trails are empty and cathedral quiet; the only break in the smooth white surface are hoof prints of mule deer, looking for the last of the green. The first time I try to ride my mountain bike in the snow and ice, I receive an unpleasant reminder about slick surfaces and gravity. I am climbing a steep hill in the mountains outside of Boulder. The road up the hill is in the shade, and despite several inches of fresh wet snow, most of the road is ice over rock. I have let most of the air out of my tires for the climb to get as much rubber as possible on the ground, and I am chanting to myself *I am balanced . . . I am balanced . . . I am balanced.* And I am balanced, right until the point that the rear wheel sheers clockwise on the ice, and I smack, face first, into the hard snow. I lay there for a minute, then pick up the bike and start up again. With the first push of the peddle, I am back in the snow, about six inches from my previous snow angel.

Things get better, though, after a long discussion with Tom Armstrong, a vice president at Cannondale.

"Yeah," says Tom, who handles that company's phenomenally successful racing team, "we get a lot of requests for bicycles to ride in the snow and ice. *Tons* of them. Let me talk to the engineers."

The result arrives a month later, a fire-engine red Cannondale with none of the frills of a modern racing mountain bike. There's no front shock absorber or rear suspension. Instead, the bike is plain as vanilla, until I pick it up. It weights nothing, each component selected as a balance between weight and durability.

"It's indestructible," says Armstrong. "It's as light as it can be without compromising durability."

The red bike is also designed for special wheels and tires, created by a bike shop in Fairbanks for winter cycling. Two normal mountain bike rims are welded together, then drilled for the spokes. The widest possible tire is then glued to the rim to keep it from slipping in the cold. When the aptly named Snow Cat is then inflated to all of 6 pounds (versus 50 pounds for a normal tire) the result is a fat, almost six-inch-wide, soft footprint in the snow. The result is a bike that rides almost as well in the snow as in the dirt.

The second part of the training equation has come in a crash course in dressing for winter. For both the Iditabike and Mt. McKinley, the challenge is the same. Temperatures will range as low as 30 degrees below zero, but because I'll be moving, especially on the bike, generating heat, "you need a clothing system," says Alexandra Cherry, whose company, Malden Mills in New Hampshire, manufactures synthetic "fleece." For lack of a better explanation, fleece is what people mean when they say "miracle stuff." I learn quickly that exercising in ultracold weather has a whole different set of problems. Besides the obvious one—freezing to death—there's the not so obvious problem of overheating. On a cold day, put on a heavy jacket and run half a mile. In no time at all, you'll be, to use technical terminology, sweating like a pig. So you stop running and unzip your jacket. For about 60 seconds, you're comfortable. But the inside of your jacket is soaked with sweat, and pretty soon you're shivering. Zip the jacket back up and walk at a brisk pace, and you're warmer. What's an annoyance on a Saturday afternoon jog is life-threatening when the bottom falls out of the temperature and you're a long way from home. Consequently, I begin the Great Underwear Search, juggling different weights and kinds of clothing, making sure there are zippers in the right place for ventilation and that I can get to them easily. Malden chips in with a couple of pair of stretch tights made of something they call Polartec.

"They're awful thin," I ask skeptically.

"Try them," Alexandra says.

And so the Ilg Treatment gets more comfortable.

The other part of the Big Finish, though, is the dive on the *Wilkes Barre*, 240 feet down off Key West. I finally catch up with wreck diver Gary Gentile in San Francisco. We have dinner at a local diner, and I outline my plans. He reacts much as Dunham Gooding from the American Alpine Institute did—"Not a good plan."

"Diving is not like mountaineering," says Gary, one of the few people in SCUBA who also has climbed mountains. "The focus for technical diving has to be the acquisition of skills, then the application of those skills."

For me, Gary Gentile was one of the gurus, if you will, of The List. Long before I knew he was a diver, I'd read his science fiction novels and logged away his name as someone I'd like to meet. Later, when I read his numerous books on diving, I knew I'd found a kindred spirit. He'd come back from the crucible of Vietnam with an insatiable desire to test the limits, whether those limits were high in the mountains, in rolling whitewater, or down the untracked powder of extreme ski runs.

In 1970, though, Gary had his first dive, and his world shifted. He found an environment where he could not only push the limits, but excel as well.

"I did not seek close brushes with death, for that is foolish," he wrote later. "I did not intend to charge blindly into inextricable circumstances. What I sought was personal challenge: to pit myself against the elements of nature, but in such a way that planning and forethought offered a strong measure of control. This was the essential difference between walking point on a search-and-destroy mission and plummeting into the depths of an unknown sea. Now I was in charge of my fate."

"How deep have you been?" Gary is asking me.

One hundred fifty feet, I say.

He nods.

"You're going to need to go deeper," he says. "You're going to need to learn how you are down there, what it's like. Then you're going to have to keep doing it, over and over."

We finally decide that my first exposure to the abyss, the world below 200 feet, should be in a controlled, supervised situation. The next week, I make arrangements to go to the horse country of central Florida, to a 240-foot-deep hole in the ground called Forty Fathom Grotto.

The drive from Ocala, the closest town of any consequence, to the Grotto is an impressionistic montage of live oaks, Spanish moss, perfect green paddocks, and thoroughbreds moving with their slow-motion gait. I have, appropriately, country music cranked up real loud, but the driving beat of Travis Tritt is not doing much to dispel my nervousness. It is, I'm afraid, much easier to talk about going where you've never gone before than actually loading up the car and heading for it.

As the horse country rolls by outside the window, I review my next few days. As Gary says, it's simple—I need to get deeper if I'm going to attempt a serious wreck dive. Going deeper though, is more than just adding a couple of pounds of lead to the wetsuit and sinking. The history of deep diving is peppered by people who did exactly that, and were never seen again. SCUBA at this level gets tricky. In other risk sports, say, climbing, you can tell immediately if what you hope to accomplish is beyond your abilities. I've stood at the base of a rock or ice climb and thought, "No way. Too steep. Too overhanging. Too exposed." The risk factor is visually apparent, sometimes too much so. But in diving, most times the surface of the water offers the same calm face, whether you're planning to go for 30 feet or 300 feet. And the limits are arbitrary, keyed to the environment and are very personal. "How deep," says my friend Michael Menduno, the editor of the technical dive journal *aquaCORP*, "is *deep*?"

How many angels can dance on the top of an 80-cubic-inch dive tank?

According to the big dive certifying agencies, 100 feet is deep, and 130 feet is the limit of what can be termed recreation SCUBA diving. Those limits have their roots back when the Navy lowered men in full dive suits with those round helmets with portholes. But the numbers are taught to every new diver, and they are, for the most part, taken as gospel.

I am really thinking about the pressure, all those atmospheres, pressing on every square inch of my body. I am thinking that a failure of the life support system at those depths will have one single consequence. It will be dark and cold. And the pressure will squeeze me . . .

I am afraid.

I think of something Gary wrote a few years back.

"What normally keeps me out of trouble on deep air dives is fear," he says. "It keeps me from being too bold, getting too far away from the anchor line or getting out of control."

I enter the Grotto through its small driveway with the international dive sign—a red square with a while slash—on the mailbox, then park beneath the live oaks that overhang everything. There are a couple of trailers, a small white outbuilding and a small building with a large deck, overlooking what could pass for any small farm pond. Forty feet across; 240 feet down.

What my plan calls for is a series of increasingly deeper dives. I'll start at 150 feet. The next dive will be to 180, then 200, then 220 and, finally, 240 feet, the back of a cavern that drops away from the surface at a 45-degree angle. There'll be two other divers with me on each dive—an instructor and a safety diver. The instructor will ask me to perform certain tasks, then record the answers on my dive slate. All this has been explained to me on the telephone beforehand. It has also been explained to me that not everybody passes the course; that some divers are so spooked, so rattled by the abyss that they don't go all the way to 240 feet—or if they do, they never go back, and they don't talk much about the experience.

Forty Fathom Grotto is the brainchild of one of diving's legends, Hal Watts, who became obsessed with the deep sinkhole decades ago, when he almost died there.

Diving in the early 1860s with a bunch of surplus gear he'd traded for and using such sophisticated diving aids as a bleach bottle, which he planned to fill up with air to bring him safely back to the surface, Watts and a friend went all the way down, 240 feet, where everything that could possibly go wrong did. While struggling with equipment and wrestling with his regulator, he actually passed out, only to come to with the regulator in his mouth at 100 feet.

"I guess you could say I've been obsessed with this place ever since," says the gentlemanly Watts, from the front porch of his house overlooking the Grotto—the abyss is, literally, home.

He has also been listed in the Guinness Book Of Records for his deep air dives, and he coined one of the basic catch phrases of SCUBA—"Plan your dive; dive your plan."

We start that morning with a classroom session about the particular monster of this deep—nitrogen narcosis, or, "The Rapture Of The Deep," for *Sea Hunt* fans. The deeper you go, the more the nitrogen in the air, under tremendous pressure, affects your mental processes. Perhaps not surprisingly—I've certainly heard it before—the exact mechanism of nitrogen narcosis isn't quite understood. It may have to do with the dissolved nitrogen interfering with the transmission of information from neuron to neuron—mental static—acting as an anesthetic gas. Think nitrous oxide here.

The result is that a diver might experience a sense of well-being, a loss of fine muscle control, euphoria (natch—that's why "rapture."). In the television shows, a "narked" diver is always trying to kiss fish or swim to the pretty mermaid. There's even the Martini Rule, which states that 100 feet of depth equals the effect of one martini; each additional 50 feet adds another drink.

Cute, but as you go deeper, you can forget the mermaids. Narcosis steadily hammers on your ability to think, to function. An activity that might be a snap at 30 feet, say doing a multiplication problem on a slate, becomes harder and harder the deeper you get. You can mentally override narcosis, I am told, but first, you've got to know what it's like.

The first dive to 150 is an excellent example of how to do everything wrong. I am uncomfortable, nervous—hey, I put the wetsuit on backwards—fumbling with equipment. When I get back to the surface, Steve Hoffman, my instructor, is optimistic.

"Well," he says, "we got the first one out of the way."

The second one the next day, to 180, goes better, except for the fact that my dive computer dies and starts feeding me incorrect information. At 180 feet, you don't need bad information. I also feel the first tendrils of narcosis. It's not so much as an intoxicated feeling as it is a sense that someone has filled your head with thick soup. Every thought seems like a baseball thrown through that soup, moving ever so slowly toward actions.

When we start down, later that day, for the 200-footer, I'm expecting more of the warm soup. Just below 180, though, narcosis slams through my head like a cyber freight train. Everything is spinning around me, and I can't make it stop. The spinning is making me queasy, and I can't think clearly. I feel the pressure, pressure,

pressure . . .

I level off and signal Steve that I'm having trouble. He nods and waits for me to sort it out. I close my eyes, and that makes the spinning worse. The nausea's getting worse, and I feel The Fear, the animal shaking the bars of the cage.

Think, think, think, but it's so very slow.

What did I do when I was afraid climbing? The thought moves glacially through my head. I focused on the rock.

There isn't any rock.

But there is the descent rope. I open my eyes and shine my light at the descent rope, a couple of feet away. At first, the rope is determined to move. But the more I focus, the steadier it becomes; the spinning in my head slows, a kid's top winding down. I blink my eyes a couple of times, and my head is clear, as if the narcosis is a storm that's blown through my head and moved on.

I signal "okay," and we finish the dive.

"The thing is," Steve is saying, "it's up to you."

We're sitting on the deck overlooking the Grotto. There is only time for one more dive, and it's up to me whether I want to go for the bottom. I don't want to go for the bottom. I don't want the dark or the cold or the "whirlies."

"Let's go," I say, with something less than enthusiasm. Again, Steve will be the instructor, and Hal Watts will be safety diver. We suit up and hit the water quickly—I didn't want a lot of chance to think. We have a very specific written dive plan. The last thing Hal Watts says to me is, "Dive the plan. That's all there is to it."

We drop quickly, the thin sunlight quickly fading into the gloom. We level off at 180 feet for a check. The plan is to stop at 220 before okaying the final drop. This time, I am ready for the storm. As I start the descent, my head spins savagely, my stomach lurching.

Focus on the rock.

The spins wind down; my stomach stabilizes for the moment.

"Okay?" signals Steve.

"Okay," I signal back.

As we go down, the pressure is like a living thing, some amoebic blanket wrapping tighter and tighter. We level off at 220, and I can tell my head wants to spin.

The rock, I think.

Perversely, instead of spinning, my head latches onto snippets of rock lyrics, blaring at full volume through my brain. Golden Earring, doing an old MTV song called "Twilight Zone." The noise is almost deafening.

I signal to continue down.

We've been angling back into the deep cave, and my light touches the edges of the rock walls. The last 20 feet are anticlimactic. I settle onto the silty bottom of the cave. I can see a wrecked car that locals parked in the old sink years ago. I see the rock walls and Hal Watts yellow wetsuit. Everything is very, very slow. I look at my gauges, and one says 2 . . . . . . 4 . . . . . . 3. I want to follow each number with my finger, reading along: 2 . . . . . . 4 . . . . . . 3. I close my eyes for a moment and think, think, think. I'm here, 243 feet. Ah. Tied to the descent line next to me, right on the bottom, is a genuine mermaid, about 8 inches long, rubber. I stare at her for a minute, then give her a squeeze for luck. Hal Watts, I think slowly, has a truly sick sense of humor. I look over, and Steve sticks out his hand in congratulations. I think for a moment, then realize he wants me to shake hands. Ah.

Are you slippin' into the twilight zone, Golden Earring sings in my head . . . *Place is a madhouse; feel like bein' stoned . . .*

I look at the gauges again. There are other numbers. My bottom timer is clicking over, 13 minutes passed.

A good number, I think.

Where am I to go, now that I've gone too far? The music continues.

Good question, I think. Right now, I want to go home.

I give the thumbs up. Steve nods.

19

The Sled and I

I FINALLY GET A CALL FROM DUNHAM GOODING AT AAI.

He's pleased with my physical training—he's heard of the ubiquitous Ilg—but I'm definitely going to need some work on technique.

"Here's what we think," he says, and I wait with my pencil poised. "If you're willing to take two weeks of individual instruction in the mountains, we'll let the instructors—who are McKinley guides—decide whether you can go."

Two weeks!

"Well," he adds, almost apologetically, "you can split the class into two one-week sessions, if you like."

Still, it's a huge amount of work (and not a small amount of expense).

"Do I have any options here?" I ask.

"Not if you want to get on an AAI trip," says the head of AAI.

"Okay," I say. "Two weeks it is. When can we schedule the first week?"

"In four days," he replies. "Our guides' schedules are tight."

Four days later, after a whirlwind pass through REI's retail stores and a visit to Boulder's legendary Neptune Mountaineering shop for mountaineering boots ("Well, we can order them . . . " "What have you got in stock that fits *right now*?"), I cross the state of Colorado to the not-so-thriving metropolis of Ouray, the Switzerland of the West, just down the mountain from trendy Telluride.

Under other circumstances, I'd be looking forward to Ouray, it being the ice-climbing capital of the United States. In fact, Ouray has an "ice park" inside its city limits. A water pipeline runs along the top of a steep, narrow canyon, and during the winter, the city fathers allow the pipe to be opened, creating a series of frozen waterfalls all along the canyon. Ice climbers come from all over the world to climb those slabs of ice.

While I might get in a day of ice climbing, I suspect that's not what my instructor has in mind.

Mimi Borquist indeed has other plans.

"Have you ever pulled a sled before?" she asks as soon as we meet. Mimi is all of five feet tall, probably weighs the proverbial 100 pounds in soaking wet fleece. In her late 20s, she already has years as a mountain guide in Switzerland and is slated to guide on Denali this year.

No, I say. I've managed to miss sleds.

"Well," she responds, "you're going to get to love your sled."

But first, she adds, I'm going to get to love my avalanche transceiver.

We are going, Mimi says, to go through mountaineering skills from the ground up. We're going to start with how to dress, how to pack a pack, what to carry, what not to carry. We're going to hammer out the details of staying alive, then staying comfortable, at 30 degrees below zero. I'm going to commit to memory the intricacies of crevasse rescue—pulling fellow climbers out of the huge cracks that crisscross the great glaciers—which knot is appropriate where, and how to tie it. I am going to become comfortable on a rope team, linked by a stretch of rope to the climbers in front and behind me. I will come to think of my ice ax as an extension of my body, combination Swiss army knife and survival tool.

But first, she says, time for a hike.

After being buried under all the things I'm going to learn, a hike seems like blessed relief. We drive the hapless rental over frozen roads deep into the San Juan mountains, parking in a snow bank just below one of the high passes. The altitude is over 10,000 feet, and the very act of lacing on the high-tech snowshoes and pulling the pack out of the car is enough to wind me.

But it is sunny and cold, and we head up, into the mountains. The first 30 minutes or so are great. The southwest Colorado mountains are the most rugged in the state. They're high and lonely, and the views seems to stretch away to the edge of forever. My pack weighs about 25 pounds, light, and I concentrate on getting the rhythm of the snowshoes. I haven't been on snowshoes since my hellish encounter with Ilg, but the rhythm is easy, and I'm using ski poles to help me hold my pace. By the second hour, the pack is starting to get heavier, as if someone has declared a slight increase in gravity and not informed me. We are steadily climbing up higher and higher ridges. The views are getting better, but the air could be a little thicker.

As I keep learning over and over again, people—including myself—were designed to live in a pretty narrow range of environments. As we go up or down, we quickly leave our comfort range. As we go up, the air is thinner. There's exactly the same percentage of oxygen in the air as there is at sea level—21 percent—but because the air is thinner, the molecules more widely dispersed, we've got to work harder to get the oxygen we need.

Huff, wheeze; huff, wheeze.

By the end of the second hour, I'm in desperate need of a third lung, or maybe a small, unobtrusive tank of pure oxygen. My body chugs and wheezes along, but it is clearly suffering decreased performance specs. My breathing has become rapid and shallow; I am sweating like a pig, alternately opening and closing zippers. None of this unpleasantness seems to affect my legs, though, which move along at about the same pace regardless of how poorly I feel. This is, I think, a good sign, so I resolve to ignore the missing oxygen molecules and concentrate on my legs. Almost four hours since leaving the car, when we grind to a stop for lunch, Mimi looks at me closely.

"So how are you doing?" she asks.

This is, I think, one of the people who will decide whether I get a shot at Denali.

"Great," I say. "I feel the altitude, but no big deal."

There is, I believe, a logic to the lie. Since I began The Big Finish, I've sensed less and less distinction between the mental and the physical. We're not talking about happy talk here, not the Little Engine That Thought It Could. It's more a feeling that if you can muster the will, your body will go along for the ride. I remember talking to a Special Forces major about physical training—"Bodies are strong; it's the mind that fails. So we train so the body will just keep going." Trainers of world-class triathletes have exactly the opposite philosophy—the mind is strong, but the body is weak. Me, I can tell the difference less and less . There are times when my brain has turned to warm cherry Jell-O, and my body keeps moving of its own accord. There are other times when my body feels like it has been doing rounds in a dryer, but my brain pulls me through. As the Ilg-Man teaches, I'm beginning to suspect we are indeed integrated systems. If I keep *saying* I'm okay, I'll probably *be* okay.

Maybe.

After lunch we begin my love affair with the avalanche transceiver. An avalanche transceiver is a little radio you wear in the back country, so if you happen to be buried alive by an avalanche, your friends can find you. When you're hiking, everyone's transceiver is set to "send." Should you be caught in an avalanche, the people above ground will set their transceivers to "receive," track down your signal, and dig you out.

This is not as easy as it might seem. The signals are weak, and you find the right direction depending on whether the signal is getting stronger or weaker, which can be amazingly hard to tell. I learn this the hard way, wandering around snow fields looking for a transceiver Mimi has buried.

The first time, it takes me 15 minutes to find the buried transceiver. Had the transceiver been, say, me, I would have become a popsicle in 15 minutes.

"Good start," she says, "but we're going to need to pick up the speed a little bit."

The drills progress from eyes open to eyes closed to blindfolded. I like the blindfolded drills best—totally focused on the high-pitched hum from the transceiver while holding a picture of a perfect search grid in your head. After a couple of hours of blind man's bluff, we head up, hiking. Eventually, I get to crawl home.

"This is your sled," Mimi says proudly. The sled is a couple of feet wide and about four feet long, created out of a pair of skis and a complex aluminum frame—sort of like the bastard mating of a cross country skier and a lawn chair. The sled connects to my climbing harness at my waist, and for the rest of the week I will carry a full pack on my back and Mimi's gear in the sled. This is not just Dunham Gooding's idea of a good time for me. On McKinley, we will not be able to carry all our gear on our backs. Each member of the team will have his or her own sled, which will follow us most of the way up the mountain. If there is a single, critical requirement of the big mountain, it's the ability to pull the sled, day in and day out.

The first day of pulling the sled is a little like learning to ride the bicycle with one hand tied behind your back. The sled has a mind of its own, and it's malevolent. The sled wants to pull to the right, but only if you need it to go to the left. If you need it to go to the right, it pulls to the left. The steeper we hike, the more the sled becomes a dragging boat anchor, 50 pounds of lead that seems determined to get back to sea level. Plus the fact that a climbing harness was designed as just that, a harness to take your weight when you're hanging. As a harness for pulling a sled, it's sadly lacking. I notice this when I feel the first cold wind creeping around my butt.

"Your pants are falling off," says Mimi helpfully.

We—rather I—pull the sled up a frozen highway for what seems like several forevers, until we come to a steep gully filled with ice, heading up to the right.

"Rope practice!" says my guide, who is altogether too excited about having me carry her load.

Rope practice consists of learning how to move up a rope that has been fixed in place by other climbers. It's really pretty simple. You have a device called a *Jumar*, an ascender, that locks on the rope. The mechanical lock allows the Jumar to slide in only one direction. As you climb up, you push the Jumar up the rope. Should you fall, the device locks and catches your fall. I like it, because my fear of heights vanishes when I'm connected to a rope.

"Then you're not afraid of *heights*," says Mimi practically. "You're afraid of *falling*. There's a difference."

As I move up the steep slope on a rope Mimi has anchored, I come to a small frozen waterfall, about six feet high. No big deal. I set my crampons a few feet up on the waterfall, then drive my ice ax in at eye level. Just as quickly, my ice ax blows back out, driven by the water pressure behind it. A perfect tube of freezing cold water arcs out of the hole, hitting me squarely in the face, running down my chest into my pants. Behind me, I can hear Mimi giggling.

Soaked, I continue on.

At the top, she has yet another surprise. About 25 feet over my head at the top of the gully is a capstone, a huge boulder that has tumbled down at some time in the ancient past. Mimi has climbed to the top and attached another rope around the boulder, leaving me a length of rope.

"You're going to climb the rope," she says, propping her pack in the sun. "I'm going to sit in the sun."

The purpose of this drill is using *prusiks*, little loops of ropes with a special knot that, like the jumars, only slides in one direction. One of the greatest dangers on McKinley will be the crevasses.

A glacier is a living thing, a moving river of ice. As the glacier pushes its way up a hill, all that unimaginable tons of ice compress. As the glacier continues to move, tops the hills, and heads down, the ice expands and cracks. Or the friction of some unseen obstacle on the ground may cause the layer of ice to move at different speeds. The result is the same, a crack in the glacier. Ideally, a climber's route should avoid crevasses altogether. On McKinley, that simply isn't possible. There are too many, and no alternate routes. So McKinley climbers are constantly crossing crevasses on unstable bridges of ice or snow. Crevasse rescue, the ability to get yourself or another climber out of these cracks in the world, is the most basic survival skill on the mountain.

Getting yourself out is where the prusiks come in.

Climbers on the mountain move in rope teams, everyone's climbing harnesses tied to a single rope. Each team member has their two loops of rope attached to the main climbing rope in a prusik knot. Should a member fall into the crevasse, they can use the two one-way knots to inch back to the surface, one loop attached to the climbing harness, the other with loops for the feet. Stand up in the foot loops, then slide the waist loop a little higher. Hang on the waist loop, and move the foot loops up. Sort of your basic inch-worm scenario.

"Up you go," she says.

Forget climbing: It takes me 15 minutes to get the stretch out of the rope. Eventually, I inch my way up (and *inch* is the operative word here). Each inch-worm move gains me about three inches. An hour of steady inching gets me about three-quarters of the way up the rope. I take a break, and the rope spins, and I can see hundreds of feet down into the valley.

"Are you afraid?" Mimi shouts from her sunny perch down below.

"Nope," I say, spinning.

"See!" she says triumphantly. "I told you you weren't afraid of heights!"

I reach the top and start to pull myself up and over, when the voice from down below alters the plan.

"Prusik down!" she shouts, then goes back to sunning.

Prusiking down involves hanging upside down to get the knots to release, then doing a sort of hanging abdominal crunch to reach the knots and move them. About halfway (and a million crunches), the knots tangle and refuse to move.

"What do I do?" I shout down.

"Untangle them," says Mimi.

Great. First I'm a sled dog; now I'm a bat.

To try this at home, put a bar across a doorway, hang by your ankles, then try to untie a piece of string you've knotted around your belt buckle.

Eventually, I once again reach the ground.

"Good thing, too," says Mimi. "I was losing my sunny spot. And your sled's waiting."

The week passes. Whether on frozen waterfalls or back up the gully, my sled is never very far away. I set up tents when my hands are frozen, knock them down when I'm exhausted, find the hidden transceiver, climb up and climb down and climb back up again. Once my sled and I race to the top of a peak well over 13,000 feet, beating another team on skis. I listen to the groaning of the snowpack and learn to avoid—as much as anyone can avoid—the avalanche slopes. One afternoon, moving up the side of a steep hill with my trusty sled, I put my foot down in the snow and watch a foot-wide crack run like chain lightning from my footprint for a hundred yards along the ridge line, the snowpack shifting, sliding, then stopping of its own accord.

'The lesson is," says Mimi, "that we just don't know. The mountains are mysteries, and all we can do is be as sharp as we can and try to stay alive."

At the week's end, at a coffee shop in downtown Ouray, I pop the question:

"Did I pass?" I ask.

"I'd climb with you," Mimi says.

Two weeks later, American Alpine Institute calls and tells me to send money, I'm on the team.

20

Mushing the Bike

BEFORE I KNOW IT—AND WELL BEFORE I'M READY—it's time to head to Alaska for the Iditabike.

I won't say I was exactly deluged with information from the race organizers in Anchorage, but each little bulletin from the Frozen North caused me to worry a little more:

"The biggest threat to life on the trail is hypothermia, commonly called exposure," reads one such bulletin. "If you get hypothermia, you will be too stupid and clumsy to help yourself. If you don't get help, you will likely die. Stay on the trail where you will be found."

Or my particular favorite, on moose. After explaining that moose are large, intractable animals with a temper and a predilection for stomping people into bloody placemats (newspaper clippings enclosed), the bulletin includes a handy passage on how to tell if a moose if attacking you:

"If a moose is moving toward you, it is probably attacking you."

The solution?

"Get out of the way."

More words to live by.

Following Ilg's psychotic training schedule, I've been spending hours alone in the mountains, riding the red Cannondale over untracked snow. I've also been sprinting the bike up hills until, as Ilg so vividly put it, I was "coughing blood." I am also aware, though, that the Iditabike is not really about bicycling. It is really about Alaska in February, where there's barely a two-story building between you and the North Pole and there's enough snow to bury your condo.

I forget where I heard about the Iditabike for the first time—the organizers don't exactly knock themselves out publicizing it. But word seeped out of the last frontier about a bicycle race on the Iditarod Sled Dog Trail, in the dead of winter. What I remembered most was the race's slogan: "Cowards won't show, and the weak will die."

That's what got the race added to The List.

Later, I learned the truth behind the race, which is every bit as weird as whatever I might have imagined. The idea was started in 1983 by Joe Reddington, Sr., the father of the Iditarod Sled Dog Race. His idea was a human-powered marathon, and the first event included skiing, snowshoeing, and a foot division. Four years later, Dan Bull added bicycles.

The race has alternated between epochs of wilderness survival and relatively uneventful rides on hard-packed snow. Temperatures have ranged from a balmy 40 degrees to a nippy 40 degrees below zero, and winds from nonexistent to howling, nightmare blizzards. But no matter what the weather, the race is always run.

"The course is doable under any weather conditions," says one of the members of the Iditasport board, Janelle Matz. "There will be no cancellations . . . so be prepared."

Two years ago, Sam Case, a professor of exercise physiology from Western Maryland College, conducted psychological and physiological studies on the race participants. Instead of the usual jocks, Case found a bunch of "creative and independent introverts," scoring on their psychological tests closest to stunt pilots and rodeo cowboys.

"Come on up!" says the ever jovial Dan Bull, the official race organizer, when I call about signing up. "You'll freeze, but we haven't lost anyone . . . yet."

By return mail he sends me the entry form and a dense, two-page liability release that reads, in part:

I fully realize the dangers of participating in a winter skiing/bicycling/running/snowshoeing race held in the Alaska wilderness during winter conditions, and fully assume the risk associated with such participation, including, but not limited to, the following dangers: hypothermia, frostbite, collision with pedestrians, vehicles or other racers and fixed or moving objects, dangers arising from surface hazards, equipment failure, inadequate safety equipment and weather conditions; and the possibility of serious physical and/or mental trauma and injury, including death, associated with winter athletic competition . . .

I sign the release in front of a notary, send my $200 entry fee and agree to show up in Anchorage with a bicycle, a sleeping bag rated to 20 below, an insulated pad for under the sleeping bag, a bivy sack to stuff myself and my sleeping bag into, stove, fuel, waterproof matches, a pot, two quarts of water, an extra day's supply of food, a headlamp with extra batteries and bulbs, a bicycle pump, spare parts for the Cannondale, and a lot of aspirin, all of which I will strap to various parts of the bicycle. Normally, I'd put packs alongside the bicycle wheels and conveniently pack everything. But I'm quickly dissuaded of that idea by the bicycling guru of All Weather Sports in Fairbanks. The Iditarod Trail can be so narrow and deeply rutted, the guru says, that the side panniers would drag. Instead, all 22 pounds of mandatory survival gear (three more pounds than the weight of the bike), have to be mounted up high, over the wheels.

Making, the guru adds, the bike handle "like a pig."

It is almost dark when I finally arrive in Anchorage. In my mind, I know there are almost as many daylight hours in Alaska in February as there are in Colorado. But Alaska seems to have this long, lingering dusk, as if the sun itself is equivocating, trying to decide whether to sink or not.

Turn up the lights, I think. *Let's have some real daylight around here!* My Cannondale's transport box looks as if it has been drop-kicked all the way from Colorado to Alaska, but when I take the bike out, all the pieces still seem to be there and the gears are working.

There are a couple of other passengers uncrating bicycles, and we look at each other with undisguised curiosity. "What sort of idiot..."

The Iditabike has sort of gotten away from me, mentally. Denali has been in my mind every waking moment, and in a lot of my dreams. Its hulking mass orbits the edges of my consciousness like some huge moon, its gravity steadily pulling the tides of my mind. From the first black-and-white picture so many years ago to the most recent book (*Mt. McKinley: Icy Crown Of North America*), I've seen hundreds, maybe thousands of images of the great mountain, and now I feel almost like a high school kid on his first date. Or maybe, more appropriately, a prisoner waiting to meet his executioner. On the way from the airport, my friends and I stop along the bay. To the north, in the dim pinkish light, Denali towers over the landscape like the avenging god of my nightmares. In the distance and fading light, the mountain is just visible, its 20,000 foot crown punching above the mists. It's freezing cold, but as I stand on the edge of the frozen bay and stare at the mountain, I feel a haze of sweat break out on the back of my neck.

I've come, I think lamely.

The mountain says nothing.

The next morning I start hammering out the on-site logistics of mounting all my gear on the bike, an event I'd entitle The Miracle Of Duct Tape. When I'm finished, the once-sleek Cannondale now looks like the pig it will ride like. The bulk of my 20-below sleeping bag, now compressed into the shape of a giant aspirin tablet, is bungeed to my handlebars. It has taken roughly an hour to come up with the right combination of straps, duct tape and bungee cords to make the six-pound tablet sit relatively still, but every time I turn the handlebars, it still bobs up and down like a turn signal dog from a '62 Chevy Impala. Next, I strap my bivy sack—a one-person tent—and a long tube containing my tiny stove, an extra pint of fuel, pot, matches, food, and what have you on the rear rack. The food is actually PowerBars, a compressed carbohydrate bar, which many people claim can hardly be called "food." One of my friends argued persuasively that PowerBars were, in fact, compressed sawdust. While I knew that the below-zero temperatures would turn the bars into some organic compound with the consistency of an iron pipe, I figured I could stuff them in my armpits until they thawed enough to chew. This is the kind of keen survival planning I knew would get me through.

As soon as I finish strapping everything down, I give the bike a shake, and, of course, everything falls off.

Several hours and rolls of duct tape later, all the gear is attached to the bike, and even my headlight is duct taped to my helmet. I look like Mickey Mouse about to go caving. On my first fully outfitted ride, all that weight high up makes the bike feel not like a pig, but as if a small child is trying to walk back and forth along the top tube of the bike. Thanks to my superior bike handling skills, though, I am able to quickly fall into the nearest snowbank. My giant aspirin tablet pops off.

Back to the duct tape.

The race itself is the soul of simplicity. Get on your bike, your skis, your snowshoes, your sneakers or a mixture of the above and ride, run, ski or slog 85 or 155 miles, through frozen swamps, rivers, hills, and moose patties. There are no rules per se. Stray too far from the course and get in trouble, and you're not going to be found until the spring thaw. You must hit each checkpoint by a certain time, or you're disqualified. After that time, the checkpoint, usually a tent, is dismantled. I have gone over and over the course on paper, gaming it out, but now that I'm in Alaska I'm struck by the foolishness of that strategy. It's lower-48 thinking and planning, whereas the actual race will be determined by the weather.

The weather has been warm, which is not good. Warm means the snow is slush, and the ice is covered with a layer of water. But, at the mandatory meeting before the race, we're told the "good" news.

"It's getting colder," the ever effervescent Dan Bull announces. "Much colder. Expect temperatures around 40 degrees below zero the first night."

That's colder, all right.

We are warned again about moose, getting yet another newspaper clipping about the most recent moose stomping, and the survival equipment is checked to make sure that we are not trying to shave a few pounds off the mandatory 15 pounds. I would have been happy to be able to get the weight of all that gear down to 15 pounds.

The other 80 or so racers are a strange mix of Athletic Gods and aging hippies. The legendary John Stamstad, who's won the race numerous times and is heavily favored to win again no matter what the weather, looks as if he's wandered in from 1968. He's a skinny, emaciated-looking protohippie who has just returned from almost dying in the Australian desert while riding across that country. He is telling me about his race footwear, which he has crafted himself. Unlike my winter mountaineering boots with insulated liner and three-sock system, he has a pair of ultralight cycling shoes with an light insulated liner.

"Don't your feet get cold?" I ask. He looks at me as if I've recently arrived from Mars.

"They freeze and go numb," he says. "It's not a big deal."

My conversation with Stamstad makes me think that perhaps there's some kind of graph of the mental states of extreme sports participants. It's a geometric curve, getting steeper and steeper as you go up it. As you head up the curve, the definition of "extreme" keeps changing. What looked psychotic a couple of years ago now looks like a good Saturday afternoon workout.

It's good, I think, that The List was drawn up when I was at the low end of the curve. I suspect I wouldn't like John Stamstad's list.

The morning of the race dawns clear and very cold. The bike is strapped and taped together, and I'm dressed in layers of long underwear, thin fleece, and jackets with lots of zippers. I've eaten a bland breakfast of bagels and something called GU, a semi-liquid food that comes in little packets and tastes like cake frosting. I've used it before in the backcountry, and I've noticed that no matter how cold it gets, it never seems to freeze. I have consciously decided to ignore the implications of this fact.

The race starts on the appropriately named Big Lake, a long frozen stretch of ice. I survive one quick crisis, a flat tire and frozen pump. I get an air fill from a loaner pump, and stuff mine inside my jacket to let it thaw. Before I have time to really think, the gun goes off, and we're under way.

The real racers are off like hares, leaving those of us at the rear to pick our way across the rutted ice. There's about five or six inches of snow over most of the lake, and the rear wheel of the Cannondale dances all over the place. I know it's "only" 27 miles to the first checkpoint, and, assuming everything goes right, I expect to be there in five or six hours.

I am about to get a lesson about assumptions.

My strategy is to cruise; as my old bicycling buddy John Rodolf would say, "Start slow, then taper off." I'll peddle easily, save my strength, I think, as I watch the other cyclists pull away. *I wonder why they're pushing so hard?*

The lake is uneventful, even fun. You have to kind of steer around looking for the hardest packed snow, but the surface is solid, and the fat tires have plenty to grab hold onto. After an hour or so on the lake, we head into the woods, and I'm greeted with the first of the "whoop-de-doos." The rolling terrain is cut with numerous creeks and streams, creating a roller coaster ride of up and down and up and down and up and down. As it happens, the roller coaster's track is covered with ice. My first approach is tentative; I baby the bike down the steepest part, lightly feather the rear break, steer carefully. This results in my sprawling on top of the bike at the bottom of the whoop as both wheels spin out from under me.

I fall a couple of time disentangling myself from the bike, which I push up the next whoop.

Forget conservative. The next whoop, I fly down, the bike shaking and quivering on the ice. We arrive at the bottom upright.

Okay, I think. *That works.*

After a period of time in the woods whooping, I come to a 15-foot drop into a frozen swamp. Ahead of me is a mile or more of smooth, flat snow, rutted by bicycle tires.

Time to make some time, I think, and head into the swamp.

I go about 15 feet, and the bike sinks up to its axles in the loose snow.

That's odd, I think. I get off and push the bike to a set of ruts made by other riders, then remount the bike. The Cannondale and I get about five feet before we're knee-deep in snow.

Every so often I can ride for a couple of minutes, but, for the most part, I'm pushing the bike in deep snow. Crossing the mile of frozen swamp takes just over an hour. I stop in the woods, eat some GU, drink some water from the pack on my back and refigure my time to the first checkpoint. I am not yet in trouble, but things are not going swimmingly. It's too cold to stop for long.

I run into a friend from Boulder, Monique Cole, an athlete and author who is writing the official history of the race. We're able to ride along together through the woods, where the snow is harder packed. We drop out of the woods to cross a wide frozen stream. On the other side, struggling up the steep 15-foot-high frozen bank, is the hapless Italian team. Hapless, because their bikes are equipped with normal tires instead of the wide, flat snow tires the rest of us are using. In the increasingly softer snow, they can't ride at all. They've come all the way from Italy with an Italian television film crew to push their bicycles across these swamps. At the moment, they're stuck at the foot of the bank, trying to get up the pure sheet of ice.

"Use your bike like an ice ax," another rider shouts from the top of the bank. "Shove your bike ahead of you, and take a step at the time!"

Halfway up the bank, one of the Italian riders loses his footing and slides back to the bottom. This goes on for many minutes, with the rest of us waiting our turn to look like idiots. Monique gets most of the way up when the Italians, ever the gentlemen, realize it's a woman on the slope and extend a helping hand. I have a couple of good falls on my own, the bike bouncing and sliding back down, until I figure out the secret, which is shove the bike in the deep, loose snow to the side of the worst of the ice, then crawl up on your hands and knees. Pure fun.

When we hit the next swamp, I'm on my own again. Monique's lighter weight lets her peddle on the loose snow I sink in.

The situation is getting progressively worse. The longer the sun shines on the swamps, the looser the snow gets and the deeper I sink. By midday, when I expected to be past the first checkpoint, I am pushing the Cannondale through ankle-deep slop. Except for shorter and shorter periods in the woods, I have given up riding altogether. As the snow gets looser and I sink deeper, it becomes harder to even make the bike roll. For long periods of time I am forced to pick the bike up and partially carry it, my own little snow anchor.

The hours pass with excruciating slowness. I try to turn my brain off, to disassociate from the whole experience, but it is obviously lodged in "record." My arms and shoulders begin to ache from the effort to shove the bike along. I respond by alternating sides, so at least my right arm and shoulder can hurt as badly as my left arm and shoulder. I occasionally start to drift off and get my ankles tangled up in the peddles—twice, I fall on top of the bike.

Mostly, I think about how even wasps learn from running mazes, but that I, unfortunately, keeping forgetting to take these events seriously enough. I get on the bike and ride about three feet before we sink.

I now understand totally why the other bikers were pushing so hard to get across the lake—to get across the swamps before the snow crust melted.

Perfect time for this revelation.

I occasionally sing songs to myself, carry on long conversations with old friends, try to remember passages from books or obscure movies.

I resolve not to look at my watch, because it's not good for me. I reflect on how time ought to be more linear than it is. Deep diving, time passes so quickly, the computer logging minutes at a frenetic pace. Out here in the swamps, time moves like an insect caught in hardening amber, agonizingly pulling each leg out of the golden resin, only to be trapped again . . . I give up and look at not only my watch, but the computer on the bicycle. I have been out for five hours, and I'm only half-way to the first checkpoint.

I am, in a word, screwed.

I resolve to pick up my walking pace, and as soon as I hit the woods, I ride hard to make up time. I also know that it's impossible to make up time. All you can do is keep going, and time will run at whatever pace it chooses. I occasionally see other racers, but most of the time I'm alone. My brain moves ahead in fits and starts, mis-firing and starting again. Unlike a long event where you can just shift into autopilot, the Iditabike is hard, the riding is tough, techni-cal, demanding. I have to be in the "here," all the time.

On-line, real time, I think, heading into the next whoop-de-doo.

Not on-line and real time enough, however. The 15-foot drop looks vertical, and before I even have time to think what to do, I am pummeling over the edge. At the bottom, I gracefully continue over the handlebars—an "endo"—and smash my right shoulder into the steep ice heading up. I lay there for a full minute, my eyes closed, waiting for the stars to stop spinning around me. Then I raise my right arm slowly, sending spasms of pain into my shoulder.

If my shoulder was broken, I reason, *I couldn't lift my arm.*

This is mentally reassuring, but my shoulder still seriously hurts. I spend a few minutes massaging it, eat a handful of aspirin and a couple of tubes of orange-flavored GU, then push the bike up the whoop. I ride stiffly to the next swamp, where I promptly sink.

Time passes, and one swamp looks pretty much the same as the next. A pink glow begins to suffuse the western sky—toward Japan, I think—and I can feel the temperature dropping. Pretty soon, I'll be on my headlight, with its battery pack hung under my jackets, against the skin of my back, where it's warm.

And I notice that I can't feel my feet.

I stop and begin the foot-swinging ritual designed to get things going again down below. I swing my legs back and forth, trying to wiggle my toes, although no toes appear to be home. I stamp out a place in the snow and stomp around like some Iron John seminar participant. All I need is a spear. After another bout of swinging my legs, the feeling begins to trickle back, and I immediately wish it *would go away*! It hurts, stings; I curl my toes, and they burn.

I begin moving again. I made the decision at the start of the race to cache my gaiters, those insulated, waterproof leggings that stretch from the top of the boot to just below the knee, at the first checkpoint. My reasoning was that I'd probably be riding steadily for the first few hours, and I wouldn't need either the extra insulation or the waterproofing. In fact, I thought the extra insulation would cause my feet to sweat too much, and I wanted to avoid wet feet at all costs.

Using my 20-20 hindsight, I saw that I'd made a fundamental mistake. Now, my feet were wet, cold and the temperature was probably already below zero. My Cannondale's computer read just 20 miles; seven more miles of shoving my bike through frozen swamps.

Seven more miles!

I consider sitting down and crying, or at the very least demanding that Scotty beam me back up to the Enterprise. Instead, I start pushing my bike through the swamp.

Here is where it starts to get weird. The sun has gone down, and I've flicked my headlight on—more for the security of the light than a need to see. The snow seems to glow, and I can clearly see the outline of the next set of woods ahead of me. I am cold, but not shivering; my feet are more or less constantly numb. A depression as deep and as smothering as the snowpack has settled on my brain, and my right shoulder aches and aches. I am almost across a swamp when I hear a voice.

It startles me so badly I drop the bike. I spin around 360 degrees, looking for the person talking, but there is nothing but the snow.

"What the *fuck!*" I shout.

Nothing, but the voice is still there.

I can feel the chemistry set of my body pumping adrenaline, my muscles gearing for flee or fight, there on the frozen swamp. Then I listen to the voice, which is talking about me. Specifically, it is my friend Sandy back in Florida, and she appears to be praying.

"I know he thinks he's alone out there, and I know he's tired and he probably hurts," the voice is saying, as clear as if Sandy were standing next to me. *"But remind him that he's not alone . . . "*

I am dumbfounded. I plop down on the bike in the snow and just sit there as the voice fades, some cosmic radio signal drifting into the background static. I sit there for about ten minutes, then I get up and push the bike. I am cold; my feet are numb; my shoulder pulses, but I feel better.

With less than a mile left to go on the computer, I come to a steep drop out of the woods onto a frozen river, the Big Susitna. I make a couple of false starts at getting down the 15 feet of ice to the river, but decide instead to throw the bike into the waist-deep snow alongside the trail. I wade through the snow to the edge, then drop the bike as gently as possible to the river. It bounces once, then slides to a stop. I then climb down to the river, using tree limbs and roots for handholds. Once on the ice, the wind is screaming and I figure it must be very below zero. I push the bike the last half mile, a blinking strobe in the distance marking the checkpoint. It takes me forever to reach the strobe. No, longer than forever. I'm shivering when I get there. Their thermometer, hanging outside of one of two tents, reads 20 degrees below zero. But there's hot water and sympathy as the last of us stragglers drag in. One of the tents is for the "refugees," frostbite victims, people suffering from exhaustion or broken equipment. There are five people in the tent, including my friend Monique, along with an old cast-iron camp stove. The tent is warm, probably around 10 degrees. I pull off my boots and start massaging my feet in front of the stove; it is like massaging a piece of steak. My toes are white and lifeless, and I feel nothing.

Monique is going on as soon as she warms up.

"If you don't go on, Michael," she says. "You'll never make the next checkpoint in time. They'll disqualify you."

I know she's right. But my will has dissolved somewhere back in those frozen swamps. I am afraid for my feet, afraid in general. I am tired—no, exhausted—and I hurt.

It is 20 degrees below zero, and everything has gone to shit. I massage my feet, and wait for the pain to come. Monique waits for my answer. I wish my brain was working faster. I wish I wasn't so cold.

"I'll stay a while," I hear myself saying. She nods, then leaves to go pack her bike. I think I have never hated myself quite so much as I do at this very instance. *Quitter! Quitter! Quitter!* the animal in my head shrieks, but I can no more go outside than I can fly. It is as if I have been inhabited by an alien being, who won't let me get on the goddamned bike, go back into the goddamned cold, get back on the goddamned trail. I break out my camping gear and claim a corner of the tent nearest the flap. I stuff my sleeping bag into the bivy, unroll my pad, then lay the whole thing on the ice. Finally, I stuff a handful of chemical heaters in the end of the bag and climb in, shucking my outer clothes as I do. It is two hours before the pain in my feet eases enough to let me fall into a dreamless, restless sleep.

"You Bane?" the first words I hear around dawn are from a race official.

"I'm Bane," I say, sticking my head out of the bag. The cold is enough to take your breath away. I breath shallow, holding each breath in my mouth to warm it.

"You can't make the next time point," she says, checking her clipboard. "At three o'clock this afternoon, you're going to be disqualified and evacuated off the course."

I nod.

"Three choices, no actually four," she continues. "You can finish the race on your own, but there'll be no support, no checkpoints and you'd better be an expert at winter camping. Are you?"

I nod negatively. It's shaping up to be a great morning.

"Three choices, then," she says. "We can evac you from here, you can ride back to the start line, or you can just keep riding until we disqualify you and a bush pilot flies you out."

"What the hell," I say. "I'll just keep riding."

"Good choice," she says, and goes on to the next person.

I get dressed, I saddle up the red Cannondale, drink a cup of cold instant coffee and hit the trail. This time, my feet are surrounded by chemical heat packs and safely laced into insulated gaiters as well as three pairs of socks and the mountaineering boots.

But I needn't have worried. It is bright, sunny and bitterly cold. The hard freeze the night before has turned yesterday's mush into pure white concrete, and the bike flies along the Iditarod Trail. Twice I pull off to let sled dog teams pass, the huskies' breath steaming in the cold air. I am actually making up time—not that it matters. The longer I ride, the better I feel mentally. My shoulder still aches, and there's no feeling in most of my toes, but I think I'll learn to live with decisions made at 20 below. In a sense, I'm free to concentrate on the frozen countryside, the mountains in the distance, their ridgelines razor sharp in the cold air. For miles the trail is lined with huge wolf tracks, criss-crossing the bicycle ruts.

They're watching me, I think, and that thought is comforting rather than threatening. I see a moose on the trail ahead of me, and

I pause for a snack until he ambles away into the frozen woods.

Almost before I know it, it's afternoon, and I emerge from the woods onto another frozen river. There's a plane on skis parked there, an antique Cessna, with a huge "Cyndi Lou" painted on the nose.

"You Bane?" the pilot asks, same question as this morning.

I nod.

"You're outta here," he says. "Take your bike apart and we'll bungee it to the plane."

The plane is parked next to a house full of people, heat, and cans of Coca-Cola. I step inside for a minute, then head back out to disassemble the Cannondale. The pilot comes and, without another word, pulls out a snake's nest of bungee cords and begins tying pieces of the bike to the little plane—the rear wheel here, the frame there, the front wheel on the other wing. When he's all done, he says, "Climb in the back seat." I look in.

"There isn't a back seat," I says.

In disgust, he points to what appears to be the gas tank. I climb on top. The plane rumbles and shakes and shudders, then starts down the frozen river. Suddenly, we are airborne, wind whipping through the partially open Plexiglas windows. For just a moment, as we bank away, Denali is suspended in the red frame triangle of my bike. I feel my stomach knot.

You're not good enough, the great mountain whispers. *This time, you go home. Next time, I'll grind your bones into powder. You'll die here.*

And then we are headed back to the start line, where I will catch a ride back to Anchorage. It will take four days for Monique to finish, and the trail will be strewn with thousands of dollars of mountain bikes, discarded by the owners in an attempt to just get to shelter. Later, another racer will ask me a strange question.

"Did you," he asks tentatively at the race banquet, "hear any voices out there on the trail?"

"What kind of voices?" I ask.

"You know," he says awkwardly. "Voices. Sometimes . . . people *hear* things out there."

"I guess it happens," I say.

21

Denali

"Hey you guys," the driver of the small van is saying, "There's your mountain!"

All eight of us—six climbers and two guides—lean to the left, giving the van the aspect of a small boat sloshing on open water. Out the left side windows, though, shining in the May sunshine, is the towering bulk of Denali, still 100 miles away.

"It's sumthin', huh?" says the driver.

We all agree, it's sumthin', all right.

After years of expectations, months of slogging through the Colorado backcountry pulling a sled, thousands of dollars on my battered credit cards, I'm in Alaska, on the way. Leading the way is main AAI guide Steve Dunbar, who spends most of his summer doing search and rescue in Antarctica, and thusly, has an interesting definition of "cold." With him, on her first trip to Denali, is Angela Hawse, late of Outward Bound.

Talkeetna, in the shadow of Denali, strikes me as, say, Dodge City around the turn of the century. It's drizzling—common, since a mountain the size of Denali makes its own weather patterns—when we get to town. The few hundred "real" residents of the log cabin slab front stores and bars are swollen by what appears to be a fashion show straight out of the pages of the Patagonia and the North Face catalogs. In the short season, from late April until the end of July, Talkeetna is filled with climbers from around the world. Everybody looks exactly like we look. Well, that's not quite true. There are actually two flavors. One group of climbers, the Newcomers, look exactly like us—brightly colored climbing shells, yellow and red predominating; matching pants; fetching fleece hats and sneakers for around town. The second flavor looks like us, except with all the happy edges sanded off. The color is faded from the shells; the pants patched with duct tape; the fetching fleece hat ragged and stinking with sweat and old sunscreen. Instead of excitement and plans, Color Two just looks tired. They eat a lot, too. In other words, it's not hard to tell whose been "up" and who's waiting to go up.

Our first stop is K2 Aviation, one of the several flight services that exist to shuttle climbers between Talkeetna and the Kahiltna International Airport, the glacier landing strip that serves Base Camp, to see if there's a chance of getting to the mountain today.

Base Camp, though, is whited out, the drizzle in Talkeetna giving way to screaming snow at 8,000 feet.

Our next stop is the ranger headquarters, a claustrophobic log cabin in "downtown" Talkeetna, where we pay our $150 "mountaineering program fee," sign in, and watch a short film that tells us 1) Denali is dangerous as all hell, and 2) to pick up after ourselves on the mountain.

Then it's back to K2, where we spend hours on the runway, checking and sorting gear; dividing bags of food and common gear; checking the tents, the medical equipment, the emergency radios; assembling the sleds. It is one last chance to race to the mountaineering store in Talkeetna for the One Last Thing we forgot (which we will, in all likelihood, discard higher up to lighten the load on our sagging shoulders). It is the last chance to stock up on Snickers bars (which are carried in amazing numbers at the Talkeetna general store); another chance to call home and assure spouses and friends that everything is fine.

If this sounds like a major undertaking, it is.

The difference between going up a big mountain, one of 20,000 feet or more, and hiking in, say, the Rockies, is more than one of just degree. It's possible—just barely, if you're a top mountaineer—to treat a 20,000-foot mountain as a hike, but you do so only at dire risks. A big mountain is a world unto itself, a microplanet with its own atmosphere, its own gravity, its own natural laws. What works at sea level, what works at 5,000 feet in the Blue Ridge Mountains, even what works at 13,000 feet in the Colorado Rockies will not necessarily guarantee your survival on a big mountain. As befits a smaller planet, the weather is violent and wildly unpredictable, as if a visitor to that planet can run through spring, summer, fall and winter in a single afternoon. Hurricane winds routinely scour the frozen landscapes, and they will remove a human presence as easily as a two-ton boulder.

Perhaps the greatest danger of the big mountains is the subtle blurring of subjective and objective dangers. As I've gone through The List, I've come to rely on the "subjective" and "objective" analysis. If you're walking down the street and a chunk of building lands on your head, that's an objective risk. Nothing you could have or should have done would have prepared you for being hit in the head by a flying gargoyle off a building. If, however, you are walking down the same street listening to your Walkman, not paying a bit of attention and step in front of a bus, that's a subjective risk. You're just as squashed, but on the subjective risk, you had some control. The game I've painfully learned is to access both risks, then focus my attention on the subjective ones, the ones I can change.

On a big mountain, the list of risks reads like a *Who's Who* (or *What's What*) of ways to die. There is the weather—the storms, the cold, the wind—avalanches, crevasses, climbing falls, failure or loss of equipment, diseases of altitude and exhaustion, and a host of minor horsemen. All of these are aggravated by the undeniable fact that, as you climb higher, you are not thinking quite as clearly as you are at sea level. As with diving deep on air, just when you need your brain to be the clearest it has ever been, it is slogging through a marsh of poorly understood chemical reactions, misfiring and sputtering. The greatest threat of the big mountains is that they blunt our most important survival tool.

And Denali is more dangerous still.

Like the Florida alligator the neighborhood kids feed, Denali's accessibility has bred, if not contempt, at least complacency. After all, the Himalayan peaks are off in some mysterious, mythical country; the South American giants are buried in the heart of the rain forests. But on a good day, you can see Denali from downtown Anchorage. Every climbing season is full of Denali "firsts"—the first summiteer under 13 years old; the first blind climber; the first "All This" or "All That" team to make the summit. At times, in fact, the great mountain has almost a circus air about it, with Talkeetna and the McKinley Base Camp jammed with people from all over the world, partying heartily, while the summit smiles down benignly from 20,320 feet.

That belies the simple fact, as restated by *Anchorage Daily News* reporter Craig Medred, who has made a career of observing the mountain and its people, "On the average, 1 out of every 100 people who head up McKinley dies."

That particular number refuses to go away.

In the cold drizzle of Talkeetna, I pause at the Climbers' Memorial, a tiny graveyard to mark the names of the climbers lost on the great mountain. Some of the names are familiar to me; some just names inscribed in stone. The newest name, from a week ago, has yet to be added, and it is a given that by the end of the climbing season, there will be more. Before I come down from the mountain, there will be more.

"Subartic Mt. McKinley, 63 degrees north of the equator, rises out of a sprawling web of glaciers whose tongues push into the lowlands to an elevation of 1,000 feet," writes Glenn Randall, in *Mount McKinley Climber's Handbook*. "In the Himalayas, at the latitude of Miami, the glaciers extend only down to 13,500 feet. The climate only halfway to McKinley's summit is as severe as the North Pole's. Nighttime temperatures two-thirds of the way up McKinley frequently hit 30 degrees below zero during May, the peak climbing season. Not until Himalayan climbers are nearly twice that high do they experience such extremes. The northern latitude means that the oxygen content in the air on McKinley's summit is equivalent to the oxygen available on the summit of a Himalayan peak that is 800 to 1,500 feet higher . . . "

On the other hand, as Frances D. Chamberlain, the second woman to climb the mountain, noted in 1963, "There are no mosquitoes . . . "

The six of us climbers—Tom Walker, Roger Kubly, Rich Davidson, Tommy Cary, Jimmy Chandler, and myself—spend the rest of the evening exploring Talkeetna, which takes about 20 minutes. The we start our waiting game, watching it drizzle and periodically checking with K2 for conditions on the mountain.

Our plan, taken at its most general, is simple. As soon as there's a break in the weather up top, we'll load into K2's blood red ski planes with all our gear and head for 7,200 foot high Base Camp and the famous Kahiltna International. Then, over the next two to three weeks, we'll walk the roughly 16 miles and 13,120 vertical feet to the summit.

Accomplishing this "simple plan" will involve building five camps as we move up the mountain—Camp 1, at 8,500 feet; Camp 2, at 10,000 feet; Camp 3, at 11,000 feet; Camp 4, at 14,300 feet and, finally, High Camp, Camp 5, at 17,200 feet. Ideally, this system will give us time to acclimatize to the altitude, and, just as importantly, to acclimatize to the mountain and to each other. We're carrying enough food, gas, tents and miscellaneous supplies to last a team of eight people a month. Because the supplies weigh so much, we'll often spend days ferrying loads from one camp to the other, then returning to the lower camp to sleep. From the moment we leave Base Camp, our lives will begin narrowing in focus. Our individual identities as writer, doctor, engineer, pharmacist will give way to being either a member of rope team one—Steve's rope—or rope team two—Angela's rope. Our daily rhythms will become simple: *carry, move, rest, wait.*

After a day in Talkeetna and a last, long shower, Angela comes out of the wooden offices of K2.

"It's clear," she says. "Time to go."

What follows is a frenzy of disassembly, stuffing, restuffing, and outright cramming as our disgusted bush pilot, who once flew F-16s, jams pieces of equipment into the four-seat red Cessna that will ferry the first half of our party to Base Camp. Before I have a chance to clearly think, even start to put my thoughts in order, I'm crammed myself, complete with my survival gear should we crash, into the right-hand rear seat, and the little plane is sluggishly snarling and growling its way down the runway, aimed at the gray-clouded sky.

"Where y'all from?" the pilot asks perfunctorily as the little plane pops through the cloudbase into the bright sunshine at 10,000 feet. We answer—*Colorado, New Mexico, California*—but we're not paying attention. Instead, we are all riveted on jagged whiteness of the Alaska Range, literally the shattered edge of a continent, pushed up by the cataclysmic collision of the Pacific continental plate and the American plate 65 million years ago. Through the front windscreen, off to the right, Denali stands above Mt. Foraker and Mt. Hunter. Soft snow, spindrift, curls in a long comma from the summit.

"Blowin' up there," says the pilot. "Not a good day to be on top."

I try to imagine what it must be like on top, the screaming winds approaching hurricane force, creating a chill so low that it no longer makes any sense—*30 below, 40 below, 60 below.* I try to imagine the wind pulling and tearing, scouring and biting, looking for the tiniest piece of exposed, fragile flesh. But the images fade quickly—*insufficient data.* Instead, I just stare at the Great God Of The North, its massive ice flows the color of hammered gold in the afternoon light. *I've come*, I think, incredulously. I can't take my eyes off the mountain.

The pilot points out a dot at the end of one of the glaciers.

"Kahiltna International," he says.

The dot rapidly coalesces into a ragtag collection of multicolored tents, bamboo pendants, and a line of cones marking the "runway," an uphill icy slope.

"Hang on," our pilot says, and he noses the red plane toward the first cone. At least the afternoon light is good. Sometimes, the pilot has mentioned, when the light is really flat, it's hard to know exactly where the ground is. So the plan is then to get the plane to where the ground more or less has to be, then cut the power. This makes for, he says, an exciting landing. The engines screams as first one ski, then the other hits the ice, and the plane skates to an uphill stop, turning 180 degrees for the downhill takeoff.

"Hurry," the pilot says as someone outside takes off the right-hand door. We clamber out and start stacking equipment to the side of the plane. As soon as the last ice ax and ski pole is out, the door is put back on and latched, and the little red plane heads downhill to a shaky takeoff.

Within minutes, the plane is gone, and the only sound is the wind.

Sixteen miles away, the summit of Denali, surrounded by a crown of light, beams down at us. It is, says one of my partners, like being in God's Own Cathedral. That particular illusion is dispelled quickly when a huge chunk of Mt. Hunter, just a few miles away, lets go, tons and tons of snow tumbling onto the glacier. Within seconds, the echoing thunder of the avalanche reaches us.

"That was a good one," says Angela.

Up the slope is the ragtag collection of two dozen or so tents that forms Base Camp. A couple of the tents are permanent, but most are expeditions either waiting for the next plane off or waiting for the weather to start up. All the tents are partially hidden by walls made of snow blocks. In the center of camp are the caches, holes dug deep and marked with the ubiquitous bamboo poles. The caches hold extra food for the return and gear that doesn't go up the mountain. The bamboo poles marking the caches are also marked with the name of the expedition and the expected return date. If your cache has been sitting around for a couple of months unclaimed, people start to get worried.

The caches are dug deep because of the ravens, huge, magnificent black birds with the ability to dig deep and rip canvas haul bags to little pieces. More than one expedition, we are told, has come back looking forward to extra food and extra clothes in the cache, only to find shreds of miracle fibers and the empty wrappers of candy bars littering the snow. If you don't presently believe ravens are messengers from the underworld, you will after an incident like that.

We begin hauling the gear of the hill to an abandoned tent platform.

"Level it out," says Steve. "Then let's build some walls."

Thus begins a routine that will, eventually, become as reflexive as walking into a room and turning on a light. The leveling is easy enough—shovel and ax; chip the ice and use the shovel to take off the rough edges. Stomp around until the platform is flat and level. Next we take hand saws, find an area of firm snow, scrape off the powder and begin cutting roughly two-foot by one-foot blocks in the snow. We use a shovel to pry the blocks out of the snow. Then we build a wall, just like a New England farmer tracking stones.

It is bright and sunny, and in no time we are stripped to T-shirts and long underwear bottoms, sweating like pigs, building a snow fortress. The walls rise quickly, and when they get a little more than four feet high, Steve calls a halt to the quarrying, and we begin pitching tents. At first, I am self-consciously clumsy. Of the team, I have far and away the least experience. Everyone else has at least one big mountain, and most members have several under their belts. Pitching winter camp is second nature to them; for me, it's trying to visualize the instruction sheet I used to put this exact same tent together on my front porch, with the temperature at a bitter 72 degrees.

But eventually the tents are set; my dreadfully expensive Marmot down sleeping bag, which I came to believe in at the Iditabike, is "lofting," fluffing up after being compressed all day, and our first dinner on the mountain is done.

"This is not so bad," I think to myself, crawling into the bag as the temperature heads toward the big zero.

Shows what I know.

We wake early, both from anticipation and from the drone of the ski planes landing more climbers. It is still sunny and bright. I hike up to one of the great "conveniences" of Base Camp, a plywood throne toilet, built over a deep hole in the ice, where you can do your business while looking across the camp and some of the most spectacular real estate on the planet. There are a couple of us waiting in line, tactfully staring in the opposite direction, when a Korean climber hikes up. His jacket is patched with a long stretch of silver duct tape, his hair matted to his head, his lips burned from the sun and festering. He looks like he's been in a war. We step off the trail and let the climber make his way to the front of the line.

"How was it?" the other person in line asks.

The Korean climber stops for a moment as if pondering, then resumes his hike to the toilet.

"Cold," he says back over his shoulder. "Very cold."

We begin breaking down camp and loading our packs and sleds for the first day. Base Camp is almost empty—most of the teams have taken advantage of this break in the weather and headed up. A few teams make their way down to Base Camp. As we watch, one team struggles up the remaining hill to Base Camp until they're within about 100 yards of the first tents. Then they just stop, as if the batteries have all finally run down to zero. Some people from camp hike down to them with energy drinks and warm water, to get them restarted for the final steps.

My rope includes Angela, the guide, who will lead; Tom Walker, an engineer for an oil company in California; Rich Davidson, yet another engineer, this one from Los Alamos, New Mexico, and me. Tom, in his early 30s, has been on big mountains in South America, and Rich—45, my age—has climbed around the world for the better part of two decades.

Basically, we line up like sled dogs. The main rope is knotted and clipped to our climbing harnesses around our waists. Our two prussics, in case we fall into a crevasse, are attached to the climbing harness and the rope. The sled has its own harness, connected to the sled by five-foot aluminum poles, which goes on over the climbing harness. My sled has somehow arrived without poles, so it's tethered to my climbing harness with lengths of parachute cord. For this first day, we'll be carrying everything—all the food, fuel, climbing gear, bamboo poles to mark our way, stoves, spares—everything, the six miles uphill to Camp 1. My share of "everything" comes to around 80 or 90 pounds in the sled. My personal pack, a giant expedition pack from Lowe Alpine, is also stuffed to the gills with my own gear and whatever joint gear I can cram in. It weights in at 60 pounds. Between the sled and the pack, I feel as if a high school student is perching on the small of my back.

"Well," says the every-cheerful Steve, "let's go."

It's hard to explain the feelings that come with actually stepping off. The anticipation mixes with the low level buzz of the fear, all dwarfed by the gargantuan scale of the Alaska Range. The further you hike, the smaller you get, as if you have entered a room built for giants. Around us, the sun sparkles off the snow. The ice falls shade through all the colors of semiprecious gems, the deep, clear blue of amethyst or the amber cat-eye yellow of topaz, a hint of pale green emerald. The snow crunches under our boots, and, often, in the distance, avalanches thunder.

I would like to tell you the hours pass quickly in this great cathedral, but the fact is the hours pass a slow 60 minutes at a time. The sled inexorably pulls at the waist, while the straps of even the best-adjusted pack gnaws into the muscles of the shoulder. It is blistering hot in the sun—all our exposed skin is slathered with sunscreen the consistency and thickness of latex paint. And, when the sun drops behind a cloud, it is freezing cold. Sometimes, I listen to the radio, tuned into an Anchorage headbanger heavy metal station that seems to defy the mountain. Sometimes, I just walk, concentrating on shutting my brain off.

Six or seven hours later, dizzy with exhaustion, we see a small cluster of tents off to the right of the trail, at the base of a steep hill.

Camp 1.

It takes two hours to dig our tent platforms, reinforce and build walls and get the tents, including our cook tent, erected. It had started snowing a few hours back, and by the time we finish camp, it is seriously coming down. After a quick supper, we dive into our tents and bags. I close my eyes, and, in my head, I'm still walking. I walk until I finally fall asleep.

The next day is a "carry" day. Camp 2 isn't that far away in miles, but it's almost 2,000 feet higher. To acclimatize to the altitude, and to ease the load on our bodies, we'll take a majority of our supplies up to within a few hundred feet of the campsite, bury them, then return to Camp 1 to spend the night. The next day, we'll strike camp and move to Camp 2.

We harness up early, the snow having broken in the night, and move out.

Somehow, I imagine that the lightened load, probably a 100 pounds total (a *junior* high student on my back), will make a substantial difference in the day's overall Pain Index. I have, of course, failed to factor in the increasing steepness of the trail. We are, after all, climbing a mountain, and, by definition, the trail goes *up*.

So does the Pain Index.

A member of a rope team doesn't have the luxury of a solo hiker. A solo hiker can slow the pace down to a barely moving crawl, or plop down on a rock and wait for either breath or inspiration, whichever comes first. A rope team, though, has to keep moving, even if it's at the pace of the slowest—me—member. On any big mountain, and especially Denali, good weather is a gift. No, make that a *loan*, to be withdrawn by any whim at any time. As long as the weather holds, we need to move, and move as quickly as we can. Breaks are measured out like water in the desert—at least, it seems that way to us, slow climbers that we are.

"Does this seem worse than yesterday?" Rich, my tent mate, asks during a break. I am too tired to speak. I just nod. "I thought so," he says. "I'm glad it's not just me."

At 9,700 feet, Steve takes a look at the two ropes, then points out a cache site. In record time, we dig the holes, stash the supplies, stick in the bamboo markers and head back down the hill. After a quick supper, we're asleep in record time, as well.

Things, including our spirits, begin picking up the next morning. I think it's the mental realization that we all are actually stuck on this mountain, and we have the proverbial long way to go. It has taken a few days for all the concerns, the worries, the day-to-day life in the lowlands to be scrubbed away by the snow. From my own point of view as an avowed nonathlete, it has taken my body a few days to get used to the idea that this pain is going to last a long time, so get used to it. Everything else on The List has been an event, of a relatively short duration. I've become confident "negotiating" with my body—*Okay, guys, we're going to need six hard hours of output, then it's Snickers and beer . . .* The mountain is different. Each day's output has been low intensity, but relentless, the extremes of heat and cold, the altitude, the heavy load—the fear—conspiring to sap strength. But I am constantly amazed by the body's ability to adapt, and to persevere.

We move quickly to Camp 2, carry the next day to Camp 3, then move to the 11,000-foot camp the following day. Superlatives fail in the great cathedral of the mountain. We hike alongside ice falls of shifting colors, through landscapes carved of rock and hard blue ice. We're still using ski poles—it's not steep enough for the ice axes yet.

I place my pole at one point, then lift the pole and look down through the hole into the dark green caverns of a huge crevasse. We hike on bridges of snow and ice, the summit of Denali emerging from its cloudy crown for minutes, sometimes hours. We hike along with other teams, talk about preparations, other mountains, plans. The mountain seems benign, even friendly, and we are lulled by its beauty.

We arrive at Camp 3 in the bright sunshine to find a stupendous series of five tent platforms unoccupied. It looks like a bunch of kids have created snow castles, connected by mazes. There's even a "bathroom," a small room walled on three sides. I promptly dub the camp Fortress Denali, and we set to work digging in the camp. Rich and I decide to take the farthest platform, near the edge of a crevasse. Although the walls are a sturdy three feet high, we decide (fueled by the fact that it's a beautiful day) to dig the platform a little deeper and get the walls up to at least five feet. After a few hours of work, Fortress Denali is something to behold. Our platform has five foot walls, benches for seating, plenty of room inside the walls for gear and a convenient side entrance to the bathroom. We decorate Fortress Denali with minarets of carved snow blocks, the entrance minaret festooned with a Happy Face of M&Ms. We finish just in time for the afternoon snowstorm, the clouds rising up from the lowlands like some huge flying saucer. We talk about the coming climb. The great rock headwall of Denali, the steepest part of the climb, is just above Camp 4, only a few days away. I have thought about the headwall for years, its 50- to 60- degree slopes of snow and ice, climbers moving slowly, a step at a time, up the ropes fixed in place. I have imagined myself stepping onto the top of the headwall, the world below me, the summit just an arm's length (well, a day) away.

"I'm worried about the headwall," says one of the other climbers. "It scares the hell out of me."

We'll spend three days in Fortress Denali, including a rest day. We're just pleased as punch.

The weather is deteriorating.

Up high, we're told by a passing ranger, it's a nightmare of high winds and stunning cold. Only four people have summited so far, and one has, as far as we know, died on the way down. Teams are trapped higher on the mountain, waiting for a weather break to move up or down. Worse for us, a weather system is forming around the mountain. The 8 P.M. weather report, delivered by Annie, the flight controller at Base Camp, is for more of the clear, cold weather we've had, but even Annie calls the weather report "bogus."

The weather gets progressively worse during our rest day, the mountain starting to show its teeth. The snow approaches white-out conditions for a while, then backs off. Steve decides that it's critical to carry to Camp 4, a much tougher climb than the hikes we've been doing, the next morning if the weather breaks at all.

Even worse for me, my tent mate, Rich, is running a fever and starting to cough badly. It is, he thinks, a respiratory infection he has brought with him to the mountain and that has blossomed in the thin air. Dr. Jim, Jim Chandler from Alabama, on Steve's rope, concurs. It goes without saying that the higher you go, the less your body is able to repair itself. Instead, the body has to throw its not insubstantial forces into maintaining heat and acclimatizing to the altitude. Listening to Rich cough scares the hell out of me. I know I'm susceptible to Acute Mountain Sickness (AMS)—I found the unfortunate proof of that during my debacle bicycling on Mammoth Mountain, at a paltry 12,000 feet. Because of Denali's reduced oxygen because of its position near the Arctic Circle, I am at the equivalent of 12,000 feet already.

While the symptoms of AMS—fatigue, headaches, insomnia, lack of appetite, nausea—are bad enough in and of themselves, the real danger, to me, is that AMS is often a precursor to the high-altitude killer, pulmonary and cerebral edema. In the pulmonary variety, there is an increase in the fluids in the lungs; in cerebral edema, there is an increase in the fluid surrounding the brain. The pulmonary variety is by far the most common.

"The unpredictable nature of HAPE, high altitude pulmonary edema, is that anyone sleeping above 12,000 feet is a potential victim," writes Jonathon Waterman in his classic book *Surviving Denali*, which we have all just about committed to memory. "[It] is dangerous because of its rapid onset. Because it isn't diagnosed in its early stages, HAPE often reaches life-threatening proportions within hours."

The only cure is to descend, and descend quickly.

There is one other fact that we have all learned: chest infections predispose a person to HAPE.

Rich coughs steadily all night.

The weather breaks in the morning, but Steve is still worried.

"We're going to have to push the pace a little," he says. "We have to be through Windy Corner before the weather turns."

Windy Corner is exactly that, a rocky "corner," jutting out like the bow of a ship, at around 13,000 feet. In a storm, Windy Corner, with its high exposure and howling winds, will be just about the worst place to be.

We have, I think, crossed a threshold here. The trail from Camp 3 to Camp 4 is steeper, more exposed. A fall along parts of this trail can have serious consequences. Instead of ski poles and snowshoes, we'll be moving on crampons—spikes that lace to the bottom of our plastic mountaineering boots— and carrying our ice axes. The axes are the mountaineer's last ditch survival tool—we've practiced over and over again falling, then jamming the sharp tip of the ax into the ice or snow, to "catch" the fall. Self-arrest. I remember my ice climbing instructor's comment on self arrest, when I asked her how well it worked on hard blue ice: "Well," she said, "if it doesn't, at least you've got something to do in those closing seconds of your life." The terrain between the two camps is heavily crevassed. "If we're going to have a crevasse fall," says Steve, "we're probably going to have it here."

We rope in and head up Motorcycle Hill, just outside of camp. How the hill got its name is a little vague, but I would give just about anything for a motorized trip up it. It's about as steep as a black diamond ski run (Thank you, Ilg!), and covered with a thick layer of powder over ice. We crunch our way up at a slow pace, but one that's more of a toll on us than any of the previous days. The hill is deceptive. Each time we get to what looks like a flat spot—a respite!—the trail gets steeper. I finally manage to shut off my brain and concentrate on putting one spiked foot in front of the other, staring down, watching the rope ahead of me move.

After a minor lifetime, we crest the hill, only to see the trail turn, every bit as steep.

"Guys, over the next section we're going to be on hard ice," Steve says. "I'm going to need you to move fast, but move very, very carefully. Some of these places, it's a long way down."

We start up again. The trail is now hard blue ice covered with snow. Each step is deliberate—set the ax, step, step . . . set the ax, step, step . . . faster now, but no less deliberate. It's still sunny when we finally round the corner that gives us a view of Windy Corner, but there are clouds building.

"Quick break," says Steve, "then back to it."

The hours drag on as we start the steep hike up to Windy Corner. At one point, the trail runs near high ridges, their tops thick with snow. Angela points at the accumulation of snow hundreds of feet above our heads.

"We don't want to spend too much time here," she says. As if on cue, there is a crack, and, on the ridge line, the snow starts to slide.

"Shit!" Angela says, and starts to sprint away. But there's no place to go.

"It's okay!" Steve shouts over the thunder of the avalanche. "We're too far away! We're clear!" The avalanche crashes into the soft snow a few hundred years from the trail, and the powder absorbs the tons of snow. A blast of freezing wind and grit pummels us. I wipe the cold, wet grit from my face.

"Let's get the hell out of here," says Angela, and we all heartily agree.

The first flakes of snow start falling as we near the Corner itself, and by the time we round the rock prow, it is snowing hard. After a quick break in the shadow of the prow, we head on.

The next section of the mountain comes to me in dreams sometimes, and I'm no longer sure how much is memory and how much is myth of my own making. Here is what I think I remember: It is snowing, but the wind has died off, leaving the mountain as still and as quiet as a Christmas morning in the country. We are entering a maze of crevasses, the trail twists and turns like a frozen python, moving up and down over bridges of indeterminate thickness. The entrance to the crevasse field is a steep traverse along a frozen hillside. The hill slopes about 40 to 50 degrees, hard blue ice. To the right of the trail is a drop into a series of crevasses; to the left, the steep ice. The trail narrows to the width of a mountaineering boot.

"Make sure you've always got three points of contact with the ice," Angela is saying, "before you move. Be careful not to hang a crampon point in your gaiters when you step."

The entrance to the crevasse field is silent, ethereal, the snow muffling even the hint of sound. The light is diffused as well, a soft gray light that seems to glow around us. We are in the clouds. As we step onto the ice traverse, our sleds drop down the slope, 60-pound pendulums pulling us toward the crevasses. With each step, the sled swings. Within a few steps, sweat is pouring off my body. My face is drenched. I try to set the butt of my ax, but it refuses to bite in the hard ice. Instead, I slip it into a hole left by another climber. Even the rasping of our breath is absorbed by the stillness. Landmarks vanish into the gray, until we are moving in a tunnel disconnected from time and space, placing one foot in front of the next, moving the ax, feeling the weights swing against our hips. The trail widens slightly, and I see ahead the outlines of snow bridges as the trail winds over the yawning crevasses.

"Keep the ropes tight!" shouts Steve, his voice flat and clipped.

It is like we're moving over a frozen Japanese garden, white bridges spanning sculpted streams of ice. I look down from a bridge, and see only gray, endless gray. I am as afraid as I've ever been in my life, and not just for my body. This is where The List has brought me, I think, to balance between in the gray between heaven and hell. *I am moving through the Burial Grounds.*

The trail turns, and, finally climbs out of the crevasse field, away from the Burial Grounds. Everyone, I realize, is spooked. "Whew!" says one of the other climbers. "Gods died there," someone else says, and I nod.

I will go through the Burial Grounds three more times, and even in the bright sunshine, the hairs on the back of my neck will stand up, and I will keep my eyes down.

Once, I will "punch through" into a crevasse, feel my right leg crash through a snow bridge, then swing around over . . . nothing. I will very slowly pull my leg out of the hole, hoping I can preserve the integrity of the snow bridge by sheer force of will. The bridge will hold.

We're excited after we get back to Camp 3. Tomorrow morning, we'll head back up. It will be hard, but we're moving now.

The storm hits that night, the winds ripping through Fortress Denali. With the wind comes the snows. For the next four days, it snows and it snows and it snows. At night, the wind is so bad we resort to earplugs just to get a little sleep. The tent shakes, pops, and snaps as the winds look for a tear, a pinhole, a way in, a way at us. The storm usually breaks in the morning for a few hours, although Steve says trying to move in the holes would be suicide. We watch one team start up Motorcycle Hill, only to retreat when a member falls waist deep into an unmarked crevasse. A pair from Norway, who've been sharing our cook tent, try to move their camp to 12,000 feet. The relentless winds hammer their tent to shreds, and they're forced to bury their remaining equipment, retreat back to Camp 3 and hole up in the cook tent, in amazingly good spirits just to be alive.

Mostly, we dig. The snow is piling up in great white drifts, and we need to keep its weight off the tents. It is as if our lives have gotten simpler still—eat, dig, wait. I wake up one morning with a nagging headache. My throat is sore, and before I can catch myself, I have a fit of coughing.

Damn! Oh damn.

Rich and I are asleep when the earthquake hits, but, like dogs, we wake up seconds before the actual impact.

"What is it? What is it?" says Rich, and I don't know. We're both looking around frantically, as if we can identify what fox has gotten into the hen house. Within seconds, the snowpack lifts and drops. Outside, despite the wind, we can hear the heavily loaded snow cornices let go and thunder down.

"Are we dead?" Rich asks.

"Give it a minute," I say. "I don't think the verdict is in yet."

We sit up in our sleeping bags and listen to the avalanches subside, and then there is nothing left but the wind. I fall back into a fitful sleep, punctuated by deep, racking coughs.

By the third day of the storm, Fortress Denali has fallen. The snow is now level with the walls, and the entire tent platform has filled up. Five or six feet of snow. The top of the tent is a few inches below the new snowline. Part of our nightly ritual is clearing the tent vents so the air doesn't go sour—"I know if you're snoring, the air's okay," Rich, who's worried that we'll finally be entombed in Fortress Denali, tells me one morning. In the morning, we burrow up, out of the tent, grab the shovels, and start digging. Once we've got the tent shoveled clear, we dig a path to the bathroom, dig out the bathroom—in other words, uncover our plastic bag—dig a path to the cook tent, dig a path to the other tents. All around us, we can see members of the other teams doing exactly the same thing.

Then we lay in our tents during the storm's many lulls, reading whatever we can get our hands on and waiting for the winds to come roaring back.

One night, Mimi, my instructor from Ouray, shows up at the

tent flap at about 3 A.M.

"You in there, Michael?" she shouts.

"Where else?" I say.

"Listen," she starts. Mimi has been trapped with another party of AAI climbers at High Camp, 17,200 feet, for a week. As soon as the weather broke, they headed down. "I'm sorry about the sled."

It's 3 A.M.

"Mimi," I answer, "what on earth are you talking about."

"The sled. If I'd known how miserable it was to pull, I'd have never made you pull my stuff all over Colorado."

"It's okay," I say. "Honest."

She straightens up, then blurts:

"I hate this mountain," she adds in a rush. "I hate the weather. I hate being sick. I'm lucky to get off it with my life . . . "

She pauses. "I guess I shouldn't be saying this to you, huh?"

"It's okay," I say. "I'm beginning to feel the same way."

The next morning, as the storm wanes, I gather up all my notes and letters and seal them in a plastic bag with a note, which reads, "Attention! In the event of an accident, please forward the enclosed material to . . . "

When the storm finally breaks, two more AAI guides, who've been climbing a different route, show up with grim news. They discovered the frozen bodies of three climbers, just off the trail near Windy Corner. At least three other teams are coming down with cases of serious frostbite and exhaustion from fighting the storm. The mountain has shown its fangs.

"We have to move now," Steve says. "Our food and fuel is shrinking from being trapped. The weather's all over the place. We've got a break now, and we have to take it."

We break camp, dig the sleds out of five feet of snow and start packing. I am feverish, with a nagging headache that won't seem to go away. I wake up feeling okay, but after three steps, I'm profoundly exhausted. I'm not sleeping, and my appetite has slipped away. I file the symptoms away. There's no where to go; nothing to be done for it.

As soon as we are harnessed up, we have to break again. Dr. Jim is sick, AMS, too exhausted to continue. Angela separates herself from the rope to take him down.

"It's like the worst case of flu I've ever had in my life," Dr. Jim tells me. He is, I think, on the verge of tears. "I'm so sick."

We pat him on the shoulder as another coughing fit rumbles up in my chest. I know what he means.

If the trip to Camp 4 was hard before, it's a living, breathing nightmare now. By halfway up Motorcycle Hill I am exhausted enough to want to just lay down in the snow, just close my eyes for a few minutes. I am burning up, dehydrated, scooping handfuls of snow into my mouth whenever I get the chance. With every step, I feel worse and worse. I imagine my body's defenses trying desperately to wage war on two fronts, fighting the infection, fighting the mountain sickness, losing on both. I know that at 14,000 feet, the body no longer has the resources to heal itself; at 20 degrees, 30 degrees below zero all the body's energies will go into making heat, shoveling whatever mean coal is left into the waiting furnace. My mind drifts, then snaps back. I have a long conversation with Ilg, who is telling me that I've forgotten that this is all a dance; that I can't dance with lead feet. *Run, Michael,* he is shouting at me. *Run up!* I wish that I had a phone, so I could call my friend Roger, Roger the windsurfer, from a hundred years ago, and tell him that I was on The Mountain, that I had let a list on a scrap of cocktail napkin lead me to some god awful frozen place . . .

And I snap back. We are halfway up the hill to Windy Corner, and Rich, behind me on the rope, is talking. "You're doing great," he is saying. "We're getting there."

My gratefulness for those words is all out of any sense of proportion.

We hear a helicopter, and, above us, the high altitude rescue copter is pulling the bodies of the dead climbers. Hanging from the skid of the fragile dragonfly chopper, a brightly colored package spins at the end of 50 feet of climbing rope.

"Gentlemen," says Steve, watching the package spin in the sunshine. "You cannot make any mistakes. None."

I go through the Burial Grounds in a haze of pain and mind-numbing exhaustion. I simply cannot be so tired, so shot. I am in good shape; I am strong; I have been in the field, dammit, and if I just . . . put . . . my . . . mind . . . to . . . it, I can make the pain go away.

One leaden step after another.

It's snowing by the time we reach the cache, which, thanks to its location, is in relatively good shape. We add the weight of the food in the cache and make the last push into Camp 4. When we get there, ten hours after we started, the sun has already dropped behind a peak, and the wind has come up. It is stunningly cold. It takes forever to dig out the platform, forever to get the tents erected forever to eat a quick supper. Steve asks me to share his tent, so he can listen to me cough. I feel so bad that I can't even bring myself to read today's note, part of the 21-card package Denise has given me for the trip. It is, simply, too great an effort.

Morning, and welcome to Camp 4, the polyglot, totally international base at the foot of the great headwall. A Russian who's been on Everest, stops by for tea; an Englishman, who remembers our tents at Camp 2, sticks his head in to see how we're making it. This is, he says, his third attempt to reach the Denali summit.

"You know," he says, "it gets better as you go along. The first time I came here, I was scared all the time—every morning, every hour, every minute. There are just so damn many ways to die here."

We are above most of the world here. There is a ranger tent and a medical tent, where various climber/doctors study the deleterious effects of altitude on people. There are maybe a dozen campsites, and most are occupied. There are even two thrones. All the conveniences of home, plus a view.

Behind us, the headwall towers 1,300 feet over the camp. I can't not look at it—it draws my eyes, captures and holds my mind. I spend most of the day resting—I get a day off while the guys retrieve the rest of the cache.

We laugh and joke, have an early supper. Roger prays for those who were lost in the storm. "Inshalla," says Tommy, who's put in time in the Middle East. *As God wills it.*

For me, sleep has vanished, a memory. I am alternately cold, even in the bag, wearing long underwear and fleece pants and shirt, a silk face mask, gloves, and two pairs of socks; then I am washed by waves of heat. My toes feel like blocks of ice. I bury my face in the wadded up jacket that serves as my pillow, stifling the coughs in piles of fleece.

Listen, I find myself saying to my body, negotiating. *I know it's been bad . . . I know we're doing our best. But I'm going to ask one more thing. Give me the headwall. Give me one more day.*

One more day.

In my head, I see the summit slipping into the mists, away from my outstretched arm. I feel the weight of the headwall, above my head.

One more day, I ask fervently, feverishly, maybe even prayerfully. *One more day.*

Around dawn, I fall into a brief, deep sleep. When I wake up, less than an hour later, it is with the absolute certainty that, on some cellular level, my body has voted, and today we will climb.

The first part of the climb up the headwall is a steep, steep hike, up to the icy gully that leads to the top of the great wall. Then we hook our Jumars—sliders that go up, not down—into the fixed ropes, ropes that were set by another team a few seasons back, for the steepest part of the climb. The idea, of course, is that the rope is protection, to catch you if you fall.

"You might not want to fall on these ropes, guys," says Steve. "Since we didn't put them in, we don't know whether they'll hold a fall or not. My guess is not."

My climbing is slow, but steady, like climbing a frozen, 600-foot ladder. We don't have the sleds, thank goodness, but our packs are heavily loaded with supplies. It is snowing and bitterly cold, but I feel as good as I have for days.

I remember a time windsurfing, before The List. I'd gone out late one afternoon, just before sunset, on a big day. For some reason, I had the beach all to myself, not a soul around. But I'd caught the wind just right, and I sailed until my shoulders ached and my legs cramped from the pressure of holding the board on course. And just before sunset, I caught one last gust, a long, carving ride across a yacht basin that seemed to go on forever. And I thought then that single ride was the best of me, that maybe a life could be captured and marked in a single line, carved on water.

I know now that the headwall is the best of me; that with each step up, each push of the Jumar, I am carving a single, fine line. There is rock and roll playing in my head, wind screaming around my face and a rope above me stretching into the clouds.

And, finally, I am at the top of the last rope. I step onto the "balcony," almost 17,000 feet high. The clouds clear, and, around me, below me, as in my imagination, my dreams, the world stretches. In one direction, further up the West Buttress, is the summit itself, achingly close. I want to reach out my hand, touch it, stand there. But I am reeling. *Remember our deal*, my body echoes.

"You okay?" says Steve. "You looked a little shaky there."

No problem, I say.

The rest is dénouement. I go down, stumbling back into Camp 4 on the last of my strength.

"Would you be willing to go to the medical tent now?" Steve asks. Sure, I say. I'll walk over there. This is all very stiff, almost formal. At the medical tent, Dr. Colin Grissom, one of the experts on diseases of altitude, is going to tell me I have AMS. That diagnosis is going to end my climb.

"You've got AMS," the doctor says. I nod.

Walking back to the tents, Steve and I joke and talk. Finally, he states the obvious.

"You know I can't take you up again," he says. I nod. "You've earned your shot at the summit, fair and square. But I can't take you up."

Down is life; up is death. So simple, so black and white. I feel dead already, inside.

"I understand," I say, and I do.

That night, the cough gets much worse. Sometime in the middle of the night, Steve begins talking.

"You have to go down in the morning," he says. "I have to take you."

I am angry—I will not kill the rest of the teams' chances at the summit. They have all earned their shot, fair and square.

"You have to go down in the morning," Steve says, calmly, but firmly, as if he is talking to a recalcitrant child. "It's your life we're talking about here."

The morning, I say, coughing. Something will come up.

And something does. At dawn, another guide shouts into our campsite—"Somebody here looking for a ride down the mountain?"

I go down.

Five days later, with food and fuel almost gone, Steve, Tom Walker, Tommy Cary, and my tent mate, Rich Davidson, reach the summit of Denali and stand on the roof of the world.

In Base Camp, I learn the full extent of the storm. Camp 1 is buried under as much as 20 feet of snow; three have died, and there are numerous injuries. At one point, two ski planes flip landing at Base Camp—luckily, no one is injured. But food and fuel run so low that the bush pilots do food drops.

I am tired, bone tired, but the worst of the mountain sickness has lifted as soon as I come down. I feel as if I am tethered to the mountain in some undefinable way, as if the line I carved on the headwall was still connected to my soul and would never be broken. Perhaps it wouldn't. I hear talk in the camp of "conquering", of "coming back and beating the bitch," and I am puzzled. There is, I think, nothing here to conquer, nothing to beat. I have come here because of a list on a napkin in a pizza joint. I am not sure what I have found here, in the cold and the snow, but the great mountain no longer makes my stomach knot with fear. The fear is gone.

In the morning, with the sound of the bush plane in the distance, I hike one more time to the throne. I have neither bathed nor shaved in 21 days. I stink so badly I can smell myself. My gloves are patched with duct tape, and I am still coughing badly. There are two young Japanese climbers, fresh off the plane, ahead of me in line. To my surprise, they step off the trail and bow slightly, waiting for me to pass.

One smiles.

"How was it up there?" he asks.

I smile back.

"Cold," I say. "Very cold."

And then I go home.

22

The Abyss

THE MOUNTAIN HAS LEFT ME TIRED and at odds, as if the best parts of me are still struggling in the snow at Camp 4. I feel a bone-weary exhaustion; a sense of failure like an endless, grinding mill wheel in my head. My sleep—in a bed; in the dark—is fitful, and I snap awake at the slightest provocation, my eyes wide open, waiting for the bite of the cold, the sound of the wind.

But it is warm and quiet in Colorado; the winds I hear all in my head.

Maybe I could have pushed harder . . . maybe I should have started the Diamox sooner . . . Maybe if I'd just wanted it more . . .

"You didn't have a choice," my tent mate, Rich Davidson, tells me over the telephone one Saturday morning. "The guide wouldn't have taken you up any higher. You were sick, man."

And I am still sick; The Mountain left its mark carved in little curlicues on my lungs. I am at a clinic, staring at my chest x-rays.

"See these curls," the doctor is saying, pointing a series of little curves, about the size of the end of your little finger's fingernail, on the film. "That's the residue of your high altitude pulmonary edema."

Will it, I ask, affect my SCUBA diving?

He pauses, squeezes the bridge of his nose.

"When?" he asks.

Couple of days, I reply. I want to finish, to see The List done. I am too tired and too depressed to care much about anything except the schedule, and am only at the doctor under duress. I am too mentally exhausted to be afraid, to be nervous. I want to get on the plane tomorrow, fly to California and dive, dive, dive.

"The day after tomorrow?" the doctor asks.

I nod.

"Well . . . " he starts, pauses, then starts again. "I think you're committing suicide."

Great, I say. What kind of risks are we talking about?

"Not acceptable," he says. "Those little curved scarrings can trap air, and that trapped air can lead to an embolism. You're just asking for an embolism here."

I go home and start making phone calls, looking for a second opinion that disagrees. Finally, a diving doctor from San Francisco sums it up neatly—"Fifty/fifty," he says when I ask for odds. "That's stupid."

I hang up, then call and cancel my deep dives. It's too late to even juggle the plane tickets, so I decide to go to California anyway and at least go through the academic portion of the mixed gas diving course.

The first thing one notices about T. Wings Stock, who's going to be my instructor, is, well, his *wings*.

Awesome, multicolored wings, tattooed wings, beginning at the wristbone of each arm and climbing to his not insubstantial biceps.

Tell me about the wings, I say, but he just shrugs it off.

"From a guy named Lyle Tuttle in San Francisco," he says. "It was a long time ago."

Only the most famous tattooist in the world. But with his huge beard and bear-like frame, T. Wings Stock does look like a remnant from the Summer of Love; it's not hard to imagine him backstage at a Dead concert, maybe working the lights. "He always gets mistaken for one of those guys in ZZ Top," says Ani Stock, who followed her sweetheart from the midwest to the Bay area; who waited for him to come back from Vietnam; who waited at home while he drove a long-haul truck after the war. But along the way, Wings Stock discovered SCUBA, and no matter how he sliced it, swimming around underwater looking at wrecks struck him as a lot more fun than permanent hemorrhoids. After discussions with Ani, Wings decided that he could indeed make a living as a dive instructor.

They settled in the tiny California community of Santa Cruz, home of the Museum of Surfing and some of the finest surf on the West Coast. Santa Cruz also anchors the top of Catalina Bay, cold, clear and deep, home of the vast, hypnotic underwater forests of kelp. While he loved the kelp and the otters and the endless, pesky seals, Wings reserved his strongest fascination for the shipwrecks that litter the sand bottom of the Pacific off Santa Cruz, Monterey, and down toward Santa Barbara.

Here's the thing about "wreckers"—they're all just a little twisted, sort of like pieces of iron and steel exposed to years and years of depth and current. Even the name has its own spin. Wreckers was the name originally given to the landlocked pirates of the early 1800s who lured ships to their deaths on rocky shoals. Key West even has a museum dedicated to the old wreckers. The new wreckers' goal is to visit many of those very ships that scattered their bones across the bottom. Almost everybody, when they start diving, spends at least a little time on wrecks, mostly because the wrecks themselves are artificial reefs, attracting all manner of blue fishes. My first wrecks were off the east coast of Florida, and I didn't get it. I mean, all that money and time, and we were looking at a sunken tugboat in 50 feet of water. This struck me as a little like paying $100 to visit your favorite wrecked car at the junkyard.

I started changing my opinion when David Feeney, my friend and dive instructor in New York City, invited me to Cape Hattaras to spend five days diving the deeper wrecks of "The Graveyard Of The Atlantic."

"You're up to it, right?" he asked.

"Sure, " I replied. *Now what*, I thought.

First was a routine I'd already gotten used to—the frenetic assembling of specialized equipment. My "dive gear" consisted of a face mask and a pair of flippers, plus my wetsuit from Alcatraz. I figured I could get by with a computer, a tank and a couple of regulators.

"Any suggestions?" I asked David.

"Get something that works," he said.

"Good idea," I replied.

Twenty phone calls, a couple of months and about $2,000 later I found myself on the Margie II, bouncing our way through rolling seas out into the Atlantic. At the helm was Captain Art Kirchner—Cap'n Artie—one of the legendary New Jersey wreckers and part of the expedition that recovered the ship's bell from the Andrea Doria, but I didn't know that.

My primary focus was on not throwing up as the little boat, awash in diesel fumes, went up and down and up and down and up and down. I'd also noticed, as people started laying out equipment, that there was a substantial difference between their equipment and my equipment, not the least of which was that they each had two tanks, and I only had one.

Huuummmmmm.

They also had dry suits, as opposed to my wet suit. The dreadfully expensive dry suits insulated the body with a layer of air between the suit and the skin. A wet suit, on the other hand, insulates by trapping a thin layer of water between the skin and the neoprene of the suit. The difference between a dry suit and a wet suit, aside from the $1000 or so in price, was that the deeper you got in a wet suit, the more the neoprene compresses and the less efficient the suit becomes—when you need it the most, the worst it works.

"You knew that, right?" says David.

"Of course," I says, vaguely remembering something from SCUBA class, wishing now I'd paid more attention.

Two hours of bounce, and we were over the first wreck.

"We're probably going to build up some hang time," David said conversationally.

I shrugged, not wanting to let on how nervous I actually was. A few years ago one of the big diver certifying agencies made the statement that SCUBA diving was every bit as safe as bowling, and they had the numbers to prove it. Statistically, that may be true, but you can bowl your entire life and never once have to stand inside the door of the bowling alley watching your watch, counting the minutes until you can step into the street without bending over double in agony, being crippled or just plain dropping dead.

That's decompression for you.

Most everybody who spent any time watching "Sea Hunt" on television or renting and rerenting *The Abyss* has some kind of idea about "the bends." Here's the deal: nothing has changed from Denali. People are still optimized to live at sea level. But as we go down instead of up, pressure increases instead of decreases. And it increases very quickly. At 33 feet of salt water, we've added the weight of an entire other atmosphere to the one already sitting on top of us. At 66 feet, there are three atmospheres of pressure weighing us down—two of water and one of air. The deeper we go, the more those atmospheres add up. Among the things happening to us physiologically is that excess nitrogen is being forced into all our tissues by the pressure. On surfacing, that excess nitrogen creates bubbles, and unless we give those bubbles a chance to dissipate— decompression—they can cause us great pain, cripple us or kill us. Or maybe not. Decompression sickness is capricious; you can do everything wrong and not get a "hit," a bubble that lodges somewhere in our body.

Or you can do everything right and end up in a decompression chamber with a $25,000 bill and a lot of serious pain.

The first mention of decompression sickness in scientific literature comes from way back, all the way to 1670, when scientist Robert Boyle looked into the eye of a snake he had depressurized in a chamber and saw a bubble. He had no idea what caused the bubble or what it meant, but he dutifully recorded the fact. Its first recorded case in man was in the mid-1800s, when doctors discovered that French coal miners digging in the world's first pressurized mine became ill when they left the pressurized environment, then got better when they returned to it. The nickname "bends" came from the unfortunate workers on the Brooklyn Bridge in New York City. The caissons on the bridge foundations were pressurized with compressed air to hold back the water, and many of the workers got sick when they left the caissons. As their co-workers twisted in pain, the other workers, ever New Yorkers, noted that the sufferers appeared to be mimicking a popular fashion pose, the "Grecian Bend." After that, everyone knew about "the bends."

If you decided to live underwater, all that devolved nitrogen wouldn't be a problem. Coming up, though, there's the problem. The pressure drops, and our bodies try to eliminate the excess nitrogen. Suffice to say that if we do not come up at a fixed, slow rate, stopping at predetermined points to let the excess nitrogen be eliminated, bubbles will form and be carried through our bloodstream to all parts of the body. Using Doppler ultrasound, you can hear the bubbles crashing through the bloodstream, transparent boulders carried along in the turbulence, waiting to do their damage.

I knew that I would have to stop at various points, determined by my computer, to let the nitrogen go away. I knew that if I "violated a stop," went to the surface too soon, I could be in trouble. What I didn't know could basically fill a boxcar, but ignorance, as they say, is bliss.

The dive itself was deeper than I'd gone before, 150 feet, with lousy visibility, cold water and currents. The whole dive, my stomach is knotted with fear, a constant list of things that could go wrong—and for which I am unprepared—running through my head. I crawl along the bottom, alternately staring at the jumbled pile of metal that used to be a ship and my computer, which is tallying my "decompression penalty," the time to the surface. It looked like the meter of a speeding taxicab.

Finally, I headed up. But I'd racked up too much bottom time, and lacked the experience (or the brains) to match my decompression time with the amount of air remaining in my tanks. At the 30 foot decompression stop, it became obvious to me that my air was going to run out before my time, leaving my with a Hobson's choice. I had already used up the air in my main tank and was breathing from a smaller "pony" tank I'd velcroed on my backpack.

I still had about eight minutes of decompression time left when I noticed that each suck on the regulator was getting less and less air. And then there was no suck left. There was one tremendous rush of panic, as I sucked frantically on the empty bottle. *I can't breathe . . . breathe . . . breathe!!!* The animal rattled the cage, shaking the bars, shrieking. A more distant part of my mind noted that I was 20 feet from the surface, didn't have that much decompression time left, wasn't at that great a risk and that there were three people on the anchor line just below me . . .

The animal abruptly stopped shaking the bars of the cage.

People below me? With *air?*

I crawled a few feet back down the line to the closest diver, then made the universal signal for "Out Of Air," a hand slashed across the throat.

I could see him laughing in his mask.

I wondered what the universal sign for, "No, really, asshole!" was.

I signaled again, and he shrugged, then handed me his "octopus," a spare regulator on a separate long hose.

I took three quick breaths, my heart rate dropping below a thousand beats a minute; the animal in my head prying his clawed hands off the bars of the cage. I smiled, signaled "Okay," then settled down to wait out the few remaining minutes.

The anchor line went limp, cut from the wreck by a diver from the boat who thought we were done. Suddenly, we were free floating, and I was underweighted—not enough lead to hold me at that depth. I took a quick look at my computer—three minutes left—took three deep breaths and handed back the octopus. Waved bye-bye and headed for the surface.

Not an optimum beginning. But I did resolve that, no matter what was on The List, I wasn't going back to the abyss until I knew what I was doing.

It's obvious everyone else is on Key West Time except Wings and me.

"You'll get used to it," says Michael Menduno, as we pace around Key West Divers' small dock. The heat is like a warm, wet blanket, the air thick and chewy enough to gather into balls and bounce. Out on the lagoon, the water has taken on the gray silver sheen of a piece of oxidized aluminum, the color of old dive tank.

"Come on," Wings says, and we retreat to the rental car with the computer to run simulations.

Dive planning software is a relatively new addition to the already gadget-laden sport, but for technical diving, the simulations created by the software are almost indispensable.

That's because, basically, there's a wing-and-a-prayer aspect to tech diving that its participants don't particularly like to hone up to.

"You diving mix?" Dr. Bill Clem, the main hyperbaric specialist at Denver's Presbyterian/St. Luke's Hyperbaric Medicine Center asked me. When I said yes, he rubbed his hands together, looking for all the world like a happy kid. "Great! You get to be part of the experiment! We'll see which decompression tables actually work."

Tech divers like to point out—ad infinitum, I might add—that people have been breathing weird gases under water for just about as long as people have been diving. According to Tom Mount and Bret Gilliam, two of the pioneers of extended range diving and the de facto historians of the sport, the first speculations on using helium to replace part of the nitrogen in air came as early as 1919. Professor and inventor extraordinaire Elihu Thompson suggested that nitrogen narcosis could be avoided if the inert gas helium was added to the mix. Unfortunately, helium at the time was $2,500 a cubic foot, making Thompson, who had merged with Thomas Edison's company to form General Electric, about the only person in the United States who could afford the stuff.

The Navy experimented with heliox, a mixture of helium and nitrogen, for years, and numerous depth records were set with the mixed gases. But Jacques Costeau's SCUBA pretty much changed all that. Most of the use of mixed gases were for divers wearing those funny *20,000 Leagues Under The Sea* outfits, with a long hose running up to the surface. SCUBA—Self-Contained Underwater Breathing Apparatuses—meant that the clunky suits with the tethers were passé. Throw on a couple of tanks and a mask, add some fins, and away you swim with the fishes. Compressed air became the gas of choice for SCUBA for a very simple reason—it's easy to compress air. Cheap, too.

The catch, of course, is narcosis. I'd already visited Narcosis World in Hal Watts's Florida sinkhole, felt the waves of nausea, the "whirlies," mental processes slowed to the speed of gooey fudge.

The difference between diving deep on air and diving deep on mixed gas," says Gary Gentile, perhaps the foremost deep wreck diver in the world, "is that on the mixed gas, you get to remember what you saw."

Of course, as Bill Clem pointed out, you also get to be part of the experiment.

The gas of choice is called trimix, a blend that replaces as much as 50 percent of the nitrogen in the air with helium. The lesser nitrogen content makes a dive to 300 feet seem more like a dive to 150 feet, narcosis wise.

"You will be amazed at how clear your head is at depth," Wings tells me. "You'll also talk like Daffy Duck on the surface."

Getting to dive with trimix isn't, I discovered, all that easy. The certification procedure is long, arduous, and as mentally painful as a college calculus class, with just about as much math.

Here's an example:

$$FN_2 = \frac{(END + 33) \times 0.79}{D + 33}$$

That's a formula for figuring the narcosis level of certain percentages of helium in the mixed gas.

It gets worse. There are sample questions in the text like: *A mix of 16% O_2 and 40% He has 1,300 PSIG remaining in it. What will be the new mix if the tanks are topped to 3,000 PSIG with air?*

In English, the question is asking what happens if leftover trimix in a tank is pumped back up with air. The answer, by the way, is 19% oxygen, 17% helium, and 64% nitrogen. Whew!

For three days Wings patiently goes over the endless calculations necessary to understand the mixed gas. More importantly, we methodically hammer away on the basics of what has been called technical diving, diving outside the range of conventional SCUBA.

"It's almost like a military operation," he says. "No, scratch that. There's no 'almost' about it. A deep wreck dive *is* like a military operation."

We have to isolate everything that can go wrong, then decide how we would deal with that problem under water—fill out the index cards, so to speak, for a whole range of new terrors. The biggest danger is neither from narcosis or decompression sickness, but, surprisingly, from oxygen. The gas necessary for our survival—even in its "normal" mix, air—is deadly below a couple of hundred feet. There's some question about the mechanism of oxygen toxicity; one theory holds that the higher concentrations of oxygen interferes with the enzymes the body uses for metabolism. There's no question about the effects, though. The biggie is convulsions, and convulsions underwater is a death sentence.

While we're diving deep, Wings says, our "oxygen clock" is running. Depending on the concentration of oxygen and the depths involved, we're getting dosages of oxygen. Once we reach 100 percent of our bodies' tolerance, we are on borrowed time. Like those nitrogen bubbles, we may exceed the limits and walk away unscathed. Or we may hit 101 percent...

"It's Russian Roulette," Wings says. "You pull the trigger, you may walk away. But if you keep pulling the trigger, sooner or later it's going to go bang."

Later that evening, just for fun, I figure my oxygen clock for the deep air dives I did preparing for these dives.

It comes to around 900 percent of maximum tolerance.

Click.

The dives in Key West will be on the Wilkes-Barre, a 600-foot long World War II destroyer, resting in 240 feet of water—well below the 130 "limit" of recreational SCUBA diving. It is considered one of the ""crown jewels" of technical diving, one of the most spectacular wreck dives in the world. Wings and I will be diving with Billy Deans of Key West Divers, who pioneered diving the wreck and who, along with Wings, has pushed out the limits of the abyss.

"The main thing," says Wings, "is that we cover every contingency and know exactly what is happening at every minute *before* we even get wet."

We begin the planning in Santa Cruz, but we finish up in Key West. The details are these: we will be diving on a mixture of 17% oxygen, 50% helium, and the balance nitrogen, which will give us the narcosis effect of around 130 feet. As opposed to a recreational dive, where you put on a single tank and jump in, our dive on the Wilkes-Barre will require four tanks apiece—two oversize tanks on the back carrying the helium mix; one tank under the right arm carrying air enriched with extra oxygen (called Nitrox) and one tank under the left arm carrying pure oxygen. The Nitrox and the oxygen are for the decompression stops, the higher concentrations of oxygen helping to flush the nitrogen out of the system. The catch, of course, is that should something happen on the bottom, at 240 feet, to the main tanks, breathing from either of the decompression tanks would likely lead to fatal convulsions. In fact, it's not safe to breath from the Nitrox tank until we're back at 100 feet; the oxygen tank is for 20 feet and less. Each tank is marked clearly, using different style breathing regulators. The oxygen regulator has a surgical tubing band stretched over the mouthpiece, so the regulator can't just be stuffed into the mouth. When we get to Key West, we learn that a diver has died recently, taking a breath of pure oxygen at 200 feet. Oh yes, the 17 percent of oxygen in the mix isn't enough to supply the body on the surface, so we plan on getting to depth quickly.

We'll also be carrying two knives apiece, an inflatable bag and reel of line to allow us to decompress on our own should we get separated from the anchor line, multiple timers, extra masks, two lights apiece, and slates marked with a series of decompression alternatives, should our bottom time be shortened or extended. The gear—like the cave gear—weighs in at almost 200 pounds.

We have run numerous computer simulations of the dive, so many that it's beginning to seem like an old friend. The intellectual challenge of the dive planning is hypnotic, tempered by the knowledge that, ultimately, your life will rest on that plan.

The computer tells us that for 20 minutes of time at the bottom, we'll spend over an hour decompressing. The entire dive will take 87 minutes.

"So with that, we can create a Run Time chart," Wings says. "We'll know where we're supposed to be, how much gas we're supposed to have, and how long we have to stay at that point. By the numbers—that's the way we'll do it."

By the numbers:

The wreck first becomes visible at just over 100 feet, Run Time: 2 minutes...

It floats up from the diffused green, at first just on the edges of the vision. We drift down, barely in contact with the down line, and the vastness of the wreck emerges from the green... It is huge, a 600-foot capital ship, a ghost from the recent past... I feel around in the back of my head, looking for the usual terror... *7 atmospheres, 8 atmospheres, 9 atmospheres... you're going to die here*..

. but the nagging feeling is absent, dwarfed by the wreck . . .

"OK?" Wings signals.

I touch thumb to forefinger to agree.

We settle onto the top deck of the Wilkes-Barre at about 155 feet. At Wings' signal, we move down a level and disconnect out stage bottles, clipping them to a section of line—a Jon line—Wings has wrapped around a crusted section of railing. The lines hooked off, he taps his wrist with two fingers—time—then signals a five. Run Time: 5 minutes—we have 15 minutes of bottom time until we have to be back at the anchor line, ready to start back up. That translates into 10 minutes of exploring time, giving me, the novice, some leeway to reattach the two additional tanks. I match Wings movements, then signal "OK," and we head over the railing, into the Lost World of the wreck.

I clear my head of random thoughts, take a second to visualize the rest of the dive—Run Time: 7 minutes—then let myself drift into the world of the wreck. We swim toward the stern of the destroyer, its massive 3-inch guns, now covered with a gilding of corals, point toward an enemy long gone. I feel the pressure in my ears as we drop down a deck, below 200 feet now. I feel around for the voice in my head, and it is still silent. Wings stops swimming, and drifts down toward the deck. Then he swings his arms wide, encompassing the wreck. "See?" he sends a message as much mental. "Do you understand now?"

And I do. We have come to one of the ends of the earth, a cathedral that will never know crowds of tourists or the swarms of recreational divers in their brightly colored matching gear. We have come to a place that will never know signs pointing to men's rooms or T-shirt sales. We have come to stand—or float—at a place where once men knew war, where now there is only the silent movement of the jacks and snappers, the razor sleekness of the barracudas, the frenetic dartings of the florescent tropicals. A blue tang, its fins tinged with bright yellow, darts up and tastes my glove, then jets back to the safety of the destroyer. A few feet away, a barracuda hangs motionless beneath one of the long barrels, its ancient computer racing to place Wings and me in the simple categories of the ocean—predator or prey.

I look toward the stern of the great ship, up toward its ghostly stacks. From a dozen flickering old newsreels, I imagine its awesome death, sliced apart, the sea thundering in through the rents and the tears, racing through the doors and the passageways, from deck to deck, level to level, until the ship shudders, then submits. I imagine the men that served on the Wilkes-Barre, wherever they are, feeling that shudder, hackles rising on their necks, as the ship dies, then settles to its final resting place.

Wings taps his wrist.

Run Time: 9 minutes.

We drop down to 225 feet, then settle into a open hold, an elevator into the heart of the ship. I kick my fins, and Wings points to a wave of silt behind me, then shakes his finger. "You're cave trained," he is saying. "You know better than to silt out an area . . . "

Run Time: 11 minutes.

In the hold, for a moment I close my eyes and envision the column of water over my head, the sheer amount of weight settled onto my shoulders. An atmosphere of pressure for every 33 feet. My breathing rate picks up, the helium-thinned gas mixture flowing easily through my regulator. Too easily—I'm off my benchmark. Not dangerously so, but something to be aware of, to take into consideration. At this depth, at this pressure, there are no "small" mistakes. Even the smallest error, the slightest deviation, can presage a disaster. *The future's uncertain*, sang Jim Morrison so many years ago. *The end is always near.*

It's time to go.

We rise out of the hold, then swim directly toward the big guns, veering off slightly to the left to move up to the deck where the stage bottles are tethered. We crouch on the old deck, rehooking the stage bottles to our harnesses. I hook the oxygen bottle under my left arm, clumsily clipping the brass "double dogs" to my stainless steel drings. The enriched air bottle on my right side goes a little easier. I add a shot of air to my BC to offset the added weight of the bottles, then check my two times.

Run Time: 18 minutes.

I feel the pull of the wreck, the urge to stay a little longer, turn on the lights and peer into the silent inner decks, drift down the great, gapping tear in the bow. I want to stay, move through the ghostly command centers, fly through the darkened crew quarters, touch the massive engines. I run my gloved hand along the railing, along the rusting, ocean crusty metal. I want to keep going.

Run Time: 19 minutes.

Wings signals toward the surface with his thumb. I match his signal, sign "OK," and at Run Time 20 minutes we start up the line, back toward the world of air and sunshine and noise.

Sixty-seven minutes and two gas switches later, we are on the deck of the Key West Diver. Billy Deans, who has come up just after us, is ecstatic.

"It's so damn cool," he says.

"So what did you think?" Wings asks.

"Worth the effort," I say, but that's not all of it. The Wilkes-Barre, the abyss, is the end of The List. I am reminded of Ken Kesey's legendary Merry Prankster bus, "Further". I have ridden, I think, my own Further for all it's worth. *I know where you're going,* Nancy Frederickson says as we walk along the frozen landscape of New Hampshire, *but how do you plan to get back?* Eighteen minutes, versus 21 days on Denali. Two days on the Iditabike. Sixty seconds of free fall. Nine minutes down Mammoth Mountain. Seconds ticked off a clock that I never knew existed.

"Are you okay?" Wings asks.

"Oh yeah, fine" I reply. I really don't know what I think. I think that some part of The Fear never really goes away—*There are so many ways to die here,* as the climber on Denali told me. The animal in your head, that screams and shrieks and cries, is always there, its hands on the bars, staring with wide, frightened eyes on a mysterious world.

And yet...

"We're going out to the Matterhorn in a month," Wings is saying. "It's a pretty cool dive, a spire rising up from the bottom. It's deep and cold, but..."

"Sounds good," I hear myself saying. "I'd like that."

On the ride back home, Wings pulls out his Doppler ultrasound sensors and places them just beneath my collarbones. There's no *pop* of nitrogen bubbles, only the steady roar of blood seeking the heart.

23

Acceptable Risks

Here is the view from the top of the mountain:

Down, a world of down.

The lift drops me off near the top of the mountain, and I step my back foot onto the snowboard and slide through the slushy snow. It is a warm July day in Colorado, and I am at A-Basin, the last hold-out to the summer's heat. Up high, though, there is snow, and it is rideable, more or less. I'm wearing waterproof pants and a T-shirt, a far cry from my usual Michelin Man expedition bundling this high up. But it is summer, and I am at odds.

I have never really considered what I would do after The List was completed. I'd never really thought that The List *could* be completed. But it has been.

"You know," my Mother tells me one day over the telephone, "I never would have thought that you'd be so good at not dying."

"It's a gift," I reply flippantly.

But it still weighs on me, a psychic lump in my head. Pieces of experiences come to me in those gray minutes before sleep: the taste of the dirty waters of San Francisco Bay; the instant the glider takes wing, when gravity releases its grip; the searing bite of the first breath at 30 degrees below zero; the sight of mercurial air pooling in the tops of underwater caves; the illusion of the frozen castles of ice, the color of jewels in the afternoon sun. But the pieces are jumbled together, like the great ice falls on Denali, crumbled and crushed as the glaciers move inexorably toward the sea.

"We can if we so choose wander aimlessly over the continent of the arbitrary," wrote Japanese novelist Haruki Murakami in the aptly titled *A Wild Sheep Chase*. "Rootless as some winged seed blown about on some serendipitous spring breeze."

I've thought a lot about the "continent of the arbitrary," because that is where we will always find the edge.

I came to the risk sports looking for Indiana Jones. Or, at least, someone like him. Some part and parcel of our mythology, cowboy or samurai, riding the edge jaggies for all they're worth. Instead, I found a group of puzzled people with a tiger by the tail, interested not so much in mythology as with touching and holding an experience as ephemeral as spider silk, ghostly as morning mist over a Montana river...

There is, I think now, even more to the edge than that ephemeral feeling. It has its own time, its own space. The edge has its own gravity, like a great dark star on the edge of the known universe. We approach that star only with the greatest of caution, because its gravity has the power to capture us and hold us in endless orbit, or even pull us into its dark heart. But we continue to approach the dark star, because its gravity has the power to rip away our preconceptions, our sure knowledge of the way things are, to let us see the way things might be. Because the dark star has the power to give us back our feelings, sometimes in exchange for our lives.

I have never met anyone who has stood, however precariously, on the flanks of a great mountain, or who has been, however briefly, to the dark world at the edge of the abyss, and not come back changed. Changed how? More humble, perhaps; more aware of the fragility of life.

I asked one of the top triathletes in the country, an expert at brutal endurance sports, for her comments on the work in process, and one day she called me, very agitated.

"What," she said bluntly, "are you going to say about death? What are you going to tell them about death? Because, if you're going to be honest, you've got to tell them something."

I started to tell her about my definition of risk, increased consequences of failure, of *flow*, of optimal experience, but she would have no part of it.

"Bullshit," she said. "What we're talking about here is *dead*. I've thought about it; you've thought about it; everybody who's been out there has thought about it."

So what, I ask, should I tell them?

"You can get dead, but it's worth it," she said.

Why?

"Because," she said slowly, "you get a chance to be different, to be a different person."

"Adventure," wrote Walt Burnett, "is a human need." And that it is.

"So," asks Steve Ilg, "what did you learn?"

I remember our conversation of so long ago, sitting in his dusty office in Santa Fe, and Ilg's great love of quotes. So I fish out a copy of an old book by Yvon Chouinard.

"Perceptions dull and we come to accept a blunting of feeling in the shadow of security," Chouinard wrote. "Drunk with power, I find that I am out of my senses. I . . . long for immediacy of contact to brighten my senses again, to bring me nearly the world once more; in my security, I have forgotten how to dance . . . "

"So," Ilg says finally. "Did you learn how to dance?"

"The feeling I get is terribly unfocused, yet very solid," Murakami's strange sheep detective muses in *A Wild Sheep Chase*. His girlfriend understands immediately: "A concentrated phenomenon based on vague motives," she replies.

The old avalanche chute is steep, the July snow as slushy as old mashed potatoes. I maneuver the snowboard to the edge of the drop, look down at the long slope. My run is off to the left, cutting across the face. Halfway down the slope, I'll cut back to the right, then drop until the slope shallows out into an easy run down what's left of the snowy part of the mountain. As I balance on the lip, I feel the machinery begin to wind up, the animal begin to pace nervously around the cage. I close my eyes and imagine the biochemical machine of my body dumping chemistry into my bloodstream. I feel the adrenaline begin to play tricks with time and space; the beta-endorphins stripping away the aches and pains. All around me, the parts of the external world that don't have anything to do with the next minutes of vertical drop are disappearing, shut out as a thick, quiet curtain falls around me. All in a millisecond, I feel sparks arc through my legs, the muscles tensing, resting. Through heightened senses, I feel the 162 centimeters of snowboard bound to my feet, feel the sharp heelside edge cut into the snow. I see my run, a glowing line overlaid on the gooey snow, see the point at which my weight will shift, initiating the turn. I think, as I always do, about the advice my friend Val, a professional extreme snowboarder, offered one day: "I know if I make the first turn," she said, "I won't die."

I smile, absently. The machine is fully on now, waiting for the datastorm to come. *Processing*, the green light blinks. *Processing*.

We are all poised there—my mind, my body, the animal created of fear and doubt and uncertainty—waiting on the edge. The feeling, when it comes, is one of calm, of joy even, beginning at the top of my head and rolling down through my body. I feel my eyes go soft; the tension in my muscles release. In the very back of my head, where my spine connects to my brain, I hear the beginning of music, the first slashing chords of hard rock and roll.

Well, it's five A.M., the fear is gone . . .

Of its own volition, without the slightest prompt from me, the board begins its run, carving a glowing line into the first turn.

Index